Contents

List of tables   iv

Acknowledgements   v

Foreword by Professor David Smith, Lancaster University   vi

Introduction   ix

one   Modernising probation and criminal justice since 1997   1

two   Durkheim, Weber, Marx and Foucault: social theory with 'the big guys'   23

three   Religious, humanitarian and personalist impulses: footprints left by   65
           'the good guys'

four   Social theory and organisational complexity: putting theories and   83
           impulses to work

five   Researching modernisation and cultural change in probation: 107
           views of solicitors, clerks, magistrates, barristers and judges

six   Modernising monstrosities and cultural catastrophes: probation   149
           trapped in a new order of things

References   167

Index   181

List of tables

1.1	Summary of significant developments, 1997–2009	18
2.1	Summarising bodies of social theory	61
3.1	Summarising the personalist perspective	80
4.1	Summarising putting theories to work	105
5.1	Evidence of modernisation and cultural change at 'Northtown' Magistrates' Court	112
5.2	Evidence of modernisation and cultural change at 'Northtown' Crown Court	117
5.3	Understandings of probation at 'Northtown' Magistrates' Court	119
5.4	Understandings of probation at 'Northtown' Crown Court	121
5.5	Age of court clerks	123
5.6	Number of years working as a court clerk	123
5.7	Age of magistrates	124
5.8	Number of years working as a magistrate	124
5.9	Criminal reports written by the Probation Service at magistrates' courts from Quarter 4, 2006 to Quarter 4, 2007, England and Wales	134
5.10	Clerks' understanding of NOMS	142
5.11	Clerks and contestability	143
5.12	Magistrates' understanding of NOMS	143
5.13	Magistrates and contestability	143

EXPLORING MODERN PROBATION

Social theory and organisational complexity

Philip Whitehead

This edition published in Great Britain in 2010 by

The Policy Press
University of Bristol
Fourth Floor
Beacon House
Queen's Road
Bristol BS8 1QU
UK

Tel +44 (0)117 331 4054
Fax +44 (0)117 331 4093
e-mail tpp-info@bristol.ac.uk
www.policypress.co.uk

North American office:
The Policy Press
c/o International Specialized Books Services (ISBS)
920 NE 58th Avenue, Suite 300
Portland, OR 97213-3786, USA
Tel +1 503 287 3093
Fax +1 503 280 8832
e-mail info@isbs.com

British Library Cataloguing in Publication Data
A catalogue record for this book is available from the British Library.

Library of Congress Cataloging-in-Publication Data
A catalog record for this book has been requested.

ISBN 978 1 84742 348 1 paperback
ISBN 978 1 84742 349 8 hardcover

Cover design by Janna Broadfoot
Front cover: image kindly supplied by www.istock.com
Printed and bound in Great Britain by Hobbs, Southampton

Acknowledgements

I have been interested in and a supporter of the moderating contribution of probation to the criminal justice system since the late 1970s. After undertaking a course of study to work as a probation officer at Lancaster University during 1979–81, I was offered employment by the Cleveland Probation Service where I remained for 26 years, until November 2007. During this lengthy period I made attempts to reflect on the nature of probation work; more recently my interests have been diverted towards engaging with the implications of profound transformations associated with the politics of modernisation. Consequently I am indebted to many people who have contributed to my work over many years. I first met David Smith at Lancaster in 1978 – he has probably forgotten this by now – when he told me I needed some practical experience before starting a period of training at university. On the strength of his advice I worked in a hostel for the homeless in Lancaster in 1978–79 before David became one of my probation lecturers. It is therefore fitting, and it also gives me pleasure, that he agreed to write the foreword to this book.

Since the early 1980s many colleagues have enriched my knowledge and understanding of probation and criminal and social justice, and I am particularly indebted to Roger Statham.

Since making the transition from the National Probation Service Teesside to being employed by Teesside University, the following people have influenced my thinking: Georgios A. Antonopoulos and Georgios Papanicolaou allowed me to become an honorary member of the Greek colony which continues to expand in the North East. They have also become very good friends and colleagues. Mark Cowling and Tracy Shildrick read and commented on a draft of the work. Jill Radford provided advice on the research. I also want to express my gratitude to Paul Crawshaw and Robin Bunton for their support and encouragement. My conversations with Kevin Dixon have been beneficial. I am also grateful for the opportunity to discuss a number of pertinent issues during two staff seminars held at Teesside University on the theme of modernisation and cultural change in criminal justice since 1997, and I am indebted to the anonymous reviewers appointed by The Policy Press to comment and provide advice on the initial book proposal and draft typescript. The research findings contained in Chapter 5 would not have been possible without permission granted by the 31 solicitors, 22 clerks and 20 magistrates. I am indebted to Judge Peter Fox QC, who made it possible for me to be provided with some quantitative data from judges, and to all those barristers who were willing to participate. Finally I want to thank my family who, understandably, have sometimes been bemused at the way in which I have been periodically distracted with the changing fortunes of an organisation. I cannot promise the distractions and obsessions will lessen during the next few years, but the subject matter is already changing its course. Therefore, and once again, I express my love and gratitude to Carolyn, Alex, Tim and Jenny.

Foreword

Professor David Smith, Lancaster University

In this book, as in his earlier work, Philip Whitehead deploys a wide range of sources to explore critical issues of policy and practice as they affect the Probation Service in England and Wales. Unusually among writers on such topics, he is alive to the insights that can be drawn from imaginative literature, as well as from philosophy and social theory. Combined with his own empirical work – interviews with criminal justice practitioners, but also a close reading of policy statements and political pronouncements – this approach produces a subtle and stimulating analysis of what has happened to the Probation Service and how this might be understood.

The focus of this book is on recent history – developments since the first 'New Labour' government was elected in 1997. Anyone who hoped that the change of government might lead to a revaluation upwards of the contribution of probation to the criminal justice process, let alone to support for a revival of its humanistic, person-centred traditions, must have been quickly disappointed. Not that such hopes could have had much empirical foundation: Jack Straw, Home Secretary in the first Blair government, was publicly committed to policies of 'modernisation' which left no room for anything that might look like sentimentality towards people who offend. While the Probation Service did not continue to suffer the malign neglect that was the most obvious feature of the Major government's attitude, from the outset New Labour's penal policy was characterised by a determination to talk and act tough. As has often been remarked, the New Labour government set new records in the pace and volume of new criminal justice legislation (for example Solomon et al, 2007), accompanied by organisational changes – notably in probation and youth justice – claimed to be necessary for the achievement of efficiency, consistency and rationality.

In New Labour's early years, however, there were grounds for optimism among those who continued to believe in the potential of the Probation Service to rehabilitate and reintegrate people in trouble. The Home Office's Crime Reduction Programme (CRP), the largest and most ambitious crime-related initiative ever undertaken by a British government, was implemented in 1999, with an intended lifespan of 10 years. Ten per cent of its £250 million budget was to be devoted to independent evaluation of the projects it supported, with the aim of improving the evidence base for effective practice (Maguire, 2004). Among the projects were a range of probation programmes designed to test the effectiveness in different contexts of work run on 'what works' principles – primarily, cognitive-behavioural group work with a focus on offending and related problems. Home Office researchers were cautiously optimistic at the start that the results would be positive (Vennard et al, 1997), but when the CRP was wound up in 2002 (after three years, not 10), little of this optimism remained. Now, it appeared, it was quite likely after all that nothing worked (the dismal orthodoxy of, roughly, 1975–90), although (supposedly) none of the research commissioned for the CRP was robust enough to show whether anything worked or not (Harper and Chitty, 2005).

Since then, the government's position on criminal justice policy, and the place of the Probation Service within it, has been defined by an odd combination of the claim that dramatic progress has been made and an insistence that much more must be done, as a matter of urgency. In a speech to trainee probation officers at the University of Portsmouth in early 2009, Jack Straw congratulated probation officers, or perhaps himself, on the 'distinct change in culture' which had come about in the past 10 years: 'Probation officers now routinely talk of the criminals they are dealing with as "offenders" – which is what they are – instead of the euphemistic language of "clients" which I encountered as Home Secretary' (Straw, 2009). He went on to give further evidence of improvement: 'More offenders are completing their orders than ever before and enforcement has improved dramatically. Now 95% of offenders are being brought back to court for breaching their orders; in 1999 this was a mere 44%'. (He meant, presumably, 95% of offenders who breach their orders.) Success is defined exclusively in terms of enforcement, not in terms of helping people change in constructive ways. In this respect New Labour's line on community penalties has been consistent: the constantly reiterated theme is that community penalties need to be made tougher, more demanding, more intensive and thus more punitive. A year earlier, the Ministry of Justice (2008a) published a 'briefing paper' which was mainly about prisons but also envisaged pilot or 'demonstrator' projects for an 'intensive control sentence' and an 'intensive punitive sentence', the latter to be made up of 'unpaid work and curfew'. All this is consistent with the overarching trends identified by Whitehead: the argument is that probation needs to become more punitive if it is to attract the support of sentencers and to build public confidence. It is thus endlessly committed to a competition with prison in which it cannot possibly win: no matter how intensive the restrictions of community supervision, they can never be as intensive as the restrictions of custody. There is no sense that probation might offer something different from custody; indeed, government statements often seek to blur the line between the two, stressing the rehabilitative potential of imprisonment, and the punitive component of probation.

Institutionally, this blurring of the boundary is represented by the National Offender Management Service (NOMS), the government's version of a national correctional service which, Whitehead suggests, will inevitably be dominated by concerns about prisons. In this organisational and policy context, he sees no prospect that the Probation Service will be able to retain the personalist, humanitarian approach which used to be seen as the main justification for its existence – although his respondents, less enthusiastic modernisers than the government, would like it to do so. Whitehead therefore concludes that if anyone is going to advise, assist and befriend offenders it will be from within the third sector, and perhaps especially from agencies representing faith communities. If third sector organisations can become embedded within NOMS (Whitehead's metaphor is that of a Trojan horse), they could provide support for offenders while whatever remains of the Probation Service attends to enforcement.

Whitehead's work reminds us that there are few new ideas in probation policy: a National Probation Service was mooted in 1962, and the idea of partnerships between the service and a range of voluntary agencies has been a recurring theme of government policy since at least the late 1980s. But there is no doubt that the pace and scale of change have both increased in the period covered by this book. As he is well aware, there still are examples of probation practice that would be recognisable as such to earlier generations of officers, but there is no doubt that they now have the air of being examples of an endangered species. This book provides an intelligent and provocative account of how they came to be so marginalised and vulnerable.

Introduction

The main purpose of this book is to explore and explain the phenomenon of modernisation and accompanying cultural transformations in probation and the wider criminal justice system since New Labour came to power in 1997. By doing so this book builds on and also develops two previous contributions within this specific field of enquiry. The first provided a historical overview of probation from 1876 to 2005 as the Probation Service approached its centenary year in 2007 (Whitehead and Statham, 2006). The second started to describe in greater detail more recent organisational and cultural mutations (Whitehead, 2007). This third and final book aims to develop a theoretical framework to facilitate the central task of exploration and explanation, as well as providing the final instalment of an empirical research project undertaken in the North East of England. Consequently this approach will help elucidate what the Probation Service has become under New Labour, in addition to allowing the research findings to articulate what it ought to be according to a number of respondents who agreed to be interviewed. Consequently the book unfolds as follows.

Chapter 1 clarifies the parameters of the book, which begins in 1997 with the election of New Labour to governmental office. It proceeds by establishing a visible index, a set of empirical indicators, of modernising features within the criminal justice system according to three continuous periods: 1997–2001, 2001–05 and 2005–2009/10. By proceeding chronologically it is possible to draw attention to some of the more salient modernising tendencies within probation contained in numerous documents that will be alluded to. Moreover, and according to one of my colleagues who reviewed the work, this chapter proceeds at a breathless pace. But, I would suggest, it needs to do so, precisely to capture the avalanche and ceaseless rapidity of those changes that have occurred in a relatively short period of time.

Chapter 2 begins by establishing the position that it is possible to construct different approaches to excavating the field of probation. The first approach constitutes a chronological description of key events. Second, one can proceed by thinking about the history of changing ideas exemplified, for example, in the work of Bill McWilliams (1983, 1985, 1986, 1987). But there is a third approach which makes it possible to consider the application of disparate bodies of social theory which draw attention to a number of insights associated with Durkheim, Weber, Marx and Foucault. In this chapter it is argued that this approach innovatively opens up rich and nuanced analytical possibilities in order to capture some of the modernising complexities that have evolved since 1997. It should be acknowledged that at certain points this chapter presents its own intellectual challenges due to the nature of the material under consideration which, it may be suggested, is difficult to avoid. Nevertheless the chapter concludes with what I hope is a helpful summary, in Table 2.1, of some of the key theoretical perspectives which will become relevant as the book proceeds.

Chapter 3 initially makes the point on the back of the preceding chapter that the Probation Service has become a complex organisation and that different social theories are useful in drawing attention to different organisational facets, for example, its heightened role in expressive forms of punishment (Durkheim), bureaucratic domination (Weber), the punishment and exclusion of problem populations under neoliberalism (Marxist) and the notion of disciplinary regulation (Foucault). However, it is not possible to remain analytically content with bodies of social theory associated with 'the big guys'. This is because one must not overlook the presence of 'the good guys' within the criminal justice system who belong to a discernible tradition supported by the lineaments of an ideology encapsulated in religion, a humanitarian outlook and social work help to individuals who offend. Here the emphasis is placed more on supportive welfare and rehabilitation rather than policies of punitisation, illustrated by what can be described as the existence of a personalist ethic. There is little doubt that the good guys have left their mark within probation, and that a vestige of personalism remains within the organisational dynamics of the National Offender Management Service (NOMS) that came into being during 2003–04. Nevertheless some of these benevolent features will be explored critically.

Chapter 4 puts bodies of social theory introduced in Chapter 2, in addition to religious and personalist impulses discussed in Chapter 3, to work. It is argued that the approach adopted in the two previous chapters can be combined to facilitate an excavation and explanation of the probation domain that has some analytical merit. In other words, it is suggested with accompanying empirical support that restyled offender managers (formerly known as probation officers) continue to operate within a modernised organisation, albeit in a restricted manner, as the good guys of the criminal justice system. But they can also be involved in expressive and occasionally illogical knee-jerk reactions, function as bureaucratic technicians, punish and exclude the residuum under neoliberal economic arrangements and operate as the disciplinary regulators and normalisers of the courts on behalf of New Labour. Therefore probation has become a complex organisation, ideologically diffuse, with traditional values compromised, which social theories and personalist impulses bring into focus. Consequently criminal justice, including probation practice, functions at levels beyond instrumental crime control. Accordingly, these four chapters constitute the first discrete part of the book.

Chapter 5 turns from bodies of social theory and personalist impulses to empirical research conducted in one criminal justice jurisdiction in the North East of England, known as 'Northtown'. In a work of this nature, it might be expected that this chapter presents research findings elicited from interviewing probation employees from *within* the organisation. However, this is not the case, which will be explained in due course. Instead I have been engaged in collecting data, both quantitative and qualitative, from a number of solicitors, court clerks and magistrates, including a more limited data set from barristers and judges, on themes pertinent to this book. Therefore there are features of this chapter that are arguably empirically innovative. Moreover tension is established between *what the Probation Service has become* (Chapters 1–4) and *what it ought to be* according to the views of some respondents. In fact some of the research undoubtedly challenges and provokes doubts about the modernising programme deemed necessary by New Labour, by retaining a place and space for pre-modern features that has significant implications for thinking about the future of criminal justice.

Finally, Chapter 6 draws the theoretical and empirical material together as the basis for presenting the view that in rebalancing probation and the criminal justice system through modernisation, the ability of the system to promote criminal and social justice has been unbalanced. In fact it is possible that modernisation has irreversibly politicised and punitised probation to such an extent that there is a new order of things, a new organisational social fact, the implications of which are considered towards the end of this concluding chapter.

ONE

Modernising probation and criminal justice since 1997

Introduction

This chapter provides an introductory and largely descriptive account of what the Probation Service has become, beginning with New Labour's manifesto of and election victory in 1997. My main area of concern is to establish a visible index of the direction of travel by alluding to a number of salient documents that bring into view a culturally transformed organisation. This approach also clarifies the operational parameters of modernisation within which this book has been constructed. However, before engaging with this task it should be acknowledged that from 1945 until the 1970s, the UK experienced a 'golden age' of inclusivist welfare and a criminal justice system majoring on rehabilitation rather than punishment (an *ideal type* construction, expounded in Garland [1985, 2001]). Nevertheless, by the late 1970s there were signs of dislocation within the post-war Keynesian schema, manifested in scaling back welfare provision and the emergence of tougher attitudes towards criminal justice (Hall et al, 1978; Brake and Hale, 1992; Cavadino and Dignan, 2006). Subsequently, from the onset of the Thatcherite era in 1979, and in the first instance until 1987, the rhetoric of law and order prevailed yet was tempered by, for example, the 1982 Criminal Justice Act, which introduced criteria to restrict the use of custody for young people (Whitehead and MacMillan, 1985; Charman and Savage, 1999). Indubitably there was a harsher melody line as the prison population continued to rise, but there were also less discordant voices. Subsequently, during 1987–92, the influence of Douglas Hurd's pragmatism moderated the Conservative motif of law and order as criminal justice became more managerialist, alongside a strategy of punishment in the community, ostensibly to hold down the prison population (Downes and Morgan, 1997). By contrast, between 1992 and 1997 the Howard–Major axis pressed the punitive law and order button in circumstances of economic difficulties and with the threat of New Labour on the horizon. Without much warning the gloves came off to expose penal hands brandishing the banner of prison works!

New Labour's election victory in 1997 signalled the evolution of a melange of contradictory penal and social forces. There was no wholesale abandonment of the links between socio-economic conditions and crime because of the salience given to tackling social exclusion, yet there would be no dilution of punitive toughness when responding to people who offended. New public management (Whitehead, 2007, p 34), inherited from previous Conservative administrations, existed alongside evidence-based 'what works' and the renaissance of a form of rehabilitation (Clarke et al, 2000). Prisons may not 'work' as effectively as community sentences, but there was no concerted policy to curb imprisonment in a climate of zero tolerance and when young people were singled out for special attention. Additionally, there remained an ongoing commitment to neoliberal economics and its complementary punitive orientation towards the individual; but then again restorative justice was part of the sentencing agenda. Consequently, New Labour has not turned back the clock to some halcyon period dominated by inclusivist welfare and anti-punishment sensibilities. Rather it has presented itself as a modern political force, pursuing a new Clintonian Democratic 'third way' (Jones and Newburn, 2004), with a mandate to modernise the country and its institutions. In other words, the political foundations of criminal justice have been expressed as: 'We must be tough; we must be modern; we must get value for money; we must be re-elected' (Cavadino and Dignan, 2006, p 75). Within this changing, modernised and modernising context, with elements of continuity reaching back to 1979, it is necessary to look more closely at the period from 1997 that established the operational parameters for more penetrating explorations and explanations later on.

New Labour and modernisation: 1997–2001

The political and electoral phenomenon of New Labour, in contradistinction to the social-democratic expression of pre-1990s' Old Labour,[1] has been associated with the overlapping themes of modernisation and cultural change. Enshrined within New Labour's manifesto leading up to the general election of May 1997, after 18 years of four consecutive Conservative administrations – *New Labour because Britain deserves better*[2] – modernisation was manifested in the way it called for a new bond of trust between the political establishment and the British people, exemplified in 10 specific commitments. These were enumerated as: education, tax, the economy, getting the unemployed into work and rebuilding the National Health Service (NHS). Importantly, at number six, was a reference to being tough on crime and its causes by halving the time it took persistent juvenile offenders to come to court.[3] The remaining four commitments were: families and communities in a modernised welfare state, the environment, the imperative to clean up politics and a statement about leadership in the modern world.

Of course New Labour's theology of 'behold I am doing a new thing' was in the process of being shaped before they were elected to governmental office. This involved setting the nation on a new course, in a spirit of rebuilding and renewing, on the solid foundation of a belief in progress and justice, values of equal worth (themes resonating with Old Labour), with no one cast aside in what would be a fairer and safer society (but see the critique in Wilkinson and Pickett, 2009). Additionally, within this latest version of the New Jerusalem, in a society rapidly approaching the new millennium, the politics of crime were constructed according to a narrative of personal responsibility that would receive a more punitive if not vindictive riposte. This approach set it apart from and also against the tenets of Old Labour, yet continued to forge a new consensus with Conservative penal philosophy since Michael Howard's right-wing lurch in 1993. In fact New Labour had already transformed its criminal justice outlook since the early 1990s so that the 1997 manifesto could claim it had become the natural party of law and order, a critical selling point if it aspired to secure electoral legitimacy. If the NHS was safe in New Labour's hands, the country could equally feel secure in the knowledge that the punishment of offenders would be as safe in the same capacious hands. Accordingly, modernising influences would fast-track the punishment of recalcitrant young people; reform the Crown Prosecution Service to convict more criminals; put more police in uniform on the beat; and crack down on petty crimes including the malaise of disorder. However, it should also be acknowledged, to maintain a sense of evidential balance, that a tougher and more punitive approach to offenders would not eschew the relationship between behavioural repertoires, differential opportunities, social deprivation and exclusion.[4]

Even though at no point in Campbell's (2007) journalistic apologia of the Blair era is there a specific reference to the Probation Service (it is subsumed beneath the reform of public services), it is difficult to entertain the view that probation was never mentioned prior to 1997 within political debates surrounding the modernising agenda. Having speculated, we are on solid ground by 1998 because the language of a modernised Probation Service was very much on the political agenda in a consultative document called *Prisons–probation: Joining forces to protect the public* (Home Office, 1998). After decades of ideological, philosophical and organisational distinctions between prisons and probation, a period of consultation was established in 1997 to explore ways in which probation and prisons could be better integrated with a view to improving efficiency and raising performance levels. In other words, according to the doctrines of new public management, could it be possible for these two organisations, which had for decades largely pursued their own distinctive penal–welfare trajectories, to work more closely together to reduce re-offending; better prepare prisoners for release; share resources, information, knowledge and skills; and reconfigure organisational structures to provide value for money?

In the second chapter of the prisons–probation review there is a reference to modernising the organisational framework of probation. It is also stated, as a matter of concern, that legislation continues to direct employees of the service to advise, assist and befriend (originally stated in the 1907 Probation of Offenders Act) which, without supporting evidence, is boldly claimed to be out of touch with the expectations of the courts and what probation work has become (but see Chapter 5, this volume). This is because the service has become more orientated towards public protection, which means that a modernised service must confront, challenge and change offenders, rather than provide advice, assistance and friendship, thus constituting a profound shift in tone. Accordingly, a harsher and more punitive discourse appears to be tantamount to the process of modernisation.[5] The document proceeds to state that there is a lack of probation accountability to central government due to fragmented governance arrangements, which at the time would have been disputed in the 56 local area services by the then chief probation officers (CPOs). Consequently, probation needed to be better organised, forging closer links with central government, the prison system, police, mental health services, local authorities and the Crown Prosecution Service. Interestingly the theme of modernisation and cultural transformation involved, the document argued, much clearer national direction and stronger national leadership, and the Home Secretary must be able to have political responsibility – in other words, centrally imposed command, power and control – over local area probation services. Windlesham concurs when stating that in the area of criminal policy, as in other areas of public administration, 'the demands of modernisation called for models of central control, rather than delegated authority and local accountability' (2001, p 245).

Finally, at paragraph 2.11 of the review (Home Office, 1998), the suggestion was made for a new organisational name to accompany the new nomenclature that would convey modernised messages. In other words, the Probation Service, with its considerable history and cachet (Whitehead and Statham, 2006), conveyed an image of tolerance towards crime and offenders that was no longer politically palatable. Therefore the organisation should be rebadged, from the Probation Service to the Public Protection Service, or perhaps the Community Justice Enforcement Agency. The 2000 Criminal Justice and Court Services Act signalled the culmination of a process beginning in the *Prisons–probation* document that saw the establishment of the National Probation Service in 2001. Consequently the word 'probation' was eventually preserved after much lobbying and deliberation between the organisation and the government. It can be argued that from 1997/98 probation was inextricably enmeshed in the politics of modernisation at the behest of New Labour modernisers (Nellis, 1999; Windlesham, 2001). This was driven home in 1999 when it was asserted that the government had a mission to modernise, to renew the country for the new millennium: 'modernising our schools, our hospitals, our economy and our criminal justice system' (Cabinet Office, 1999). Probation was therefore relaunched on a new trajectory based on the many changes that had already occurred since 1979 (Statham and Whitehead, 1992; Whitehead and Statham, 2006). Before moving on, it is interesting to acknowledge Raynor and Vanstone's analysis of this period because even though the prisons–probation review gave due consideration to the merging of two organisations into a single service, with a view to *reducing the cultural divide*, at this stage it was considered to be a step too far (Raynor and Vanstone, 2007, p 71). A step too far in 1998 but not by 2003, as we will see later.

A new urgency: 2001–05

By 2001, after a four-year term in office, New Labour's manifesto, *Ambitions for Britain*, included a number of pledges for the next five years on economics, schools and health. There was also a pledge for 6,000 extra police recruits to tackle drugs and crime and to build on the claim that crime was down by 10% compared with 1997 (in fact crime had been falling overall since the mid-1990s; see Reiner, 2007a, for an assessment of the relevant data). Once again attention was drawn to an agenda for more radical public service reform that included renewing public services to provide frontline staff with the freedom to respond to the needs of the public, particularly nurses, doctors, teachers and police officers (probation officers were not included in this list). The language of 'tough on crime' was repeated, as were the related themes of punishment and individual responsibility for one's actions, seemingly regardless of differential social circumstances. In fact, outbursts of criminality were constructed almost in millenarian–apocalyptic terms as a battle that had to be fought and won by government on behalf of the people. In other words, this was a war against crime, or, more specifically, a war against certain impoverished sections of the community waged by government in support of the law-abiding. It has been pointed out that the war on crime, including the war on terror and war on poverty, became a cogent motif of political governance in the US that helped legitimate the expansion of governmental power, punishment and authoritarian control. By doing so it helped drain away the real causes of social conflicts rooted in the 'asymmetrical effects of power' (Simon, 2007, p 14). This tone was duplicated in the UK when, in the Casey report, it was stated that crime was tackled most effectively when the law-abiding majority 'stand together against the minority who commit it' (Cabinet Office, 2008, p 4).

Reforming and modernising impulses towards the criminal justice system were also the subject of a White Paper that would speed up the prosecutions of offenders, take victims much more seriously and continue the fight against crime, in addition to the development of crime and disorder reduction partnerships (CDRPs). The fight would also continue against anti-social behaviour and what was emotively referred to in 19th-century terms as a 'yob' culture. It should also be acknowledged that there was a greater sense of urgency to reform and modernise after the election victory in 2001, encapsulated in the political gimmickry of the benefit sanction and rigorous enforcement procedures (Windlesham, 2003). Therefore, at this point, we need to explore this White Paper in a little more detail. *Criminal justice: The way ahead*, published in February 2001 (Home Office, 2001a), begins by acknowledging in structuralist, social exclusion mode that the increase in crime over the past 25 years was partly a result of unemployment and lack of opportunities for the unskilled, the increasing blight of drugs and the availability of consumer goods. Consequently, even though the mechanisms for the creation of a responsible and law-abiding society do not inhere solely within state criminal justice systems – in other words, socio-economic and wider structural factors must be factored into an analysis of human behaviour which balances structure and agency – nevertheless, a modernised criminal justice system must function instrumentally to prevent crime and reduce re-offending, be efficient at dealing with cases, respond appropriately to victims and be more accountable for its decisions. Fundamentally, what was desirable was a criminal justice system that delivered justice for all (Home Office, 2001a, p 5).

Parts 1 and 2 of the White Paper summarise the reforms introduced since 1997,[6] in addition to expatiating on the theme of modernisation. It is explained that the criminal justice system would continue to be modernised in response to marked changes in society and associated patterns of crime. This would be effected by catching and convicting more of the hard-core persistent offenders and dealing with them expeditiously (according to *Criminal justice*, 100,000 hard-core offenders could be responsible for half of all crime); and by tough and effective punishments which would become more intense for persistence. This meant that the more you offended the tougher it would be, a theme contained in the 2003 Criminal Justice Act which reflected a different penal philosophy to proportionality underpinning the 1991 Criminal Justice Act. Modernisation is also associated with giving the police, Crown Prosecution Service, courts and other agencies what they required to do the job defined by central government, and to build public confidence in the work they did. Moreover, modernisation encapsulates the Auld (2001) review of and reforms to criminal law (begun in 1999); the Halliday review of sentencing practices (begun in 2000, but see Home Office, 2001b); reducing delays in the system; bringing more people to justice; a better deal for witnesses and victims; and facilitating more effective partnerships with a view to enhancing delivery of services. It also involved the creation of the National Probation Service that occurred in 2001. Again attention is drawn to the political importance attached to enforcement practices, a theme resonating throughout many of the documents under consideration (Home Office, 2001a, para 2.78). But if these changes were not challenging enough for the criminal justice system to absorb, along came another set of reforms that established what was to become the National Offender Management Service (NOMS) as the veritable exemplar of modernisation.

In 2002 Patrick Carter was asked to undertake a review of correctional services. Subsequently, while the year 2003 witnessed the arrival of the latest Criminal Justice Act, which had significant implications for the work of the National Probation Service (based on the Halliday review but not implemented until 2005), it also saw the appearance of Carter's deliberations: *Managing offenders, reducing crime: A new approach* (2003). This report included an analysis of the state of the prisons, overcrowding and the lack of help available for short-term prisoners associated with the fact that no one agency had responsibility for offender services. Consequently Carter proposed the linear concept of end-to-end management of offender services and the creation of a single agency to deliver it in the form of NOMS (Hough et al, 2006; Gelsthorpe and Morgan, 2007). There would be a chief executive and national offender manager and 10 regional offender managers who would be responsible for commissioning services – both custodial provision and in the community – for the management of offenders in that region. Moreover and importantly, the goals of effectiveness, better performance and target achievement (see Whitehead, 2007, which includes a critique of targets) would be sharpened up via a mechanism of contestability in what would be a marketised mixed economy of provision. In other words, it is possible that the work currently being undertaken by probation could be awarded to other organisations within the public, private and voluntary sectors. This was not a novel policy development because during the early 1990s, a decade before the arrival of NOMS, the monopoly position of probation was being challenged by the rise of a pluralism of offender services providers (Fullwood, 1994).

It is important to confirm that impulses towards help and support for offenders remain part of NOMS in that services exist to respond to problems in relation to accommodation, education, training and employment, finances and addictions. By contrast, the new organisation has been criticised for sustaining a politics of punitive controlism, depersonalisation, deprofessionalisation and promoting a responsibilisation strategy. On the theme of punitive controlism, the retributive penal agenda, fuelled by punitive populism, radically threatened to shift the purpose of probation 'from one of caring control to one of punitive control' (Burnett et al, 2007, p 228). Furthermore, the National Association of Probation Officers (NAPO) and the Probation Boards Association (Gelsthorpe and Morgan, 2007) have raised a number of concerns in response to developments associated with NOMS, specifically privatisation and contestability.

By 2004 the strategic aim of *Confident communities in a secure Britain* (Home Office, 2004a) was boldly articulated in terms of social change to achieve enhanced security, whatever this meant. Additionally the objectives of the Home Office for a safe, just, tolerant society included helping people to feel more secure in their homes and communities. It was therefore stated that the interests of the law-abiding citizen would come first and that they would be protected from the threat of terrorism, illegal immigration and crime on the streets. The theme of modernisation continues to reverberate throughout this document when it turns to address ongoing reforms within the criminal justice system, the programme of structural and organisational changes that commenced in 1997, and elevating the status of victims. Moreover, there were supporting references to Halliday and the 2003 Criminal Justice Act, the delivery of effective punishments, the creation of NOMS, enforcement and crime prevention. But it is also important to acknowledge that offenders would not be left without support to respond to the requirement to change behaviours. Nevertheless, if offenders did not respond positively to the offer of support, negative consequences would follow in the form of tougher enforcement, thus drawing attention to the complex relationship between support and rehabilitation, enforcement and punishment, inclusionary and the menacing threat of exclusionary forces. The prevailing discussion on criminality is very much directed at low-level street crime rather than, for example, at the social harms inflicted by the powerful, even though a number of documents under discussion in this chapter have sections on the phenomenon of organised crime.

Next, according to *Cutting crime, delivering justice* (Home Office, 2004b), published concurrently with *Confident communities in a secure Britain*, the vision for the criminal justice system during the next five years was articulated by the following language: increased public confidence in the system; victims and witnesses should receive a high standard of service; bring more offenders to justice; rigorous enforcement receives yet another mention; joined-up services; and reducing delays within the system – these constitute the formal elements of modernisation. Once again, modernising reforms that had occurred since 1997 were reprised and there was specific reference to probation within the context of more resources being allocated to the police, Crown Prosecution Service and prisons. In fact, when turning to probation it was lamented that the training of new probation officers had ceased under the Conservatives between 1995 and 1998, with the result that no newly qualified staff had entered the profession for several years in the 56 local area services (Whitehead and Statham, 2006). Moreover, breach/enforcement action had been a particular problem until the system was tightened up in the 2000–02 National Standards.[7] It is also important to acknowledge that these documents published during 2004 signalled an end to the so-called 1960s' liberal consensus on law and order. Therefore, creating safer communities would be pursued through a punitive war on crime, rather than ameliorative social policies to reduce the deleterious effects of inequality (Wilkinson and Pickett, 2009).

Since 2005

New Labour's 2005 manifesto, *Britain forward not back*, repeated the message of tough on crime and its causes, and proudly acknowledged that sentences had become tougher, illustrated by the fact that there were 16,000 more prison places compared with 1997. It is also stated that the newly created NOMS would ensure that every offender would be individually case-managed from the beginning to the end of their sentence. Furthermore, the Respect agenda was increasingly important but, in his book on *Penal populism*, John Pratt (2007) persuasively argues that the notion of respect had contingent social conditions. These were enumerated as commitment, trust, tolerance, loyalty, stability and security, which were being eroded by neoliberal economic conditions that favoured the few rather than the many (2007, p 121). Additionally, the manifesto referred to Anti-social Behaviour Orders (ASBOs), which resulted in the criminalisation of low-level disorderliness; a proper focus on victims and the law-abiding majority; and the commitment to cut crime and send dangerous offenders to prison. There was also a reference to making community sentences more effective, a persistent theme over the last two decades.

On 19 September 2005 Charles Clarke, former Home Secretary, made a speech to the Prison Reform Trust on 'Where next for penal policy'. While sentencing within the reformed criminal justice system was conducted according to various and incompatible sentencing philosophies,[8] the introduction to this speech continued to affirm that the government would be tough on crime and criminals, particularly dangerous and persistent offenders. The Home Secretary proceeded to refer to a contract between the offender and the state that would involve a commitment not to re-offend. Additionally, the provision of help and support to offenders should be provided not only by the statutory services, but also the voluntary/faith sector in the form of community chaplaincies. In other words, the provision of help to offenders and families on release from prison could be enhanced by building links between churches and communities[9] as an integral part of the NOMS strategy. However, when turning to discuss prison Clarke naively states that the central strategy must be to take all possible steps 'to encourage prisons to become colleges for constructive citizenship rather than recruiting sergeants for crime'. This is naive rhetoric, utilised for symbolic effect, because the prison service has not managed to achieve this in 200 years.[10]

Importantly the Home Secretary's speech addressed NOMS within the context of organisational change and the way in which this part of the strategy would deliver the modernisation agenda in the criminal justice system, by bringing prisons and probation closer together. The central priority was articulated as the reduction of re-offending by 5% by 2008 and then 10% by 2010. The role of the new offender manager was considered – note the change of job designation from *probation officer* to *offender manager* – as was the plan to develop a mixed economy of provision, thus breaking up the monopoly position of the Probation Service in the delivery of offender services. It was stated that NOMS was committed to rehabilitation, but it was also acknowledged that while a number of prison and probation areas had made a positive response to the prevailing challenges and improved, there were other areas that had not achieved as much as the government considered necessary. This was the reason Charles Clarke was personally committed to the creation of a vibrant mixed economy within NOMS. The policy being reinforced was that to utilise untapped resources that existed outside the public sector there would be a system of contestability in which the public, private and voluntary sectors would contest with each other for the contracts to deliver offender services. Consequently, the vision for the future consisted of regional offender managers purchasing services from different providers (which may no longer be a probation organisation), who would be expected to achieve targets and provide value for money, the rationale being to drive up standards of performance within a market-driven criminal justice system. Once again there is a message on the importance of rigorous enforcement that has become a deeply symbolic cause célèbre during the modernising programme of New Labour.

During 2005, then updated in 2006, the Home Office was involved in the production of the NOMS offender management model (NOMS, 2006). Included within this document was guidance to probation areas on the tiering (stacking) of cases, the rationale being to relate resources to the assessed category of risk – low, medium, high and very high risk. Consequently there were four substantive tiers, all of which would deliver some form of punishment to the offender, even though the document also articulated the importance of social work relationships: tier 1, punish; tier 2, punish and help; tier 3, punish and help and change; tier 4, punish and help and change and control. It should be clarified that tier 1 cases comprised low- to medium–risk categories; by contrast tier 4 contained high- to very high-risk categories, including public protection cases. Tiers 3 and 4 would attract most of the resources and be the preserve of trained and professionally qualified staff. Next we consider a spate of documents that appeared during 2006.

Notwithstanding the complexities involved in obtaining an accurate picture of crime statistics, *A five-year strategy for protecting the public and reducing re-offending* (Home Office, 2006a) restated the claim that while crime was decreasing, the strategic aim remained to cut re-offending, protect the public, keep the right people in prison and manage the risks posed by offenders. In fact the offender manager was responsible for the punishment and rehabilitation of offenders including the promotion of closer links with the prison system via the newly emerging NOMS structure. This document therefore underlined the political message that while the language of punishment, reparation and rehabilitation were interrelated, punishment was a legitimate activity in prison and the community and that both organisations should help prevent re-offending. In fact the context remains one of being tough on crime, illustrated by the assertion that we are 'catching and convicting more criminals' (Home Office, 2006a, para 1.4). It is imperative that the public must be kept safe from serious, violent, dangerous and persistent offenders. Risks must be identified and managed via the offender assessment system (OASys; but see Mair et al, 2006), which is considered one of the most advanced systems of its kind in the world (Home Office, 2006a, para 2.2). Once again certain key political messages were delivered about enforcement (para 3.12): the document states that when offenders breached their community orders, over 90% were enforced (the process of returning them to the sentencing court normally after two failed appointments) within 10 working days. Nevertheless, managing offenders to prevent re-offending and improving compliance could be enhanced by confronting and resolving factors related to obtaining work, housing and drugs (para 4.3). In other words, there remained an uneasy alliance between the discourses of punitive toughness and ongoing support for some of the underlying causes of unlawful behaviour, which OASys was expected to identify.

Much had been achieved since 1997 when the reforming modernisers came to power. Nevertheless, the dominant message of *Re-balancing the criminal justice system* (Home Office, 2006b) was that the modernisation of the criminal justice system was not yet complete. It was claimed that crime had fallen by 35% since 1997, and the risk of becoming a victim of crime was the lowest since the British Crime Survey began in 1981. Public confidence in the criminal justice system was on the rise, and worry about anti-social behaviour had fallen since the commencement of the Respect programme, alluded to earlier. Modernisation, which had assumed the quality of a permanent revolution, was constructed positively by recourse to the provision of more resources for criminal justice agencies, investment, improved performance, partnerships, NOMS, stricter enforcement, new laws, ASBOs and bringing more people to justice. In fact, while so much had been achieved, the system must nevertheless be rebalanced in favour of victims rather than offenders themselves. On compliance and enforcement (para 2.32) it was reinforced that in addition to ensuring appropriate sentences were imposed, the public continued to expect the criminal justice system to enforce them effectively, with robust measures to secure compliance. Accordingly, the 2003 Criminal Justice Act and accompanying National Standards introduced a system of more onerous requirements. In other words, offenders are currently punished for non-compliance with extra requirements or even a custodial sentence (para 2.34). Paragraph 3.29 addresses probation specifically by stating that resources should target serious offenders rather than work with minor offenders, a point underpinned by the new tiering system. The intention also remains to break up probation's monopoly by creating a mixed economy of provision through the NOMS structure that would require new legislation to enable other potential providers to get involved. Finally, the document turned to the aspiration of *Delivering simple, speedy, summary justice* (Home Office, 2006c), and its potentially serious implications for the Probation Service are now considered.

This document, another integral component of the modernising agenda, was an attempt to push ahead with a more effective but also efficient criminal justice system, particularly within the operational dynamics of the magistrates' courts that deal with 95% of all criminal cases. It is further clarified that the latest vision for the criminal justice system must include the following categories:

- *Simple:* dealing with some specific cases transparently by way of warning, caution or some other effective remedy to prevent re-offending without recourse to the court process.
- *Speedy:* those cases that need the court process will be dealt with fairly but as quickly as possible.
- *Summary:* a much more proportionate approach still involving due process – for example dealing with appropriate cases the day after charge or during the same week – which would constitute a change in the way cases are currently dealt with in the magistrates' courts.

This agenda has profound implications for the work of probation, primarily because the pressure to deal with more and more cases expeditiously touches the organisation critically at the point where reports (written documents) are being prepared for the courts, particularly the magistrates' courts. In other words, one of the aims of the triple 'S' agenda (simple, speedy, summary) was to reduce the average number of hearings before a case was finally sentenced from five/six to an expectation of one for guilty pleas, which would effectively eradicate costly adjournments, and if the court required more information on the offender then this would be in the form of a fast delivery report (FDR) rather than a full and detailed pre-sentence report (PSR). Therefore modernisation could at one level be construed positively in terms of effective and efficient case management (the application of new public management principles: see Whitehead and Statham, 2006). By contrast, speed may have moral implications in relation to the delivery of criminal and social justice (Cook, 2006). This is an area of development that will be considered in some detail in Chapter 5 when I turn to discuss the research findings on this specific area of probation work.

By 2006 it was over two years since the Carter report resulted in the emergence of NOMS, and progress had been made, even though it needed to continue in the direction of using the talents of public, private and voluntary agencies. As John Reid stated in *Public value partnerships*, the public sector is valued and will have a continuing role to play. 'However, all current providers should be open to challenge and able to demonstrate that the services they offer are the best available' (Home Office, 2006d, p 3). The rationale of this document was therefore the development of NOMS principles, primarily the creation of a mixed economy of offender services. In fact if the Probation Service was failing under the reconstituted arrangements it could be taken over by another organisation to deliver effective and efficient services. It was clearly stated that government plans for extending contestability were not to cut costs or even to have competition for its own sake. Rather it was about improving standards of service and encouraging innovative practices that would result in less crime and getting the best mix of services and service providers.

Moving on, the Prime Minister's Strategy Unit (PMSU) (2006) produced an interesting document, *Policy review: Crime, justice and cohesion*, initially confirming that there had been a regime of tougher sentencing since 1997. For example, the average length of custodial sentences at the Crown Court increased from 20 to 30 months between 1994 and 2004. Moreover there had been an increase in the use made of community sentences that were also more demanding, but they displaced fines rather than being direct alternatives to custodial sentences. Therefore a more punitive culture had been deliberately created within the criminal justice system. Equally important was the assessment that recent decreases in crime were due to positive economic factors, but alternatively we read how the Home Office is predicting that crime will begin to rise because the economy is slowing down (PMSU, 2006, p 13). This point raises important questions which touch directly on the efficacy of the criminal justice system, contrasted with an inclusive and protective social policy response, during adverse socio-economic conditions (Garland, 1985, 2001, p 90; Young, 2007; Wacquant, 2008, 2009). This point is reinforced by Zedner when she persuasively argues that the 'social, economic, and cultural sources of crime control thus extend deep into social policy and cannot be supplied by the criminal justice system alone' (2006, p 153). Additionally, during September 2008 a leaked Home Office letter – 'Responding to economic challenges' – warned that the global economic downturn was expected to result in more crime, fewer police and more illegal immigration coupled with far Right extremism. After studying previous recessions and effects on crime and policing, Home Office computer modelling indicates that an economic downturn 'would place significant upward pressure on acquisitive crime and therefore overall crime figures' (reported in the *Telegraph* on 1 September 2008; see also Reiner, 2007b, and his analysis of how the rise in crime since the 1970s and accompanying law and order responses must take account of neoliberal policies).

As we progress towards the end of this introductory chapter, *Ten years of criminal justice under Labour* (Solomon et al, 2007) is a significant publication because it constituted an independent audit of significant events since 1997. One can recapitulate by saying that since 1997 the intentions of New Labour were clear in relation to being tough on crime and its causes, introducing modernising reforms across the public sector, which included the criminal justice system manifested by more investment, a new (harsher) nomenclature, resulting in cultural transformations and ideological dislocations (Whitehead, 2007). The priorities of the New Labour phenomenon have been narrowing the justice gap (bringing more offenders to justice), reducing re-offending and dealing with anti-social behaviour. Moreover, the big issues have drawn attention to policing, reforms to youth justice and tackling drugs. Indubitably more resources have been pumped into the criminal justice system[11] but the critical question remains – has it all worked? The audit results are somewhat mixed, notwithstanding the many modernising reforms which have been implemented and pushed through at a relentless pace. Significantly, and this echoes the aforementioned Cabinet Office document (PMSU, 2006), questions remain about the efficacy of the criminal justice system to achieve its objectives. In other words, is it the right instrument to respond to illegal forms of behaviour particularly when some of these are associated with socio-economic structural factors?

Next, the importance of the Carter review of prisons, published in December 2007, was not so much the proposal for Titan prison establishments to expand the capacity of the prison estate (in fact Titans were abandoned in April 2009). Rather I am interested in the analysis of those *drivers* behind the 60% (more than 30,000) rise in the prison population in England and Wales between June 1995 and November 2007, by which time it stood at 81,547. First, Carter touches on changes in public attitudes and the political climate, from the law and order themes of the 1980s; break-up of consensus, economic decline, rising crime and retreat from rehabilitation; the Jamie Bulger and Stephen Lawrence murders in 1993 and accompanying media responses; and developments within community punishment and the prison works debate in the 1990s. Consequently, there was a much greater public preoccupation with crime, fuelled by media reporting, accompanied by a heightened emotional tone in the way crime issues were presented (Freiberg and Gelb, 2008). Second, legislation and the sentencing framework, including the drift towards more punitive sentencing, were alluded to, particularly the 66 pieces of legislation since 1995. On this point it is interesting to refer to the comments of Lord Justice Auld when he said that the public's confidence in the criminal justice system was damaged if, as had happened all too often over recent years, legislative reforms were insufficiently considered and 'hurried through in seeming response to political pressures or for quick political advantage' (Auld, 2001, p 19). Third, custody rates and sentence lengths have increased along with greater sentencer demand for probation and prison. In fact, the number of community penalties at all courts increased from 129,922 in 1995 to 190,837 in 2006. Fourth, and as already alluded to earlier, there has been a much greater focus on harsher enforcement practices and more emphasis on risk, harm and public protection. When turning to the newly created Suspended Sentence Order, introduced by the 2003 Criminal Justice Act, Carter states that a significant number of suspended prison sentences were currently being given for summary offences and it appeared that 'a significant number of these would previously have received non-custodial sentences' (Carter, 2007, p 51).

A new Ministry of Justice was created in May 2007, which assumed responsibility for probation and prisons following the shake-out within the Home Office. By the end of 2007 Patrick Carter, as we have just seen, published his review on prisons. One of the proposals contained in the review was for a reappraisal of the headquarters function of NOMS that would have implications for both prisons and probation. In other words, the restructuring of offender services associated with the creation of NOMS during 2003/04 was itself now being restructured. This was initiated during January 2008 with a view to improving the efficiency and effectiveness of managing offenders and the refocusing of resources to enhance frontline delivery. By March 2008 this amounted to bringing probation and prisons even closer together within a streamlined headquarters function, and the rationalisation of regional structures. With this latest bout of restructuring Phil Wheatley, who was Director General of Her Majesty's Prison Service (HMPS), became Director General of NOMS. Consequently there have been material changes to the upper managerial and strategic reaches of the organisation. One significant outcome of this restructuring is that probation no longer exists separately from, or even on equal terms with, the prison system. Instead it has been subsumed beneath rather than standing alongside the Director General. In fact the organisational map of the restructured NOMS, produced in July 2008, revealed that the Director of Probation, Roger Hill, no longer occupied a position standing shoulder to shoulder with Phil Wheatley. Rather he was relocated below the Director General and set alongside seven directors who were in turn responsible for operations, high security, finance and performance, human resources (HR), the capacity programme, commissioning and offender health. By the autumn of 2008 it became clear that the Director of Probation would not be replaced when Roger Hill became the Director of Offender Management in the South East region. Therefore, streamlining appears to have greater implications for probation than prison, even though, at the NAPO Conference on 17 October 2008, the Minister of State, David Hanson, denied this was a merger or even the prison takeover of probation. Accordingly, both agencies would remain as individual delivery services with their own governance and employment structures. Nevertheless it is difficult to square these disarming ministerial comments with the latest NOMS organisational structure.

It should be acknowledged that changes at the national level were established on 1 April 2008 and that further changes to regional structures were introduced by April 2009. This means that each of the 10 regions will appoint a director of offender management (from regional offender manager to director of offender management, and an advert was placed in the *Sunday Times* on 2 November 2008) to coordinate and commission all probation and prison services from the public, private and third/voluntary sectors consistent with the legislative provisions contained in the 2007 Offender Management Act. In fact such arrangements were put in place in London and Wales during 2008, which meant that the Prison Service London Area Office and the office of the regional offender manager were formally merged in the office of director of offender management. It may be suggested that these latest changes are largely cosmetic, primarily concerned to save money, and will hardly be noticed lower down the organisational structure by prison officers and probation offender managers when working with offenders. On the other hand, senior managerial and organisational reconfigurations within NOMS could culminate in the declining influence of the probation ethos throughout the whole of the criminal justice system. If this is the case then the following reflections on restructuring the restructuring are offered for consideration.

First, the wide-ranging changes that have affected probation during the last decade in particular were not a result of slow evolutionary processes *initiated from within*, but rather swift and decisive revolutionary changes *imposed from without* by central government for political more than sound penological reasons. Moreover, these were not the kind of changes which necessarily would have been chosen by the organisation itself, then slowly introduced over a period of time after a careful analysis of their likely implications. Rather they were a series of convulsive events that rapidly transformed the character of the organisation, which continues with the latest phase of restructuring. There was opposition to many of these enforced changes, particularly from NAPO. Nevertheless, it may be asked to what extent the *leadership* of the organisation itself has been complicit in (because it has largely gone along with) the many changes that have occurred.

Second, it may be suggested that initiatives designed to encourage organisations to work more closely together to reduce cultural divides (the language of partnership arrangements) could be perceived as a laudable objective with more attendant positive than negative features. By contrast, when organisations are 'forced' to move closer together at the behest of political and strategic imperatives, the end result could be that the distinctive contributions of each institution are considerably diluted. Such developments can, for example, damage those necessary checks and balances within the criminal justice system that rely on the disparate influences and contributions of its component parts. In other words, competing and sometimes discordant voices heard from within different organisations can be a sign of health rather than malaise (from prisons *and* probation, magistrates *and* judges, police, court clerks *and* defence solicitors), particularly when developing policies that respond effectively to offending behaviour. The necessary mechanisms for maintaining the strength of different organisations and democratic institutions are: the testing out of cogent arguments; the challenge of different perspectives; listening to and learning from each other's organisational perspective, values and responsibilities; and steering a course through contrasting positions which includes critiques of central government policies. Intriguingly this perspective finds some support from a barrister in the North East of England who participated in a research project, the results of which are produced in Chapter 5. He made the insightful point that:

> "The Probation Service has changed beyond recognition over the course of the last 10 years. The shift of the Probation Service has left the criminal justice system unbalanced. There is too much emphasis on punishment and a void where there should be an agency dedicated to values of befriending and assisting."

In other words, probation should have a clearly articulated and different organisational rationale to other criminal justice organisations, and arguably this difference should be strengthened rather than diluted through streamlining and coalescing.

Third, at one level it can be argued that rationalisation and streamlining organisational functions to conserve limited financial resources is another laudable objective. It is reasonable to suggest that organisations should not be allowed to become bloated on the back of taxpayers' money, and the principles of economy and efficiency can be compelling. However, the view can be advanced that criminal justice should not solely be guided by fiscal principles, encapsulated by the new public management. Dealing with people who offend, justifying punishment and recourse to community or custodial sentences raises profound moral issues taking the debate beyond financial, bureaucratic and managerial priorities. Probation, until relatively recently, constituted a challenge to punishment and imprisonment and by doing so made a distinctive contribution throughout the 20th century to criminal and social justice. But this distinctive sphere of influence is being eroded by further restructuring that, increasingly, could see the prison agenda dominate probation's historic mission. Those features that set probation apart have been denigrated, and a discourse of punitive excesses has displaced sociological understanding and explication. Therefore it may be suggested that what is currently taking shape is not in the interests of either prison or probation. This is because a strong probation service, which has a distinctive and separate voice within NOMS, and which is allowed to promote the probation ideal,[12] could help to ensure prisons are used as a last resort for more serious offenders, to save on costs and reduce pressure on hard-pressed staff within overcrowded prisons without compromising on the goals of efficiency and effectiveness.

Conclusion: behold a new heaven and a new earth

This chapter has defined the operational parameters of modernisation and accompanying cultural shifts, in addition to introducing the supporting language of change within probation and the wider criminal justice system. Of course it would be possible to suggest that the first bout of modernisation could be traced to the 1948 Criminal Justice Act, or perhaps later to the 1980s, which have a better claim on the term. Nevertheless, the starting point was deliberately established at 1997, with earlier periods covered in previous work (Whitehead and Statham, 2006; Whitehead, 2007). Towards the end of 2008 the Justice Secretary, Jack Straw, gave a speech to the Royal Society of Arts in London on the theme of punishment and reform (27 October 2008). The speech was constructed as a justificatory reprise of what New Labour had done in the field of criminal justice, which included an unseemly boast about the policy of punitive toughness that had been pursued towards offenders – the new criterion of success. There was also a litany of predictable themes: 14,000 more police; 30% more prison places; but even this is not enough because 12,500 additional places will be required by 2014 to increase capacity to 96,000, even though adult offending is down by 23% and youth offending down by 19%. However, there is an analytical drought when it comes to explaining the circumstances in which many of these features were deemed necessary, and there was little in this speech that was novel. In fact it is a case of more of the same (Goodman, 2003).

In another speech the following month (17/18 November 2008), this time to the influential Magistrates' Association, Straw made it clear that the Comprehensive Spending Review of 2007 meant that by March 2011 there should be £1 billion worth of savings across the Ministry of Justice. The aim remained to deliver a fair system of justice, but could this be achieved if there were 10,000 job cuts in probation, prison and court services? Nevertheless the expansion of punishment talk, organisational restructuring associated with NOMS, new public management principles, centralisation and accompanying deprofessionalisation within local probation areas, and the end of social work encapsulated within advise, assist and befriend, remain as some of the talismanic fixtures of the new penal heaven and earth.

Finally, modernisation is being manifested in fluorescent vests adorning offenders on community payback, only one small step from US-style chain gangs. As the Jews were ghettoised in Renaissance Europe (Venice being a stark example) and much later forced to wear the distinguishing yellow star as the mark of a racially excluded and denigrated *other*, so offenders undertaking unpaid work in the community bear the mark of Cain as a deviant and exclusionary *other*. The New Jerusalem of modernisation and cultural change, *extraordinarily cemented in place by the political Left rather than Right*, has taken a nastier turn. But there could be more to come because the Justice Secretary, in a speech to trainee probation officers at the University of Portsmouth on 4 February 2009, stated that community sentences still had an image problem by appearing too 'soft' (Straw, 2009). Does this mean that probation employees will be transmuted into 'soft cops' to enhance their credibility with the public (Goodman, 2003, p 219); or perhaps muscular attack dogs of the penal state snapping at the heels of offenders in the community? Some of the key events since 1997 are summarised in Table 1.1.

Table 1.1: Summary of significant developments, 1997–2009

1997	Labour Party manifesto: *New Labour because Britain deserves better*
1998	*Prisons–probation: Joining forces to protect the public* (Home Office)
1999	*Modernising government* (Cabinet Office) Lord Justice Auld's review of the courts commenced
2000	Halliday review of sentencing began, which culminated in the 2003 Criminal Justice Act National Standards (revised 2002) introducing stricter enforcement
2001	*Criminal justice: The way ahead* (Home Office) National Probation Service commenced on 1 April New Labour manifesto: *Ambitions for Britain*
2002	Patrick Carter asked to review correctional services
2003	Criminal Justice Act (partially implemented 4 April 2005) Carter report: *Managing offenders, reducing crime: A new approach*, signalled the beginning of NOMS
2004	*Confident communities in a secure Britain: The Home Office strategic plan 2004–2008* (Home Office) *Cutting crime, delivering justice: A strategic plan for criminal justice 2004–2008* (Home Office)
2005	New Labour manifesto: *Britain forward not back* National Standards revised NOMS model
2006	*A five-year strategy for protecting the public and reducing re-offending* (Home Office) *Re-balancing the criminal justice system in favour of the law-abiding majority* (Home Office) *Delivering simple, speedy, summary justice* (Home Office) *Improving prison and probation services* (Home Office) *Policy review: Crime, justice and cohesion* (PMSU)
2007	*Ten years of criminal justice under Labour: An independent audit* (Solomon et al) Ministry of Justice created National Standards updated Offender Management Bill received Royal Assent on 26 July Carter review of prisons published in December
2008	NOMS restructuring undertaken Louise Casey report: *Engaging communities in fighting crime* David Hanson's speech to the NAPO conference on 17 October Jack Straw's speech during October on punishment and victims *Punishment and reform* (Ministry of Justice)
2009	NOMS strategic business plans 2009–11 Jack Straw's speech to trainee probation officers at the University of Portsmouth

Notes

[1] A clear distinction should be established between Old and New Labour. It is worth recalling that the Labour Party was out of office for 18 years between 1979 and 1997, a period in which there were four consecutive general election defeats at the hands of the Conservatives. Consequently it has been argued that a critical factor in the reconstruction of Labour, particularly after 1992, was a significant change in the direction of penal policy. What had been an antipathy towards the police and a predisposition for explaining offending behaviour by reference to socio-economic disadvantage were now seen 'by the modernisers as being increasingly out of step with the public demand for greater protection from the consequences of criminal acts' (Windlesham, 2003, p 61). It is also helpful to be acquainted with the material contained in Robert Reiner's *Law and order* (2007a) on this theme.

[2] For more information on party political manifestos since 1945 see: www.psr.keele.ac.uk/area/uk/man.htm. Another useful resource is the excellent chapter in *The Oxford handbook of criminology* by Downes and Morgan (1997).

[3] There is a collection of useful texts on the subject of youth justice, for example Muncie, *Youth and crime* (2004) and Burke, *Young people, crime and justice* (2008). Moreover the assessment by Solomon and Garside (2008) *Ten years of Labour's youth justice reforms: An independent audit* is particularly instructive. My book primarily explores and explains modernisation and cultural change in probation. Nevertheless, it should be acknowledged that one of the first acts of modernisation by New Labour was undertaken in the field of youth justice. Prior to 1997 the youth justice system was deemed to be uneconomic, inefficient and ineffective. After 1997 the system was reformed, which can be illustrated as follows: a number of consultation documents were produced and the 1998 Crime and Disorder Act established the new youth justice system, youth justice board and youth offending teams in local authorities. It was also stated in Section 37 of the 1998 Crime and Disorder Act that 'It shall be the principal aim of the youth justice system to prevent re-offending by children and young persons'. Therefore reform was a key priority from 1997 to 2001, but modernisation is also associated with: a punitive turn (Pratt et al, 2005); more resources accompanied by performance indicators; National Standards; value for money; and economy, efficiency and effectiveness (the new public management agenda). There has been a focus on system management, procedures and processes, including target setting, some of which have not been met. All these matters are critically reviewed in this document (Solomon and Garside, 2008). Furthermore for an exploration of modernisation in the prison system, see Sim (2009), particularly Chapter 5.

[4] Jock Young (2007, Chapter 6) touches on New Labour politics and the creation of the Social Exclusion Unit. He argues that New Labour acknowledged the structural causes of crime, but this has not resulted in changes being made to the structures of society. Rather the focus has been placed on 'managing the problem' rather than initiating necessary transformations. The 'analysis of crime, therefore, emphasises agency over structure, and management and the administration of life's difficulties over the structural inequalities

which generate these difficulties' (p 112). This analysis resonates with the arguments contained in Wilkinson and Pickett (2009).

[5] The text prepared by Norman Fairclough (2000), *New Labour, new language?*, is worth consulting. It contains an interesting thesis that, among other things, looks at the way in which changing the culture of an organisation is inextricably bound up with transforming its language. It is also worth noting how Fairclough provides examples of modernising features associated with New Labour, some of which resonate with what has occurred within probation: introducing an annual report on the progress of government; devolution; the centralisation of power and the role of special advisers; bypassing the cabinet; coordinating the presentation of policies across government departments; discipline and control within the party in addition to public sector organisations; and focus groups, spin and media manipulation.

[6] Some of the key features contained in the White Paper *Criminal justice: The way ahead* (Home Office, 2001a) should be alluded to. First of all it acknowledges that the increase in crime over the past 25 years is associated with unemployment, lack of opportunities for the unskilled, drug taking, the availability of consumer goods and changes within social attitudes. Therefore even though the formal structures of the criminal justice system cannot, on their own, create a law-abiding and cohesive society, nevertheless the system must prevent crime and re-offending, effectively deal with criminal cases, be responsive to victims and the law-abiding and be accountable for its decisions. Accordingly, it should deliver 'justice for all' by catching, trying, convicting, punishing and rehabilitating offenders. Furthermore some of the reforms since 1997 are reprised, primarily those to the youth justice system and Crown Prosecution Service, including establishing 376 crime and disorder reduction partnerships (CDRPs) in England and Wales. There is also a reference to: Neighbourhood Watch Schemes, 160,000 separate local schemes involving six million households; victim support; additional resources; and expressions of concern for minority ethnic groups being over-represented in the criminal justice system. Significantly modernisation is juxtaposed with being *tough*.

[7] National Standards were initially introduced into probation in 1988 with a view to creating a more consistent and accountable service. Since then they have been periodically reviewed and new versions produced in 1992, 1995, 2000–02, 2005 and 2007.

[8] The 2003 Criminal Justice Act was the first piece of legislation to set out the aims of sentencing, of which there are five:

- Punishment
- Reduction of crime, including deterrence
- Reform and rehabilitation
- Public protection
- Reparation.

The discussion contained in Taylor et al (2004, p 173), on what are deemed to be incompatible philosophies of sentencing, is worth consulting.

[9] Additional material on encouraging faith communities to participate more fully in the delivery of services to offenders will be considered in some detail in Chapters 3 and 4. Suffice to say at this point that this constitutes an important development within NOMS because of the way in which the third sector is attracting a degree of prominence.

[10] Foucault's thesis that prison does not prevent recidivism (in fact the reverse is the case) can be found in *Discipline and punish* (1977). Some data indicate that the re-offending rate following short custodial sentences was 59.7% compared with 37.9% for community sentences (Straw, 2009, p 3). For more information on Foucault see the discussion towards the end of Chapter 2 that covers this subject in rather more detail. Additionally see the critique of the carceral boom, primarily in the US, in *Punishing the poor* (Wacquant, 2009).

[11] *Ten years of criminal justice under Labour: An independent audit*, by Solomon et al (2007), is an important document. It explores a number of issues including spending on the criminal justice system since 1997 and Labour's record on crime reduction. The document proceeds to look at three New Labour priorities: the justice gap (bringing more people to justice), re-offending and anti-social behaviour; before turning to the police, youth justice and drugs. In relation to political intentions and targets, this independent audit comes to the conclusion that the results are mixed after 10 years. The criminal justice system has been overhauled since 1997, major changes imposed and more resources provided, particularly since 2000 when probation has done quite well (an increase of 70% in real terms since 1997; see Straw, 2009, p 3). By contrast the Ministry of Justice is pursuing savings of £1 billion between 2008 and 2011 that will affect probation, prisons and the courts. One observation of the independent audit is that 'Questions remain about whether government is placing too much emphasis on finding criminal justice solutions to complex social and economic problems' (Solomon et al, 2007, p 13).

[12] In a previous publication (Whitehead, 2007) the main features of what can be described as the probation ideal were summarised as follows: take victims seriously; offenders have the potential to change; work with other agencies to keep offenders out of the criminal justice system and custody because of the labelling effects of both; a clear set of values rooted in tolerance, decency, care, compassion and *sociological* understanding; the importance of social work relationships; an awareness of the adverse effects of social circumstances on human behaviour; and the promotion of criminal and social justice.

TWO

Durkheim, Weber, Marx and Foucault: social theory with 'the big guys'

Different approaches to probation

It is possible to construct different approaches to explore and explain the organisation of probation throughout its long association with the criminal justice system. The first approach, which utilises a descriptive methodology, sequentially presents a number of significant events beginning in late Victorian society with the missionary forerunners of probation officers. This approach can be found neatly illustrated in the works of Joan King (1964), Fred Jarvis (1972) and Dorothy Bochel (1976). The second approach locates a series of largely discontinuous ideologies which can be slotted into definable time frames: 1876–1930s, a theology of saving souls; 1930s–70s, 'scientific' curing by casework to rehabilitate offenders; 1980s, alternatives to custody; 1990s, punishment in the community; after 2001, bureaucratic managerialism and the politics of more expressive forms of punishment (McWilliams, 1983, 1985, 1986, 1987). Arguably this is of greater interest compared to the first approach because it is more analytical than descriptive, and draws attention to the significance of changing ideas and accompanying discourses within probation practice. These changing ideologies are also related to transformations within state formations in support of different socio-economic systems that, in turn, shape penal responses (Garland, 1985, 2001; Cavadino and Dignan, 2006).

A third approach, utilised in this book, is grounded in bodies of social theory that have profitably been applied within the sociology of punishment to such illuminating effects (Garland, 1990; Hudson, 2003). Accordingly, as there are different approaches to and understandings of the phenomenon of punishment that draw theoretical inspiration from Durkheim, Weber, Marx and Foucault, similarly it may be suggested that the modernised probation domain since 1997 can profit from an exploration as theoretically diverse. The Probation Service is not, nor has it ever been, some monolithic structure, a self-contained entity, immune to influences pressing in on it from the *outside* of its organisational parameters, such as changing public attitudes and responses to crime; the politics of power and latest fashions in managerialism and bureaucracy; government centralisation and the problem of maintaining order in circumstances of increased risk; emotive crime stories generated by the media on an almost daily basis which fuel a fear of crime, and so on. Rather it is a complex organisation, operating at more than one level, involved in a multitude of tasks, which bodies of social theory can help to explore and explain. Therefore to capture contemporary and modernised complexities introduced in the previous chapter, a nuanced approach is required which, in turn, begins to establish a solid basis for insightful understanding and sustained critique. For my purposes a predominantly descriptive approach is singularly ill equipped for the exploratory and explanatory task of Chapters 1–4. Moreover, even though it could be argued that 1997–2010 can be constructed as a discrete period shaped by the political effects of modernisation, thus discontinuous with previous manifestations, my purposes are best served by allowing bodies of social theory to do their work. However, I do so by employing the metaphor of a loose rather than tight-fitting jacket.

A brief note on the role of theory

Social theory constitutes an essential tool in scholarly activity to approach, then explore and analyse, some features of social phenomena, which include institutional practices. Institutional practices located within the criminal justice system cannot sustain a single approach or interpretation any more than the phenomenon of crime (whatever one means by crime) can be embraced by a single criminological theory. Consequently it has been suggested that theories involve constructing 'abstract interpretations which can be used to explain a wide variety of empirical situations … they represent attempts to explain particular sets of social conditions or types of occurrence' (Giddens, 1989, pp 17, 711). It has also been suggested that theories are the 'conceptual means of interpreting and explicating information. They come into competition only when they offer alternative and incompatible explanations of the same data' (Garland, 1990, p 13; see also Duffee and Maguire, 2007, on criminal justice theory). Therefore if it is possible to theorise, for example, the work of the police and the prison system from different perspectives (Zedner, 2004), a similar approach can be adopted towards probation. But first it is important to establish some of the theoretical tools that will be used to accomplish this task in this and the next chapter, before their application in Chapter 4.

Emile Durkheim: 1858–1917

Introduction and some biographical references

It was Auguste Comte in France (1798–1857) who constructed the term 'social physics' to describe the newly emerging science of society. Later he supplanted social physics with sociology because he thought the former construction had been purloined by Adolphe Quetelet (1796–1874).[1] Accordingly, to Comte the newly emerging science of society was to follow the pattern of the natural sciences not only in its 'empirical methods and epistemological underpinnings, but also in the functions it would serve for mankind' (Coser, 1977, p 3). Sociology offered the prospect of extrapolating from the past a predictable future by the appliance of positive science which would provide indubitable benefits (Simon, 1963). Consequently Durkheim could not claim to be the founder of the intellectual discipline concerned with the science of society. Nevertheless, even though Comte is the acknowledged founder, Durkheim cultivated the discipline as one of his descendants. At this stage attention can be drawn to the way in which Durkheim's sociological approach influenced the Chicago School of Criminology and the thesis that the level of crime is linked to social organisation or rather disorganisation (Smith, 1988; Newburn, 2007, p 170). Furthermore, Durkheim's anomie later assumed the hue of strain theory in Robert Merton (Sztompka, 1986), and crime was defined as a social phenomenon that offended the collective conscience, which required a sociological rather than psychological explanation. It is also important to emphasise that Durkheim had much to say about crime and punishment, to which we will turn later as the first substantive section unfolds. For what probably remains the definitive biography of Durkheim covering details of his life, academic interests and outputs, the reader can be guided towards Steven Lukes (1973). Nevertheless, if new to the subject an excellent place to begin is Kenneth Thompson (1982). Both texts provide detailed information on Durkheim's contribution to the following thematics: the family, morality, law, crime and punishment, education and religion. Durkheim was also the founder of the journal *L'Année Sociologique*, which was published between 1898 and 1913. This journal is the source of a significant paper on crime and punishment, 'The two laws of penal evolution', which will be examined later.

Some key sources: primary

The division of labour in society (1893 [1984])
The rules of sociological method (1895 [1938])
Suicide: A study in sociology (1897 [1952])
The two laws of penal evolution (1899)
The elementary forms of the religious life (1912)

Also texts on Montesquieu; *Moral education* (2002); published lecture courses including 'The two laws of penal evolution'

Lukes (1973, p 561) provides a comprehensive bibliography of all Durkheim's publications. Thompson provides the reader with a similar service (1982, p 167), but in this text by Thompson there is a bibliography of Durkheim's major original works in French and their English translations.

Secondary sources

Simon (1963)	Giddens (1971, 1972, 1989)
Taylor et al (1973)	Coser (1977)
Garland (1990)	Morrison (1995)
Hudson (2003)	

Some themes in Durkheim

Arguably the scholarly contributions made by Lukes (1973), Thompson (1982) and Morrison (1995) provide excellent introductions to the variety of sociological themes running throughout the Durkheimian corpus. Nevertheless Morrison's exposition and critique, which is particularly pertinent for my introductory purposes, begins with an account of some of the major intellectual influences at work on Durkheim's thought. This is a good place to begin.

First, and as indicated earlier, Comte could be discovered in the background casting a long positivistic shadow (Simon, 1963). What this amounts to is the application of the methodology located within the orbit of the natural sciences to the social realm. It therefore purports to be the scientific study of society, comprising human beings and their social arrangements, rather than the world of inanimate objects and things. This is a methodology which pursues the so-called independent/objective 'facts' based on empirical observation, the search for law-like regularities and patterns with a view to establishing causal, predictive and invariant laws of how things work and will continue to work into the future. Mazlish underlines this point by stating that it follows from the 'scientific' nature of Comte's work, just as it does not follow from that of Hegel's, that Comte's sociology is an attempt to predict future social phenomena (1968, p 210). Consequently if, by the 19th century, human beings were well on the way to establishing laws that account for natural phenomena, so the newly emerging discipline of sociology was expected to render the same intellectual service for social phenomena. This substantiates the claim of the unity of the scientific method, or what was also known as the orthodox consensus between the natural and social–human sciences (Giddens, 1982).[2] Moreover, in *The rules of sociological method*, Durkheim expressed the point as follows:

> Since the law of causality has been verified in the other domains of nature and has progressively extended its authority from the physical and chemical world to the biological world, and from the latter to the psychological world, one may justifiably grant that it is likewise true of the social world. (1895 [1938], p 159)

Put simply, social phenomena become an object of positive knowledge using the methodology that underpinned the natural sciences.

Second, it should be clarified that Durkheim (in addition to Weber, Marx and Foucault) was working against the intellectual background established by the 18th-century European Enlightenment. Some of the main characteristics of this enlightened age of reason have been sketched as follows. Initially it is the replacement of supernatural by natural explanations; religion by science; divine decree by natural law; and priests by the critical thinking contained in the philosophers. The second point is the exaltation of human reason and experience as the instruments that could be used to solve human problems. Next is a belief in the perfectibility of man as a consequence of scientific progress, perhaps along the lines of the Comtean stages of progression from theological, then metaphysical, through to scientific positivism that would benefit mankind. Finally one should refer to those humanitarian concerns for the rights of man that culminated in the French Revolution of 1789. Another manifestation of this was the Liberal crusade and accompanying pursuit of justice associated with Beccaria and the application of reason and humanity to penal policy in *Dei delitti e delle pene* (for additional information on all these Enlightenment features see Sampson, 1956; Mack, 1962; Gay's excellent two volumes, 1967, 1969; Porter, 2000).

Another tenet of the Enlightenment was that man was assumed to be a free, responsible, equal, autonomous, rational and self-directed individual. This can be further elucidated by resorting to the doctrine of utilitarianism, man as rational calculator, which influenced the classical criminological perspective in which man was psychologically constructed as someone who pursued pleasure and avoided pain, thus weighing the costs and benefits of various repertoires of behaviour prior to selecting a specific course of action (Garland, 1985). Therefore it can be advanced that the utilitarianism of Beccaria and Bentham gave prominence to an individualistic perspective when accounting for criminal behaviour.[3] By contrast, the sociological theorising of Durkheim advocated the position that human beings could not be reduced to a set of biological–psychological explanations. By doing so his work constituted a discernible break with 'analytical individualism' (Taylor et al, 1973) because he questioned the degree to which individuals were the free, rational calculators of utilitarian theory. In other words, when turning to the tensions between structure and agency, according to Durkheim, the latter was curtailed because of the constraining force of social facts that imposed themselves on the individual. It should be recalled that in *The division of labour in society* the defining characteristics of a social fact were externality, constraint and generality.

Third, and to expand on the last point, Durkheim did not concur with Hobbes, Rousseau and Spencer that social order was based on the free decisions and motivations of self-seeking individuals. Consequently, and as alluded to earlier, he rejected the utilitarian view that the pursuit of one's own economic self-interest formed the basic unity of society. In other words, a social contract between autonomous individuals was not the basis of social solidarity and cohesion. Of course the social world is comprised of individuals, but these individuals were also influenced and constrained by, as well as being the product of, social forces. Therefore, consistent with a tradition which can be traced through St Simon, Comte, Renouvier in France (Simon, 1963), Schaffle and Wundt in Germany, even English and North American influences if the discussion is extended to religious phenomena (Thompson, 1982), according to Durkheim there is a discrete realm of social facts which can be studied empirically just as the objects of nature can be studied empirically. Moreover, these social facts constitute a discrete realm of social phenomena that exists independently of individuals. It is therefore possible to talk about the social realm as an artefact, in opposition to a more phenomenological perspective that embraces the notion that it is something constructed by the individual (the social as object rather than product). On this point Lukes (1973) arrives at the view that Durkheim's epistemology follows that of Descartes.[4] This means that phenomena are purported to exist independently of the observer, yet that the mind can grasp clearly and with certainty. Descartes' rationalism expatiated on the relationship between the content of the human mind and the external world being reliable (Grayling, 2005). In other words, the contents of the human mind mirror that which exists outside of itself accurately, producing a mirror-like image of what objectively 'is' the case. This thought will occupy us further when this chapter turns to discuss Weber, Marx and especially Foucault.

One issue that can be raised at this point concerns the way in which the individual is purported to be constrained by Durkheimian social forces and facts. In other words, to what extent are individuals free and responsible human beings? We have already alluded to this conundrum, albeit in passing, when reflecting on the tension between structure and agency (philosophically expressed as determinism versus free will) and how the role of individual human agency is circumscribed in Durkheim's sociology. Later on, this subject will be further explicated when considering the positions of the remaining social theorists. Suffice to say at this juncture, and by way of illustration, that Durkheim turned to suicide rates and proceeded to explain them by referring to social phenomena such as religion and economic conditions, rather than the predilections of the individual. Consequently suicide rates were higher during periods of economic recession, caused by a lack of moral-social regulation.[5] In fact it was the lack of organisation, the decline of moral regulation and solidarity in the 19th century – associated with the Industrial Revolution, egoistic individualism, rapid urbanisation and class divisions under transformed social arrangements created by capitalism – which constituted a central theme in Durkheim's sociology. Moreover, these are some of the very factors that established the background for the rise of social-theoretical perspectives associated with Durkheim but also Weber and Marx. There are other Durkheimian themes which are worth alluding to prior to turning to crime and punishment: the division of labour; mechanical and organic solidarity; anomie; collective conscience; individual versus social facts; the constraining influence of morality; religion and the sacred; and repressive and restitutive sanctions. Some of these will surface in what follows as the focus of concern is narrowed.

Crime and the sociology of punishment

According to Durkheim, the discussion surrounding and understanding of crime is rooted in the collective feelings and sentiments prevailing within society. One implication of this is that crime should not be approached as a fixed artefact, nor is it a phenomenon that possesses some inherent, objective, definable and unchanging essence (which finds an echo with the labelling perspective of the 1960s).[6] On the contrary, it is a phenomenon that changes over time, more social product than unchanging object, and as a consequence crime and law can be argued to provide valuable insights into the changing nature of society, the prevailing forms of social solidarity. In other words, law constitutes a visible symbol or index, an empirical indicator, of the nature of society, moral phenomena and type of social solidarity, the collective conscience and social change.

Furthermore, according to Durkheim, the perfect social order, that is, a form of order based on a spontaneous rather than a forced division of labour that characterised 19th-century capitalism, is conducive to producing social solidarity. This can be explicated as a set of arrangements in which occupational status accords with individual abilities or, to put it another way, roles distributed according to biologically endowed talents. However, the lack of such socio-economic perfection during the 19th century created conditions that conduced to deviance. Therefore, following the detailed exposition contained in the work of Taylor et al (1973), Durkheim's typology of deviance can be outlined as follows:

- *Biological deviant:* it is argued that even if there was in existence a spontaneous and therefore perfect division of labour, if deviance did occur it could be explained by genetic and psychological malfunctioning. Having said that it is extremely difficult to conceive of a perfect and therefore completely deviance-free society.
- *Functional rebel:* a form of behaviour that constitutes a response to the forced division of labour. Consequently this response is a challenge to the lack of fit between biological faculties/talents and occupational status.
- *Skewed deviant:* if the preceding category is a consequence of a normal person responding to a pathological division of labour, by contrast the skewed deviant is an un-socialised person within what can be described as a sick society. According to Durkheim, there are two sources for this condition: anomie, that is, a lack of normative moral-regulative framework; and egoism, associated with excessive individualism.

It is worth repeating how the Durkheimian thesis explicated that during the 19th century rapid socio-economic developments ran ahead of moral regulation, which had formerly been provided by the cohesive nature of religion, thus creating anomic conditions. It can therefore be argued that anomie involves a 'lack of social regulation, and a situation in which the unrestricted appetites of the individual conscience are no longer held in check' (Taylor et al, 1973, p 87). In what follows I want to expand on Durkheim's understanding of crime and punishment. This enables me to begin to establish one of the theoretical tools that can be applied to the excavation of the probation and criminal justice domains later on. The three main texts for consideration are: *The division of labour in society* (1893 [1984]); 'The two laws of penal education' (1899); and *Moral education* (2002; course delivered at Bordeaux between 1889 and 1912; see Lukes, 1973, p 110).

The division of labour in society

In Book 1 and Chapter 2 of *The division of labour in society* Durkheim turns his attention to mechanical solidarity, or solidarity by familiarities. This prepares the ground for a discussion about crime. According to Durkheim, the word 'crime' applied to those acts that elicited a punitive response from society. He stated that 'Universally they strike the moral consciousness of nations.... All are crimes, that is, acts repressed by punishment' (1893 [1984], p 31). He proceeded to argue that the phenomenon of crime 'disturbs those feelings that in any one type of society are to be found in every healthy consciousness' (p 34). Then, in a passage familiar to those acquainted with Durkheim's work, and often quoted, he explained that crime was tantamount to a form of behaviour that offended the collective consciousness. Consequently we should not say that an act 'offends the common consciousness because it is criminal, but that it is criminal because it offends that consciousness. We do not condemn it because it is a crime; but it is a crime because we condemn it' (p 40).

Durkheim advances the discussion by stating that under conditions of mechanical solidarity there were a number of distinguishable features: a homogeneous population (sameness rather than difference); most of the population will be engaged in the same form of employment (for example hunting); minimum specialisation in the division of labour; strong religious sentiments; uniformity of beliefs; and strong values conducive to social cohesion. Accordingly the system of punishment under these specific social arrangements equates to repressive sanctions expressed as emotion, outrage and vengeance. In other words, criminal behaviour elicits a strong reaction that serves to re-establish and promote social solidarity. Consequently, and this is a significant point, the punitive-passionate response primarily functions to restore the collective conscience which has been adversely affected by actions designated as criminal. Durkheim put it like this when he said that 'punishment constitutes essentially a reaction of passionate feelings, graduated in intensity, which society exerts through the mediation of an organised body over those of its members who have violated certain rules of conduct' (p 52).

This implies that the main function of punishment is not primarily directed at the guilty individual with a view to deterring future criminal acts, or even as a means of deterring others (not philosophically justified on the grounds of either individual or general deterrence). In other words, the purpose of punishment should not primarily be understood in terms of its instrumental utility or transformational efficacy as a means to achieving individual correctionalism.[7] Rather, its expressive quality and emotional content culminates in a passionate reaction towards the offender, and it is also possible to suggest that expressively passionate outpourings could contain a vestige of the illogical and irrational. But in doing this its fundamental purpose is to 'maintain inviolate the cohesion of society by sustaining the common consciousness in all its rigour' (p 63). Furthermore, the nature of crime and associated systems of rules, laws and punishments, provide an important clue to the nature of society and type of underpinning social solidarity. We have just considered Durkheim's theorising about crime and punishment under conditions of mechanical solidarity, but what of organic solidarity?

'Organic solidarity' is a term which describes a more advanced and complex form of society which can be contrasted to mechanical solidarity as the following features exemplify: a larger population; more complex division of labour with specialised functions; individuals become more dependent on each other's specialised roles; a society marked more by difference than sameness; legal contracts rather than obligations; individualism and differentiation; and occupations in a more secular society and their associated status. The nature of law and punishment associated with organic solidarity is more restitutive than repressive. Instead of repressively punishing offenders it restores things and human relations to what they once were prior to the crime being committed. As Durkheim explained in *The division of labour in society*, the nature of the restitutory sanction was sufficient to demonstrate that the social solidarity to which that law corresponded was of a completely different kind (p 68). Therefore, from expiation to restoration constitutes a visible index indicative of a more advanced, specialised, contractually based form of society and corresponding relations between people. Arguably this is constitutive of post-Enlightenment, capitalist and emerging industrialised society in the 19th century, which required relations to be restored between individuals rather than promoting individual–group solidarity, as in more primitive forms of social arrangements. However, and importantly, this ideal-type construction of organic solidarity and its constituent elements may not be possible under conditions of a dysfunctional and anomic division of labour. When reflecting on Durkheim's discussion of law, crime and punishment, in relation to differential forms of mechanical and organic solidarity, one of the criticisms levelled against him is that he did not allow sufficiently for the existence of restitutive sanctions under the former social arrangements or repressive sanctions as a feature of the latter. From a functionalist perspective Durkheim considered that crime could be understood as a normal phenomenon in society because it made a contribution to the promotion of social solidarity and stability. In fact the benefits of crime, articulated in *The rules of sociological method*, can be summarised as follows: it can serve to heighten collective sentiments; integrate the community in opposition to the transgressor; it has an adaptive function in that crime can promote social change thus preventing social stagnation; and it also has a *boundary maintenance* function in that it reinforces social values and helps to differentiate right from wrong (Newburn, 2007, p 170).

By way of summary it is helpful to refer to the exposition of Durkheim's sociology of punishment in the work of David Garland (1990). According to this reading, Durkheim's sociology was primarily concerned with the nature of social solidarity (see also Coser, 1977, p 133, which adds support to this position), and those deep moral structures at the heart of social life which have a claim on the individual, and which can elicit a strong reaction when violated. Accordingly, as Durkheim turns to expatiate on crime and punitive responses, it can be viewed as a 'moral phenomenon operating within the circuits of the moral life, as well as carrying out more mundane social and penal functions' (Garland, 1990, p 24). It may well be the case, as Garland argues, that the contempory nature and forms of penality at work within the criminal justice system could be approached from the standpoint of their utilitarian and instrumental efficacy, and judged accordingly. However, Durkheim drew attention to a different set of impulses which included the moral basis of penality, the involvement of those looking on beyond the individual offender, the symbolic meaning attached to penal rituals, the relationship between punishment and moral sensibilities and, importantly, the emotional nature of punishment as the expression of community disapproval through the formal mechanisms of criminal justice (Garland, 1990, should be considered closely). Additionally, punishment was a 'communicative device', a language that delivered messages into the social body (Wacquant, 2009, p 108). Society may well develop over time from simple to more complex forms, which corresponds with changes in penality, but punishment continues to communicate passionate responses.

'The two laws of penal evolution'

This was not the subject of a book but rather an essay written after *The division of labour in society*, when Durkheim was at Bordeaux between 1887 and 1902. The essay was originally published as 'Deux lois de l'évolution pénale' in *L'Année Sociologique*, vol IV, pp 65–95 (1899–1900). In what follows I have used the paper translated from French into English found in M. Traugott (1978) *Emile Durkheim: On institutional analysis*. At the beginning of the paper the two laws are stated as follows:

- *The law of quantitative variation:* the intensity of punishment is greater as societies belong to a less advanced type and as centralised power has a more absolute character.
- *The law of qualitative variations:* punishment consisting in privation of freedom – and freedom alone – for lengths of time varying according to the gravity of the crime, tend more and more to become the normal type of repression.

Where the first law is concerned, Durkheim referred to the form and intensity of punishment being greater in a less advanced type of society. By contrast, as society became more advanced, punishment became correspondingly more lenient. By establishing this point he repeated the basic argument surrounding mechanical and organic solidarity explicated in *The division of labour in society*. Nevertheless it can be said that Durkheim is at work in this essay refining his earlier thesis by introducing an important qualification to his general position, which is the absolute character of centralised power (Lukes, 1973, pp 257–65; Thompson, 1982, p 88; Garland, 1990, pp 35–41). Additionally, Durkheim argued that both of these elements – the nature of social arrangements and absolute political governments

– could operate independently of each other. Accordingly, as society passed from a less to a more advanced state, from mechanical to organic solidarity, punishment became less repressive. However, it happens that in 'passing from a lower species to other, more advanced types, we do not see punishment decrease, as could be expected, because at the same time the governmental organisation neutralises the effects of social organisation' (Traugott, 1978, p 175).

Durkheim expanded the argument by introducing a historical analysis that explored a number of hideous punishments, beginning with ancient (pre-classical) societies. For example Egypt resorted to hanging, beheading and crucifixion, in addition to other excruciating physical torments. In Assyria malefactors could be thrown to wild beasts or roasted in a basin over a fire. Intriguingly strangulation and decapitation were considered insufficiently severe! Syrian offenders could be crushed under the feet of animals. But when arriving at the Hebrews of the Old Testament, arguably not a more advanced social type in Durkheim's analysis, he made the assessment that they were in possession of a less severe Mosaic law. Next he proceeded to consider more advanced city-states where a more marked regression of penal law could be observed. For example Rome had a less repressive system of penality, but it became more severe when the Empire became an absolute power. When turning to Christian societies, Durkheim explicated how penal law evolved according to the same law in that 'the facts' indicated punishment was milder. However, from the 14th century royal power escalated and penal law strengthened, so that the 'apogee of absolute monarchy also marks the apogee of repression' (p 163). This persisted until the humanitarian protestations of Beccaria and suggested reforms to the ancien régime in the 18th century (but for an alternative reading see Foucault later).

Therefore the argument is played out throughout this historical excursion that during the course of penal evolution the *form* of punishment experienced changed, yet its essential *function* remained the same. Furthermore, in less advanced societies the intensity of penal measures was associated with, and can be explained by, the religious and collective permeation of society. Crime thus constituted an offence against the sacred moral order that elicited a passionate response marked by vengeance and outrage. By contrast, as societies advanced and became less religious, more morally diverse and individualistic, the force and passion of punishment was attenuated as the distance between offenders and offended-against reduced. Additionally these two types of criminality differed profoundly because 'the collective sentiments which they offend are not of the same nature. As a result repression cannot be the same for both' (p 172).

This quantitative shift in the form of punishment was complemented and accompanied by a qualitative shift as the prison, rather than physical punishments, became the normal type of repression. For Durkheim such a qualitative transformation represented a discernible change in human sensibilities, away from bodily mutilation and torture towards the restriction of liberty. In fact the prison, from being initially a place of detention for those awaiting trial, to assuming its role as a discrete form of punishment within penal systems, produces a second historical survey in the two laws. In more advanced organic societies it has become necessary to ensure miscreants do not evade punishment, which was less difficult in primitive societies given the closer-knit nature of families and communities, who would exercise group-clan oversight responsibilities for the individual. Thus the prison, in the way it has emerged, can be interpreted as a further illustration of the attenuation of severity because of the change in the collective conscience and corresponding social arrangements. Towards the end of this chapter I will provide a different perspective on the role of imprisonment when turning to the analysis of Foucault.[8]

Moral education

Durkheim delivered a course on moral education that was initially offered at the Sorbonne during 1902–03, yet apparently sketched earlier at Bordeaux. (When considering Durkheim's text on moral education it should be noted that I have used the 2002 Dover edition.) In two substantive parts containing a total of 18 chapters, Durkheim addressed 'The elements of morality' and 'How to develop the elements of morality in the child'. Pertinently, in three consecutive chapters, 11, 12 and 13, he discussed the theme of punishment within the context of education and role of the school in socialisation: 'The use of punishment in the school' (for additional expositions see Giddens, 1972; Lukes, 1973, pp 110–19; Garland, 1990, pp 41–6; and Chapter 3, this volume).

   In Chapter 11 Durkheim posed the question: why do we punish? He answered by saying that to punish a child to prevent misbehaviour, to exact retribution, even atonement, were all possibilities. In fact to engage in such a discussion touched on the instrumental function of penality in addition to philosophies, theories and justifications of punishment. Nevertheless, for Durkheim, if someone committed an offence, or violated a rule in school, this was tantamount to breaching something inviolable. Consequently the law that was violated 'must somehow bear witness that despite appearances it remains always itself, that it has lost none of its force or authority despite the act that repudiated it' (p 166). He continued by saying that the essential nature of punishment 'is not to make the guilty expiate his crime through suffering or to intimidate possible imitators through threats, but to buttress those consciences which violations of a rule can and must necessarily disturb in their faith' (p 177). Accordingly, he reinforced the position contained in earlier contributions to this subject. Once again Durkheim advanced the position that the real purpose of punishment was not to be conceived in terms of its instrumental efficacy directed at individual offenders. Rather its expressive nature was directed towards restoring the sacred moral order that had been violated and for the benefit of the law-abiding. Punishment remained concerned with the expression of feeling because it was 'a notation, a language, through which either the general social conscience or that of the school teacher expresses the feeling inspired by the disapproved behaviour' (p 176). A breach of social morality elicited a passionate reaction that restored the sacred moral order that was deemed to exist independently of the child in the classroom, and this could be extended to the individual appearing in court.

Therefore Durkheim is drawing our attention to a number of themes within the orbit of crime and punishment which are of interest in themselves, but which can be easily overlooked by approaching the phenomenon through a narrow lens of utilitarian and instrumental efficacy. Additionally, it is being suggested, in anticipation of a later discussion, that Durkheimian themes have a contemporary relevance when excavating the complex and multifaceted nature of probation practice within the modernised criminal justice system. It is the Durkheimian corpus, as Garland helpfully elucidates, which draws attention to a troubling dilemma illustrated by the outpouring of punitive passions deemed to be politically necessary – expressive nature contained in the politics of punishment – yet at the same time penologically inefficacious and therefore to some degree irrational for controlling crime. And yet there is no shortage of punitive impulses; such impulses continue to grow in their intensity and they are arguably futile yet seemingly destined to persist. For Garland this constitutes a clear illustration of punishment's 'tragic quality' (1990, p 80). After considering a number of Durkheimian themes we now turn to a very different set of ideas located within another tradition, which are just as relevant for my exploratory purposes.

Max Weber: 1864–1920

Introduction and some biographical references

It is interesting to point out that, as far as one is able to determine, Weber did not apply himself to a systematic treatment of crime and punishment. This, of course, is in marked contrast to Durkheim above and Foucault towards the end of this chapter. A close scrutiny of the extensive index to *Economy and society* (Weber, 1922 [1968]) provides evidence to support this claim. Nevertheless, it is important to state that there are a number of Weberian themes that are relevant when excavating developments in probation and criminal justice. As such this perspective constitutes another conceptual lens that brings into focus certain facets that belong to the complex and multifaceted modernised domain of probation. In particular there are two areas of interest I want to draw attention to in this chapter. Prior to expatiating on what these are, the following biographical references are worth pursuing: Bendix (1960); MacRae (1987); Gerth and Mills (1948).

Some key sources: primary

The Protestant ethic and the spirit of capitalism (1904–05 [1958])
Economy and society, three volumes (1922 [1968])
Selections from Weber in Gerth and Mills (1948)

Secondary sources

Albrow (1970)	Giddens (1971)
Coser (1977)	Garland (1990)
Morrison (1995)	Ritzer and Goodman (1997)
Hudson (2003)	Whimster (2004)

Some themes in Weber

In the three-volume edition comprising *Economy and society* (1922 [1968]), Weber addresses a number of sociological themes. Accordingly he was looking at the various types of social institutions that would best serve the interests of a modern capitalist state (Hudson, 2003, p 105; Whimster, 2004, p 300). In volume 1 Weber referred to a number of sociological terms and provided a definition of sociology, types of legitimate domination, status groups and classes. In volume 2 he turned his attention to religion, the sociology of law and political communities. Lastly, in volume 3, the themes of domination and legitimacy, bureaucracy, patriarchalism, feudalism, charisma and the city were explored. Of course there are other thematic points of interest too: *verstehen*, ideal types, the zeitgeist of the modern world, the process of rationalisation and how the spirit of Protestantism was conducive to the emergence of capitalism.

Where the orientation of my book is concerned I want to bring into focus two specific Weberian themes that have resonance for an analysis and critique of contemporary probation and the operational logic of the criminal justice system. The first is Weber's use of the concept *verstehen* within the context of his understanding of sociology (1922 [1968], volume 1, pp 4–24). The second is *bureaucracy* (volume 3, pp 941–1003). Furthermore, it is possible to suggest that the notion of *verstehen* is particularly relevant when thinking about the rationale of probation in relation to the division between the natural and social sciences. The following question may be posed at this stage: should the organisation of probation have a role to play in understanding, analysing, then explaining the human condition and associated offending behaviours, or is the primary task the bureaucratic management of individuals? The following discussion has a bearing on this question, which will be explored in more detail later.

Verstehen *and debates surrounding the natural and social sciences*

Verstehen is a German word meaning *human understanding* and as such draws attention to human subjectivity that includes the inner states and motivations of individual human actors. According to Outhwaite (1975), its origins can be traced to theological hermeneutics concerned with the meaning of written texts. Weber, influenced by the work of Wilhelm Windelband and Heinrich Rickert on the *Methodenstreit* (controversy over methods in the social sciences during the 1880s), focused on the unique individual rather than forms of knowledge 'afforded by the physical sciences, which was abstract, general and capable of being stated in the form of invariable natural laws' (MacRae, 1987, p 63). Gerth and Mills (1948, p 46) supported this point when they stated that it was within the context of conflicting intellectual currents that Weber worked out his distinctive orientation, which included the individual as the primary unit of analysis. Consequently there is an important point of contrast between Weber's focus on the individual human actor, associated with one of the themes which helped to define the Enlightenment, and the Comtean-Durkheimian sociological approach which elevated social structures acting on and constraining the individual.

Following Rickert, Weber expressed the view that sociology should concern itself with the interpretation of social action in addition to which it is interested in the concept of values because acts of evaluation and judgement were a precondition of social action (Morrison, 1995, p 274). Moreover social action has four main concepts, one of them being *verstehen* which embraces how people assign meanings to their own and each other's actions. In the first volume of *Economy and society*, Weber said there were two types of understanding within the context of social action – one was direct and the other exploratory or interpretative. Where direct understanding is concerned he talked about a level of comprehension based on the direct observation of an act. To illustrate this point he referred to the formula $2 + 2 = 4$, which is readily understood. Additionally, if we observe someone chopping wood, or being angry, it should be clear what is occurring. By contrast, when turning to exploratory understanding the emphasis shifts from what is going on to an interpretation of why. In other words, we may observe and clearly understand *what* someone is doing by their actions, but this is very different to understanding *why* the action is being performed. For example $2 + 2 = 4$ is being used to demonstrate a mathematical formula, and someone is chopping wood to use as fuel in winter. As such, exploratory understanding proceeds to put the 'what' of an action into a framework of meanings and motives. This is a more complex form of understanding because it requires additional work to explain the link between the activity being observed and its meaning for the actor. For Giddens it involves elucidating the motivational link between the observer observing the behaviour, and understanding what it means to the actor (1971, p 148). Barbara Hudson, in a passage that helpfully contributes to elucidating Weber, says that human beings interpret each other's actions and from this they build up 'patterns of identity, behaviour and meaning which becomes generalised within their own lives and within society. These stable patterns become the customs, social roles, laws and institutions that we call culture' (2003, p 107). This means that for Weber and those sociologists who followed in the *verstehen* tradition, the route to studying culture was through observing the actions of individuals.

Consequently, and this is a salient point to extrapolate when operating within the Weberian tradition, the social or human sciences have as their orbit of concern empathic understanding, the actions and associated motives, meanings and consequences of individual human action. Accordingly, a distinction is required between an *understanding and interpretation* of individual behavioural inner states (human science) and *prediction* (associated with the domain of the natural sciences). At this point it is possible to drop the hint that such a distinction has relevance when considering the rationale of probation and clarifying its discrete contribution to the competing professional logics operating within the institutions of the criminal justice system. For those organisations that purport to work with people within the context of humane–professional relationships, the future could never assume the status of an exact science. Predicting the future based on previous behavioural repertoires, albeit taking seriously the possibility of discernible behavioural patterns, does not operate within an uncontentious epistemological sphere. Therefore it is important to distinguish conceptually between *inferentially predicting* the future based on the totality of evidence at our disposal in the spirit of induction, and *knowing* what will occur which is beyond our epistemological compass (Buchdahl, 1969, p 339). This is a distinction which should be clarified in light of inflated claims attached to risk technologies, for example the efficacy attached to OASys. Furthermore operating within the human science of *verstehen*, Weber, in *Economy and society* (volume 1, pp 21–2), expressed the view that it could well be the case that the vast majority of human beings behave in a state of half-consciousness. As such they are not acting in full self-knowledge of what they do or why they do it. Rather, behaviour can be a consequence of impulse, force of habit, thus constituting an unthinking rather than rational response. If this is the case, how difficult it is for the probation officer, social worker or youth worker to engage in an interpretation of the 'other's' behaviour with a view not only to understanding but also predicting future events in the contingent social world.

The position being established is that the human sciences are more concerned with hermeneutics, the complex meanings and interpretations of human action, than the causal, predictive and invariant laws associated with the natural sciences, which was at the heart of the *Methodenstreit* debates. Morrison develops the point and in so doing provides a helpful clarification by stating that Weber came to the conclusion that the natural and social sciences operate within different domains of knowledge. This is because in the natural sciences knowledge is of the external world that is accounted for in terms of valid laws, whereas within the social sciences knowledge must be internal or subjective in the sense that 'human beings have an inner nature that must be understood in order to explain outward events' (1995, p 337, also p 276). Furthermore Turner said that Weber 'reintroduced the discussion of meaning to the analysis of human action, thereby serving as a major, though by no means comprehensive, resource for later schools of interpretative sociology' (1996, p 43). As such this constituted an epistemological challenge to the positivistic domain of science, thus offering a more substantive inspiration to study the meaningful viewpoints of human actors and consequences for action. Additionally, Coser (1977, p 217) contributes to this discussion by saying that Weber did not follow the Durkheimian schema in terms of applying the methodology of natural science to the newly emerging social sciences. Consequently there is no unity of the sciences in terms of a consistent methodological approach embracing both disciplines. Coser supports the view that the natural and social sciences are ontologically and epistemologically different. By contrast it can be argued that what they have in common is that neither can claim to provide a total explanation of the phenomena under investigation. The world is too rich, complex and unpredictable, both in the realms of nature and history, so that even in physics it is simply not possible to predict with certainty what will happen in the future (Coser, 1977, p 219). Moreover Gerth and Mills say that in drawing a clear distinction between understanding and interpreting people, and the natural sciences, Weber drew the line between his interpretative sociology and the 'physique sociale in the tradition of Condorcet, which Comte called sociologie and Durkheim worked out in such an eminent manner' (1948, p 57). Because of the centrality of this theme, in addition to which it prepares the ground for a later discussion, it is necessary to explore the matter in more detail at this point.

There is a long and strong scientific tradition that, particularly since the period of the 15th-century European Renaissance, has been utilising mathematics to explain the world (Hall, 1954). For example by utilising combinations of numbers it was possible to predict the movement and future positions of the planets. Copernicus advanced his heliocentric principle, and Newton established the laws of motion and gravity. Moreover this impulse to utilise numbers to measure the world, that mathematics could account for things as they were 'in reality', continued into the 1700s with Alexander von Humbolt and Carl Frederick Gauss. It was during this period that von Humbolt acquired various measuring instruments for the task, from a barometer for measuring air pressure and a hypsometer to measure the boiling point of water to a theodolite for measuring the land and a Leyden jar for capturing electrical charges. In fact everything must be measured if it is to be explained (Kehlmann, 2007, p 29). Concurrently Gauss was pursuing his own researches and in Kehlmann's book on *Measuring the world* we read that:

> Again and again he laid his quill aside, propped his head in his hands, and wondered whether there was a proscription against what he was doing. Was he digging too deep? At the base of physics were rules, at the base of rules there was laws, at the base of laws there were numbers; if one looked at them intently, one could recognise relationships between them, repulsions or attractions. (2007, p 73)

Additionally, the French tradition encompassing Montesquieu, Condorcet, Turgot, St Simon, Comte and Durkheim approached social facts as thing-like objects in nature to establish the scientific and predictive laws of society. What von Humbolt and Gauss did for measuring objects in the natural world, Comte and later Durkheim attempted for the social world, as we saw earlier.

By contrast there is an alternative German tradition, to which Weber belongs, which questioned the idea that the methodology of the natural sciences could seamlessly be extended to the social, historical world of human beings. This is the tradition that acknowledges that human beings are complex actors, with complex histories, who cannot be reduced solely to passive objects being acted on by the world's forces, its repulsions and attractions. Nor is it possible to reduce human beings to combinations of numbers. Rather individuals possess the capacity to act on the world, to alter their immediate environment, in order to change themselves and the course of events that elevates agency over structure. Consequently it can be reinforced that objects and mechanistic events in the natural world are not of the same order as the social world of individual human beings with their various behaviours and complex meanings attached to actions. Therefore in the scholarly literature (Giddens, 1978, 1982; Bryant, 1985) there are rich debates on the differences between the domains of natural and social sciences. Giddens drives the point home when he says that neither the formulation of laws, nor causal analysis, have any place in social science. This is because social science is a hermeneutical endeavour and, as such, 'a logical gulf separates such an endeavour from the logic and methods of the natural sciences' (1982, p 4). It is possible to suggest at such an early stage in this book that probation work should be concerned with the language of human events, behaviours, meanings, possible understandings and interpretations; in other words, *verstehen*. This is in marked contrast – ontologically, epistemologically and axiologically – to an aggregately based and positive science of risk prediction supported by an array of numbers that is what it has become (Whitehead, 2007). The tradition and application of *verstehen*, as Giddens concedes, does not provide a basis for scientific research. Nevertheless it does provide a basis for empathic understanding, which is required when working with, in order to explain, human beings in all their individual complexity (1978, p 277).

Positivist orthodoxy, with its scientific embrace, adopts a particular view of the natural and social worlds. This view, replete with objectivity, theoretical and value neutrality, proceeds on the basis of observation, induction, the collection of 'facts' and of course the assumed certainties of quantitative measurements to reveal the nature of 'objective' reality. However, this view does not exist unchallenged because it can be acknowledged that such a positivist-scientific approach to the world, purported to exist outside our minds, is ontologically and epistemologically complex. In other words, it is extremely difficult to disentangle those features that belong to objects and those imposed by the active mind of the human observer. Therefore it is possible to advance the position that the world does not have an innate meaning, a given essence, which can be discovered by assiduous scientific endeavour and captured by numbers. Rather reality, and the knowledge that goes with it, are to some degree constructed and imposed by our cognitive faculties. Accordingly there are many realities created out of the subjective experiences of different individuals. There is no objective social reality 'out there', but rather a bewildering collection of interpretations and opinions that get projected onto the world (Tarnas, 1991).

This anti-positive and pro-humanistic perspective, which arguably resonates with the organisational rationale of probation with its people orientation, should be concerned to understand the realities of clients' lives not from the standpoint of the expert practitioner, but clients themselves in all their complexity. This is a form of *verstehen* which conduces to an emotionally empathic level of understanding of the person; it has an appreciative quality; it is more art than science, qualitative rather than quantitative. This is not so much a calculated or even definitive description of human action, but a holistic exploration, excavation and interpretation of the human condition. Not scientific prediction based on aggregated data sets, but a rich, nuanced and appreciative understanding of the individual located within the broadest parameters. Not measurements by well-tuned instruments producing systems and combinations of numbers, but often ambiguous meanings defying risk scales and precise classification. However, this is not an account of the place the Probation Service currently inhabits within the criminal justice system. Nevertheless these are pertinent themes that can be developed within a Weberian framework consistent with *verstehen*.

Bureaucracy

If *verstehen* is a concept with pertinent applicability to the functioning of the criminal justice system in terms of the qualitative understanding it brings to the behaviour of people who offend, equally applicable is bureaucracy. Martin Albrow (1970) explains that the word 'bureaucracy' is of 18th-century origin and means rule by officials within organisations. In an interesting aside Albrow refers to von Humbolt in 1792, the same von Humbolt who appears in Kehlmann's book alluded to earlier, who made reference to the mechanisation of human life. Nevertheless, when turning to Weber, Albrow establishes the point that the idea of bureaucracy was associated with changes in German administration during the 19th century, and links are forged between bureaucracy, administration, organisations and power. The argument is also advanced that bureaucracy constitutes the most efficient form of organisation exemplified by precision, continuity, discipline, strictness and reliability. According to Weber, bureaucracy is an inevitable process in the modern, post-18th-century Enlightenment world, and it gathers pace and power as it develops. But, as Albrow states, the problem Weber addressed was how the inherent tendency of bureaucracy to accumulate power 'could be prevented from reaching the point where it controlled the policy and action of the organisation it was supposed to serve' (1970, p 47).

Albrow proceeds to explore seven modern conceptualisations of bureaucracy along the following dimensions: bureaucracy as rational organisation; organisational inefficiency; rule by officials; public administration; administration by officials; the organisation; and modern society. Consequently bureaucracy has been employed in a wide variety of theories about modern society. As such it has been linked 'with the growth of tertiary occupations, with the differentiation of social functions, with the alienation of man from work, with the growth of oligarchy and with a general process of rationalisation' (1970, p 85). Additionally, in *Economy and society* the defining characteristics of the Weberian ideal-type bureaucracy can be summarised as follows:

- a specialised division of labour where different individuals/officials undertake specialised tasks in pursuit of organisational goals;
- a hierarchical chain of command and offices, with higher offices supervising lower ones;
- actions of officials governed by rules and administrative regulations, so there is little scope for individual initiative, discretion, autonomy, even human feeling;
- appointment to office is based on merit;
- there is a clear separation of public role and private life;
- a uniform organisation replete with documents, files and knowledge contained in technical experts.

Additionally the Weberian analysis of bureaucracy takes place within types of domination that correspond to three types of legitimation:

- rationally regulated with a structure of domination that is bureaucratic;
- traditionally prescribed social action is represented by patriarchalism;
- charismatic based on the authority of the individual.

Weber advanced the view that a major feature of the modern capitalist world was the trend towards rationalisation. This means it was planned, technical, calculable and efficient; but also depersonalised, lacking in human feeling, and because of this could be described as the disenchantment of the world. Consequently bureaucracy is an illustration of the modern trend by which law, rules and prescriptive regulations come to dominate charismatic and affective elements. Bureaucracy may well be the most technically efficient form of domination in a modern, capitalist, industrial society. However, there is a price to pay in terms of its dehumanising tendencies. Weber, with Nietzsche lurking in the background (Tarnas, 1991; Safranski, 2003), was concerned with the way in which, during the 19th century, those human values associated with the affections of the human heart were being damaged by the cold penetrating light of reason and science. On the one hand, rational and bureaucratic tendencies produce the technically efficient organisation and society. On the other, the same impulses create an oppressive iron cage where human beings are reduced to cogs in a vast impersonal machine from which there can be no escape. For as Weber himself says, 'Bureaucracy develops the more perfectly, the more it is "dehumanised", the more completely it succeeds in eliminating from official business love, hatred, and all purely personal, irrational, and emotional elements which escape calculation' (1922 [1968], volume 3, p 975). It is within this context of Weberian thinking on the meaning of bureaucracy that, in previous work on modernising trends within probation, I resorted to distinguishing the notions of *bureaucratic technician* from the exercise of *therapeutic imagination* (Whitehead, 2007). Consequently it may be suggested that the categories of *verstehen* and bureaucracy constitute a different set of critical tools for exploring and explaining what probation has become within the contemporary criminal justice system, particularly since 1997.

Karl Marx: 1818–86

Introduction and some biographical references

The first substantive section of this chapter explored how the Durkheimian perspective drew attention to the way in which punishment functioned to maintain social order and promote the bonds of social solidarity. In other words, punishment buttressed the collective conscience, the moral basis of society, the prevailing social consensus. Therefore Zedner succinctly summarises the Durkheimian position by saying that the function of punishment is less concerned to control crime than to provide a vehicle for the 'expression of outrage when crime is committed and thus to reaffirm the social value transgressed. The subject of punishment is, therefore, less the offender than society as a whole' (2004, p 77). Next, Weber did not, as Durkheim clearly did, address the themes of crime and punishment directly. Arguably, however, there are Weberian themes which resonate with and which can be developed within the overlapping domain of probation work, namely *verstehen* and bureaucracy. It will be argued in more detail later that both of these perspectives can be put to work as functioning exploratory tools that draw attention to a number of contemporary and modernising features.

When training the spotlight on Marx it can be seen that he, like Weber, but in marked contrast to Durkheim, had little to say directly about crime and punishment (Tierney, 2006, p 186; Cowling, 2008).[9] Nevertheless the view can be advanced that it is possible to identify a discernible Marxist tradition which incorporates the sphere of crime and punishment. Consequently this constitutes the third body of social theory that will later be applied to the criminal justice domain. It represents another analytical tool for exploring and excavating its complex and multifaceted undulations. This is the body of social theory that operates with the view that technological change, specifically to the mode of production, is a necessary condition of social change. This set of events has, in turn, implications for the operational logic of punishment (McLellan, 1986, p 41). Therefore (and this point was raised when exploring the Durkheimian position) law, crime and methods of punishment can be approached as relative phenomena. In fact they constitute a set of institutional forms and expressions that change over time as the economic system transmutes. Notwithstanding criticisms of the

Marxist tradition,[10] one can turn again to Zedner, who alludes to the enduring nature of Marxist analysis. This is because it provides a framework for thinking about the nature of punishment as a government strategy 'inherently linked with power relations, economic struggle, and social conflict' (2004, p 80). Accordingly it draws attention to the notion of class-based justice in the way that the existence of rules and laws promotes the interests of the rich over the poor, strong over weak, thus maintaining the vested interests of the few over the many (see also Reiman, 1998). Helpful biographical texts for consultation are McLellan (1976, 1986).

Some key sources: primary

The economic and philosophic manuscripts of 1844 (1932 [1964])
The communist manifesto (1848 [1967])
The German ideology (1845 [1947])
Capital: A critique of political economy, Volume 1 (1867 [1976])

Secondary sources

Rusche and Kirchheimer (1939 [1968])	Coser (1977)
Giddens (1971)	Taylor et al (1973)
Bailey and Brake (1975)	Hall et al (1978)
Walker and Beaumont (1981)	Garland (1990)
George and Wilding (1991)	Morrison (1995)
Hudson (2003)	Cowling (2008)

Some themes in the Marxist tradition

It should be acknowledged that Morrison (1995) provides the reader with a succinct overview of some of the key themes in the Marxist corpus, which constitutes a voluminous literature. These are alienation (which resonates with rationalisation in Weber); the industrial capitalism of the 19th century and how the newly emerging mode of production associated with it shaped class relations in the post-feudal period; the dialectical idealism of Hegel transformed into the dialectical materialism of Marx (Morrison, 1995, p 316), that is, history with a purpose and the law of historical development; political economy; surplus value; and the base and superstructure metaphor.

McLellan, a biographer of Marx, expands on some of these themes by reminding us that Marx was influenced by German-Hegelian idealism, French political theory and English classical economics. In fact McLellan proceeds to clarify that the intellectual background of Marx's home and school was the 'rationalism of the Enlightenment, a pale Protestantism incorporating the virtues of reason, moderation and hard work' (1986, p 24). For Hegel, the philosopher who followed in the footsteps of Kantian idealism with its postulation of an active rather than passive mind in the construction of reality, advocated a view of history which is unfolding according to a plan. In other words, through a dialectical process of thesis, antithesis and synthesis, what is referred to as reason-spirit-absolute is unfolding itself within the historical and evolutionary process.[11] Moreover the entire Hegelian philosophic edifice is raised on the assumption that the nature of reality is *ideal* in content and that 'human reason as part of that reality, of the Ideal whole, is capable of direct, intuitive knowledge of the world in which it operates' (Sampson, 1956, p 191). By contrast Marx eventually emerged from Hegel's metaphysical abstractions to advance a materialist rather than idealist conception of the historical process. In other words, Marx transformed the dialectic in the shape he received it from Hegel. Rather than beginning with the ideal and then moving towards the material world, Marx inverted the Hegelian conception and in the process it was turned right side up again. Mazlish elucidates by stating that Hegel's emphasis on consciousness, on what was inside the human head, was correct. However, what was erroneous was the attribution of consciousness to ideal rather than material forces and movements (1968, p 225; Chadwick, 1990).

According to Marx it was the economic system – the way in which societies are founded on the fundamental requirement to produce in order to sustain life itself – which was determinative of the social system as well as being the locus of power. This is the often-cited base–superstructure metaphor as the fundamental economic base and the dependent non-economic superstructure. The latter includes, for example, a society's legal and political institutions. Additionally the education system, family, religion and the criminal justice system can be included, conditioned by the demands of the economic system and thus promoting the interests of those who own and control the means of production, distribution and exchange. Morrison takes this further by saying that in resorting to the concepts of base and superstructure, Marx demonstrated that the system of economic production shaped social relations and therefore the very structure of society. Additionally, the economic system shaped the class structure and the corresponding ideas that were related to the roles that people performed in production (1995, p 313). Of course this base–superstructure relationship has been interpreted in terms of a crude economic determinism, with recourse to causal terminology. However, McLellan questions this by saying that the most that can be said is that, for Marx, 'technological change was a necessary, though not sufficient, condition of social change' (1986, p 41). Therefore with these preliminary thematic points in mind I want to continue the discussion by exploring a number of perspectives that are located within the Marxist tradition. I begin with a criminologist during the early years of the 20th century, and conclude with a probation commentator in the 1980s.

Marxist tradition, from Bonger to a reference in McWilliams

During the early years of the 20th century, Willem Bonger (1916), according to the re-evaluation of Reiner (2007b, p 352), was one of the first criminologists to develop a Marxist analysis of crime. Even though Taylor et al were critical of

Bonger (1973, pp 222–36), Reiner adds a more charitable encomium by saying that such criticisms signally fail to acknowledge Bonger's position as a pioneer of the political economy of crime. According to Bonger's analysis crime should not be understood as a fixed or absolute concept, following Durkheim and Marx, in that it has no ontological reality but it is a variable phenomenon (see the discussion in Cowling, 2008). Additionally, it was the structure of capitalism that generated conflict and exploitation, which were themselves criminogenic in the way they conduced to egoism and avarice. It was this destructive melange of capitalism and egoism which can explain the motivations of working-class, or perhaps more accurately sub-proletarian, crime, in addition to the crimes of the powerful in society. Consequently one of the key perspectives within the Marxist tradition is that the phenomenon of crime is rooted within the organisation of capitalist social and economic arrangements, rather than individual pathology.

Next, Rusche and Kirchheimer, in *Punishment and social structure* (1939 [1968]), examine the relationship between the economic system, labour markets and punishment. These authors, within the context of engaging in a historical analysis commencing in the medieval period, seek to demonstrate that prevailing productive relations shape penality. Therefore as changes occur within the economy, so changes correspondingly occur in the nature of penality, a thesis advanced to support the contestation that economic forces determine punishment. In other words, one should not talk about punishment in general terms, but rather a specific form of punishment related to the means of production. This can be exemplified by saying that when labour is in plentiful supply, penal responses can be harsh and reckless with human life, as in the late Middle Ages when capital punishment was prevalent. By contrast when the demand for labour in the economy exceeds supply, the state is less disposed to exercise excessive punishments. Consequently the labour market determines the social value placed on human life, and the form taken by punishment corresponds with the demand for labour. Rusche and Kirchheimer state that 'Every system of production tends to discover punishments which correspond to its productive relationships' (p 5). According to this reading, *there is no direct or unambiguous relationship between crime and punishment. Rather the system of penality is involved, beyond the narrow crime–punishment nexus, in controlling surplus populations (always the poor) under specific economic conditions.* On this point Rusche says that criminal laws and the daily work of the criminal courts 'are directed almost exclusively against those people whose class background, poverty, neglected education, or demoralisation drove them to crime' (quoted in Garland, 1990, p 91). Wacquant would agree that penality is a strategy for controlling the poor (2008).

David Garland (1990) and Barbara Hudson (2003) remind us that there are diverse perspectives within the Marxist tradition, in addition to the economic determinants of Rusche and Kirchheimer. Pashukanis (1978), Hay (1975) and Ignatieff (1978) refer to the role of punishment within the politics and ideologies of conflicts and struggles between classes, and as a way of maintaining and promoting the power of the state and hegemony of the ruling class. Therefore it can be argued that the operation of the criminal justice system, of which probation and social work are constituent elements, functions as part of the state's strategy for controlling the poor located at the margins of society, sub-proletarian populations who lack the rudiments of socio-economic security and who form the backbone of probation's caseload of some 250,000. Under capitalism and its contemporary manifestation within neoliberalism (Harvey, 2005; Reiner, 2007a), certain sections of society are rendered economic casualties who become surplus to the requirements of the state, veritable social junk (Box, 1987), sand in the machine (Mathiesen, 2006), deregulated populations (Parenti, 1999), which the state, through its penal agents both in prison and the community, seeks to manage, control and contain, but also punish, discipline and exclude. Therefore there is some veracity attached to the claim that the rich get richer and the poor get prison, or other penal dispositions, in a criminal justice system that neutralises the threat of crime represented by the recalcitrant poor (Reiman, 1998).

It was during the late 1960s that radical criminological perspectives, influenced by Marxist theory, surfaced in the United States (Cowling, 2008). Subsequently an outbreak of radical and Marxist theorising occurred in the work of Taylor et al (1973), who took issue with the prevailing orthodox consensus expressed in terms of its functionalist perspectives, scientific positivism, determinism and predominantly individualistic explanations of and responses to crime. In fact they engaged in a ground-clearing critique of major criminological theories (classicism and positivist paradigms; Durkheimian anomie and Mertonian strain; the Chicagoans; as well as Marx, Engels and Bonger) before making a case for their *fully social theory* of deviance which, they argue, must take account of the class-based political, social and economic structures of capitalism. The authors argue for a politics of social reform, in contradistinction to the traditional panoply of positivism, quantification, measurement and prediction, which are associated with a criminal justice system predominantly in pursuit of correcting the pathological and maladjusted individual understood as embodying an essential 'otherness'. Consequently, to do otherwise than to work for the collapse of capitalism and the transformation of society to one of socialist diversity is to become implicated in correctionalism, that is, 'the coercive use of the criminal sanction to "correct" behaviour on a personal basis when its roots lie in social structural inequalities of wealth and power' (quoted in Downes and Rock, 1988, p 247). It is also important to acknowledge that this criminological perspective embraces the following themes: human action is meaningful and voluntarily chosen rather than being positivistically determined; a conflict rather than consensus view of society; socio-economic arrangements must be factored into an analysis of crime which can be interpreted as a legitimate and rational response to these arrangements; and the state through the criminal justice system draws attention to certain forms of behaviour (working-class benefit fraud) rather than other more serious social harms (tax evasion) – white-collar crimes and the crimes of the powerful. Finally, moral panics can be generated by the media in conjunction with the politics of power which serve to mystify the real source of people's problems located within the political economy.

Arguably, *Policing the crisis* (Hall et al, 1978) provides a good illustration of what a fully social theory of deviance would look like. Within the context of exploring the phenomenon of mugging during the 1970s, and associated moral panics generated by the media, one argument advanced is that it is not possible to detach human behaviour and repertoires of offending from wider political, socio-economic, macro-structural and cultural variables. In other words, a holistic approach is required. Consequently Hall and his colleagues during the crisis decade of the 1970s analyse mugging and crimes of violence in relation to a number of factors, including the role played by the media in fabricating rather than simply reporting the news. Therefore the state, faced as it was with massive social and economic dislocations during the 1970s (a crisis of hegemony), engendered moral panics, which diverted attention away from the real source of problems located in class relations and a fundamental crisis within capitalism. Accordingly, crime is utilised by a state rocked onto its heels as a 'symbolic source of unity in an increasingly divided class society at a time when traditional modes of providing consensus were diminishing' (Valier, 2002, p 122). Consequently a veil of ideological mystification is thrown over the real source of the problem; capitalism is restructured at the expense of the working class to maintain profitability for the few; and problems that are fundamentally rooted within class conflict are shifted onto authority relations as crime and politics are separated. During a crisis of hegemony the crime card is dealt by a state supportive of capitalism to restore its hegemony at the expense of the working class and its youth.

It was also around this time that the National Deviancy Conference (NDC) was making its presence felt (Zedner, 2003). Beginning in 1968 and associated with Stanley Cohen, David Downes, Ian Taylor, Jock Young, Paul Rock et al, objections were raised against a criminological orthodoxy in league with positivism that, among other things, denied meanings to human actions. It is of interest to note, as an aside, that it was Leon Radzinowicz, when pondering the activities of the NDC and its radical Marxist orientation, who referred to the advocates as 'naughty schoolboys' (1999, pp 229–30). Furthermore it was during the early 1970s that a group of radical social workers published their Case Con manifesto. After reflecting on the creation of the welfare state, a combination of altruism and political expediency, it also constituted a strategic-political response to the threats posed by the militant working class. Therefore it can be theorised that the welfare state was a concession made by the capitalist state during the 20th century in the interests of stability and social order, as well as contributing to the provision of a fit and efficient workforce that would be supportive of a capitalist economy. The radical critique of Case Con draws attention to the practices of casework that can be seen as a *con* in the way it blames the individual for problems which are largely rooted in capitalism such as poverty, inequality, homelessness, economic exploitation and differential life chances. Indeed the professionalisation of social work encouraged by Seebohm in the 1960s (Whitehead and Statham, 2006) resorts to casework as a tool that pathologises behaviours, demanding individual responsibility within conditions of socio-economic inequalities. Consequently:

> Case Con believes that the problems of our 'clients' are rooted in the society in which we live, not in supposed inadequacies. Until this society, based upon private ownership, profit and the needs of the minority ruling class, is replaced by a workers' state, based on the interests of the vast majority of the population, the fundamental causes of social problems will remain. (Case Con manifesto, quoted in Bailey and Brake, 1975, p 144)

Case Con's emblematic status for radical social work was complemented in probation circles by the publication of *Probation work: Critical theory and socialist practice* (Walker and Beaumont, 1981). This text, after exploring the current state of probation practice in relation to the following dimensions – court work, prison-based work and the assimilation of new developments – proceeded to pick up on themes already alluded to above as Walker and Beaumont worked out their radical critique of probation within a Marxist analytical framework. By doing so they theorised that the organisation was involved in the reproduction of capitalist social relations, individualising crime and promoting consensus within society that was basically conflictual. During the course of their book they arrive at the point that 'A fundamental conclusion of our analysis is that Probation Officers are paid to do a particular job for the state and that this role is generally supportive of capitalism' (p 160). Accordingly, they advocated a form of socialist practice characterised by the following elements:

(a)   Defending clients from the worst forms of punitive excess within the criminal justice system, minimising the use of custody and recourse to breach proceedings as a last resort.
(b)   The provision of help consistent with the position taken by Bottoms and McWilliams (1979) in their explication of the non-treatment paradigm.
(c)   Educational work and the provision of useful services to meet the varied and complex needs of clients.
(d)   Community involvement in addition to campaigning action for social change and also changes within the criminal justice system.

In conclusion it is of paramount importance for Walker and Beaumont that there are probation officers prepared to state publicly that prison is indubitably destructive, that laws can be unjust, that law enforcement is discriminatory and that the Probation Service 'cannot cope with the poverty and hardship our work uncovers' (p 169). They also invite magistrates, police officers and prison staff to share responsibility with probation officers in articulating dissent at the system they describe (which of course was a very different slant on multiagency arrangements!).

Finally, and succinctly, Bill McWilliams, in a quartet of papers published in the *Howard Journal* (1983, 1985, 1986, 1987), analyses the history of changing ideas in probation since the period of the police court missionaries towards the end of the 19th century. It should be acknowledged that McWilliams was an important thinker within and contributor to the literature on probation over many years, both as a practitioner, researcher and also academic at the Cambridge Institute of Criminology. In the paper published in 1987 he identified three significant ideologies underpinning practice during the 1980s. These are explained as personalism (see Chapter 3); managerialism; and radical–Marxist approaches mainly represented by the work of Walker and Beaumont. McWilliams argues that all three approaches, notwithstanding clear philosophical differences between them, located people who offend within a framework of government policy and that they were united in pursuing alternatives to custody within a decade committed to this objective. In fact it can be suggested that the 1980s were thematically emblematic of alternatives to custody, rather than rehabilitative optimism, an objective politically supported until the events of 1993 put the policy into reverse gear under Howardian reactionism for political rather than penological reasons.

After reflecting on various perspectives within, and numerous illustrations of, the Marxist tradition, I conclude this overview by alluding specifically to its presence within probation in the 1980s. Valier (2002) summarises the perspective by reminding us that three main claims emerged from this tradition from the 1960s: criminalisation is a central feature for maintaining capitalism; criminals can be seen as proto-revolutionaries who see through the injustices generated by their class position (Left idealism); and there is a focus on working-class crime rather than the crimes of the ruling class, white-collar workers and the powerful. Furthermore Barbara Hudson ties the key elements together within the Marxist perspective by stating that the functions served by social institutions are described by Marxists as 'regulatory (mechanisms to keep the system working), repressive (penalties for workers who do not accept the rules of capitalist production), and ideological (making workers believe that social arrangements which in fact serve the interests of the capitalists, are in the interests of all)' (2003, p 115). Consequently it is suggested that probation is implicated in these functions as it comes into contact with some of the poorest individuals within society in relation to the following variables: problems within the family home; underachieving educationally; unemployment; low income; and impoverished life chances. If supporting evidence is required, beyond perusing statistics produced by the Ministry of Justice, then an ethnographic visit to a local magistrates' court can be instructive. These are the individuals who predominantly make up the supervisory caseloads of probation, particularly within inner-city areas, in addition to occupying prison cells. Additionally these are the people who are currently subjected to the new regime of punitive responses towards offending behaviours but also, in turn, at the receiving end of additional punishments in the form of the benefit sanction and rigorous enforcement policies (Whitehead and Statham, 2006).

Having made these observations it can be argued from within a radical frame of reference that the criminal justice system has been modernised (see the discussion in Chapter 1) to crack down mainly on deregulated populations from whom probation derives the majority of its clients. In fact the argument is advanced in the United States, the United Kingdom and France, for example, that the police, prisons and probation have been restructured to deal with the crisis created by the pursuit of neoliberal-capitalist economics (Parenti, 1999; Young, 1999, 2007; Harvey, 2005; Reiner, 2007a). Neoliberalism is conducive to hardening attitudes towards the urban poor that have culminated in structural violence being imposed 'from above' by the state (Wacquant, 2008), thus producing its inevitable casualties. But the creation of such casualties has its roots in relative deprivation and the material insecurities of late-modern living. This is the new context within which probation operates and therefore its judgements and decisions must be appraised accordingly, particularly if it involves itself in the penalisation of poverty and its potential for exclusion.

Michel Foucault: 1926–84

Introduction and a biographical reference

The history of Western philosophy is as rich and diverse as it is complex (Russell, 1946 [1996]; Tarnas, 1991; Magee, 2001). It is argued that the nature of philosophical enquiry has largely been preoccupied with the question of the constituents of reality (what is real? – *ontology*) in addition to what is real and how we know what is real (routes to knowledge – *epistemology*). Consequently both ontological and epistemological preoccupations have a prestigious heritage, precipitating a multiplicity of world views. Furthermore, and beginning with the Greeks, the dual legacy of rationalism and empiricism represent different approaches to knowledge. As Tarnas succinctly states, the 'secular scepticism of the one stream and the metaphysical idealism of the other provided a crucial counterbalance to each other' (1991, p 71). These competing but also complementary impulses of the dual legacy handed down by the Greek intellect during the *first Enlightenment* (Gay, 1967, 1969) work their way through the Western philosophical tradition, sometimes one acting as a corrective to the other. This can be illustrated by picking up on this preliminary discussion as we move towards the *modern* era and ending with Foucault.

The Renaissance of the 14th and 15th centuries is associated with the development of scientific method that was primarily concerned to establish the laws underpinning the natural world. This is the context for the challenging world views of Copernicus, Galileo and Kepler and later Newton's mechanistic and mathematically derived formulations. In fact the scientific revolution was such a significant event that Copleston is convinced it constituted a clear dividing line within the history of European thought (1953 [2003], volume 3, p 421). It was also around this time that Francis Bacon (1561–1626) promoted the empirical outlook associated with observation, the search for 'facts' and induction. Bertrand Russell designates Bacon as the father of modern empiricism and scientific method (1946 [1996]).

However, prior to building on this empirical orientation a brief diversion is required exemplified by the Continental rationalists – Descartes, Spinoza and Leibniz – who affirmed the efficacy of the human mind's reasoning and deductive powers over reliance on sense experience and empirical observations. It was considered that the human mind innately constituted the source of certain truths about the world. This can be expressed by articulating the position that one could proceed from innate ideas through a process of deductive reasoning, mathematics offering the pre-eminent paradigm, thus relying on one's cognitive faculties to establish knowledge based on a correspondence between thought and object. In other words, it is rationally possible to say what the furniture of the world is really like (Buchdahl, 1969; Descartes, 1988), rather than how it appears to be. Consequently, and prior to Kant in the 18th century, Descartes was responding to challenges fostered by Renaissance science, including truth and certainty surrounding the claims of metaphysics. In fact Descartes wanted to provide for philosophy a degree of certainty analogous to that which it was considered could be located within mathematical and therefore deductive reasoning. Accordingly, Continental rationalism proceeded from the nature and content of ideas within the reasoning mind to an external world that, according to Descartes, was underpinned by a level of truth and certainty guaranteed by a good God who would prevent human beings from being deceived about the nature of reality (Grayling, 2005).

Now if we return to an earlier point, the British empirical tradition – beginning with Bacon and then continuing with Hobbes, Locke, Berkeley and Hume – relocated the basis of knowledge in sense experience *not* the innate ideas of the rationalist perspective. Therefore rather than building a deductive system from innate ideas, now the mind is claimed to be a blank slate, thus passively receiving sense impressions. This implies that ideas or impressions are like the objects that form the basis and source of the sensations it receives. However, and significantly, it was Locke who recognised there could be no guarantee that human ideas of things genuinely resembled the external objects they were supposed to represent (Buchdahl, 1969; Tarnas, 1991, p 334).[12] In other words, when attempting to establish objective and certain knowledge (whatever this means), such claims to knowledge are always influenced, if not contaminated, by the subject's experiential point of view.

Set against the ontological and epistemological positions represented by the Continental rationalists, and later British empiricists, it was the Kantian synthesis in the 18th century that advanced the position that it is not possible to know the world *as it is in itself* in an unmediated fashion. What this amounts to is that the world we experience, and proceed to make knowledge claims about, is shaped and structured by a priori cognitive categories located under the headings of 'quantity', 'quality', 'relation' and 'modality' (see the explication in Copleston, 1960 [2003], volume 6, p 250). These are the a priori mental categories which impose a structure on experience so that the mind is not a passive onlooker or receiver, but instead is actively involved in constructing reality. Kant was operating against the background of Descartes' search for objective knowledge, and came to the conclusion that knowledge is arrived at by synthesising rationalism (Descartes and Leibniz) and empiricism (Humean scepticism). Consequently Roger Scruton, summarising Kant's position, states that while it is possible to know the world independently of one's point of view on it, 'what I know (the world of appearance) bears the indelible marks of that point of view' (2001, p 27). Therefore the Copernican revolution in Kantian philosophy is not that knowledge conforms to objects as in mirror-like thought–object correspondence, but rather objects to knowledge supplied by a priori categories.

Subsequently it is possible to trace a post-Kantian, metaphysical-idealist philosophical system in the work of Hegel. Interestingly Copleston says that with the death of Hegel in 1831 a specific philosophical epoch came to an end signalled by 'the collapse of absolute idealism and the emergence of other lines of thought' (1963 [2003], volume 7, p 2). One such line of thought in the post-Hegelian period is the retreat from speculative metaphysics and emergence of positivism in the 19th century that has already been mentioned. Located within the mindset of the empirical and scientific tradition, it can be underlined that positivism is associated with what can be described as a reductionist ontology and epistemology. Accordingly, it was a philosophical position that denied any validity to knowledge claims outside of and therefore not derived from scientific methodology – observation, facts, experience, induction and empirical verification.

The term 'positivism', associated with Comte in the 19th century (Simon, 1963), conveys the position that positive science constitutes the only reliable source of knowledge about the world. For Comte, arguably indebted, as we saw earlier, to the tradition of Renaissance science – Bacon, Turgot, Condorcet, Montesquieu and St Simon – knowledge had progressed through the law of the three stages from theological, and then metaphysical, to the positive sciences. Moreover, and this point bears repetition, just as laws govern the world of nature, similarly there were those who claimed the social realm of human activity is also governed by discoverable laws. Later, in the 20th century, logical positivism was defined by a number of reductionist features which included: statements claiming to be factual have meaning only if it can be shown how they can be verified; metaphysical speculation is meaningless because unverifiable; and statements about moral, aesthetic and religious values, which are not scientifically verifiable, are also basically meaningless (Simon, 1963). Nevertheless, the exalted claims made by science, as the only reliable route to truth and epistemological certainty, have themselves been questioned. In other words the viewpoint is expressed that the nature of reality, knowledge and truth are just too complex to be encapsulated within any one intellectual paradigm. Perhaps another way of putting it is that all human understanding is provisional and therefore perspectival rather than being absolutely fixed, and that no one single interpretation can ever be definitively final, which includes the scientific paradigm (Tarnas, 1991, p 397).

One such interpretation during the 20th century brings us to the work of Michel Foucault. We have already seen how, notwithstanding the claims made by science to describe the world as it is in itself, Kant questioned whether it was possible for the human mind to acquire this kind of knowledge. Furthermore, the *second Enlightenment* during the 18th century, and its associated modernist project with its faith in science and humanity, believed in rational progress and the power of human reason to establish truth and certainty. By contrast, since the 1970s late or post-modernity has expressed disenchantment with the modernist project by drawing attention to a series of interconnected impulses which can be touched on as follows: globalisation, post-industrialisation, consumerism and the contingent nature of what is real and what we can know. There is no longer any overarching master narrative but a plethora of competing opinions, interpretations and relativities (Belsey, 2002). Moreover, meaning does not inhere within or is given up by the world itself (essentialism), but is existentially contested and constructed. Even though it is extremely difficult to categorise the complex contributions of Foucault, it is argued that his intellectual contribution can be located within a post-modern reaction to the tenets of Enlightenment modernism (Tarnas, 1991, pp 351, 418).[13] This is a position that questions the scientific and progressive assumptions underpinning the age of reason, particularly man as an autonomous and rational subject. One biographical text that can be alluded to before proceeding further is the helpful introductory text by Didier Eribon (1989).

Some key sources: primary

The order of things: An archaeology of the human sciences (1970)
Discipline and punish: The birth of the prison (1977)

Secondary sources

Garland and Young (1983)	Cousins and Hussain (1984)
Merquior (1985, 1986)	Garland (1990)
McNay (1994)	Gutting (1994, 2005)
Hudson (2003)	Scheurich and McKenzie (2005)

Some themes in Foucault

Garry Gutting (1994, 2005) warns us of the danger of distorting the Foucauldian corpus because of its many complexities. Perhaps the main reason for this is that he produced such a diverse body of work that defies categorisation. This warning indubitably applies to *Les mots et les choses* (*The order of things*), the first of two texts I wish to draw attention to because of their relevance for theorising modernising changes within probation. According to Didier Eribon, *Les mots et les choses* is an extremely complex work (1989, p 156) as well as a masterpiece (Merquior, 1986). Nevertheless Eribon assists with the book's interpretation when he says it addresses the point at which man became an object of knowledge within the context of

Western culture with the appearance of the human sciences. The argument is advanced that every period is characterised by an 'underground configuration that delineates its culture, a grid of knowledge making possible every scientific discourse, every production of statements' (Eribon, 1989, p 158). In other words, Foucault appears to be saying that a historical a priori exists which constitutes an episteme governing the parameters of knowledge and thought, so much so that human agency becomes an obviously questionable concept. This is the first theme for consideration.

The order of things (Les mots et les choses)

Before considering *The order of things* one should not rush past the revealing subtitle to Foucault's work: *An archaeology of the human sciences*. Scheurich and McKenzie (2005) address Foucault's archaeological methodology (see also Merquior, 1986; Gutting, 2005) by explaining that it is predominantly qualitative because of its interest in texts and archive material. These authors proceed to elucidate that Foucault was indebted to Georges Canguilhem, Gaston Bachelard and the theme of discontinuity (caesuralism is an epistemological break or rupture). In fact, discontinuity, along with disorder and non-linear development, constitutes a post-modern perspective that stands in opposition to the optimistic modernist position of the linear development of history with a purpose (for example Hegelian, Marxist, Christian teleologies and the Comtean idea of progress). Consequently the archaeological method encapsulates the way in which numerous elements in a society at a given period, from philosophical ideas to everyday opinions, as well as institutional practices, determine its prevailing knowledge base. This can be articulated as the epistemological unconscious of a given era. Scheurich and McKenzie proceed to explain that Foucault's archaeology is a complex set of concepts including '*savoir, connaissance*, positivity, enunciations, statements, archive, discursive formations, enunciative regularities, correlative spaces, enveloping theory, level, limit, periodisation, division, event, discontinuity, and discursive practices' (2005, p 845). With this reference to the archaeological method in mind that, it can be suggested, has affinities with a structuralist perspective (Piaget, 1971; Merquior, 1986; Gutting, 2005), *The order of things* subjects four historical periods to critical analysis:

- pre-classical, up to the end of the 16th century (Renaissance);
- classical, up to the end of the 18th century (Enlightenment);
- the modern period of the 19th century;
- the contemporary age since 1950.

First, the 16th–17th-century pre-classical period is described by Foucault in the language of correspondence, similitude or resemblance between language and the thing it names, a unity or mirror-like images between words, ideas and objects. By unpacking the following terms – convenientia, aemulatio, analogy and sympathy – Foucault seeks to elucidate that this episteme draws all things together in one continuous chain of being, thus providing a knowledge of things which is unmediated. Furthermore Merquior refers to this episteme as 'the prose of the world defined by unity of words and things' (1985, p 43). This is but one of the Foucauldian constructions for ordering things which was stimulated by his chance encounter of Borges' discussion of a Chinese encyclopaedia.

Second, Don Quixote's adventures mark the end of the Renaissance and the beginning of the classical episteme because words and things no longer resemble one another (Foucault, 1970, p 48). Consequently the excavation is advanced that there was a discernible cultural and epistemological disruption (caesurae), underlined when saying that within the space of a few years 'a culture sometimes ceases to think as it has been thinking until then and begins to think other things in a new way' (p 50). Accordingly, the pre-classical age of resemblance is coming to an end in that classical knowledge excludes mirror-like resemblance (similitude) and a new, discontinuous approach based on representation, comparison, measurement and order emerges. Foucault elucidates the differences between the two epistemes by stating that the mind's activity no longer consists:

> ... in *drawing things together*, in setting out on a quest for everything that might reveal some sort of kinship, attraction, or secretly shared nature within them, but, on the contrary, in *discriminating*, that is, in establishing their identities, then the inevitability of the connections with all the successive degrees of a series. (p 55; emphasis in the original)

Additionally mathesis is the basis of a science of measurement and order, the attempt to render phenomena calculable, and Foucault proceeds to say that the fundamental task of classical discourse is to 'ascribe a name to things, and in that name to name their being. For two centuries, Western discourse was the locus of ontology' (p 120). Cousins and Hussain contribute to this discussion by stating that a radical change has occurred because interpretation 'has been replaced by analysis. Resemblance has been replaced by the representation of identity and difference. The entire mode of knowledge had changed' (1984, p 33). Even though Foucault describes these different epistemes, he does not say how one is replaced by another.

Next in the Foucauldian schema is the modern 19th century and beyond, from the natural and physical sciences to the rise of the social and human sciences. Foucault seems to suggest that prior to the emergence of the human sciences in the 19th century man did not exist as an object of scientific knowledge. Nevertheless they made their appearance – biology, economics, philology, and one may add psychology, sociology and criminology – occasioned by the demands of an industrial-capitalist society and the attendant norms of order and normality required. Once again this created a new episteme associated with the demands of capitalism as opposed to feudal arrangements. Therefore it can be argued that systems of thought, the production of knowledge, discourse, language, from a post-modernist perspective constitute the products of power relations. As Foucault himself explains, the human sciences are not:

> … an analysis of what man is by nature (essence); but rather an analysis that extends from what man is in his positivity (living, speaking, labouring being) to what enables the same being to know (or seek to know) what life is, in what the essence of labour and its laws consist, and in what way he is able to speak. (1970, p 353)

The concept of discourse is important because it constitutes an institutionalised way of thinking, imposing limits on what can be said about a subject. Accordingly, forms of discourse are involved not in revealing or *discovering* 'truth', but rather in the *production* of 'truth' that may, of course, be misleading.

Therefore the subject matter of *The order of things* is the way in which *fundamental cultural codes* impose order on experience (Merquior, 1985, p 35), which change over time and are discontinuous with previous epistemes, or, in other words, the existence, at different periods of history, of epistemes that can be approached as paradigms, a mental infrastructure or conceptual grid, which functions as a historical a priori 'almost a historical form of Kant's categories' (Merquior, 1985, p 38). Significantly these discontinuous blocks of knowledge do not advance human beings in some Comtean-linear or progressive fashion nearer towards absolute truths or discoverable forms of objective knowledge of how things are in themselves, either in the world of objects or the category of human existence. Accordingly, the human subject is not the sole origin of meaning, which means for McNay that 'the subject is in fact a secondary effect or by product of discursive formations' (1994, p 5). This perspective not only takes issue with the assumption that meaning inheres within the human subject, but it also calls into question associated notions of truth about human beings, and what constitutes knowledge and progress. As such it can be constructed as a clash between modernist and post-modernist ways of thinking about the nature of man, reality, knowledge, thus raising profoundly complex issues surrounding ontology, epistemology and particularly language (Belsey, 2002), in relation to conflicting perspectives on *discovered* contrasted with *imposed* meanings. The human sciences are not science in the sense that they increase knowledge and truth about human beings. For Foucault knowledge is not geared towards the truth 'but to the everlasting skepsis of endless random interpretations – and his Nietzschean soul refuses to be depressed by it' (Merquior, 1985, p 75).

As a corrective to this Foucauldian-structuralist and somewhat anti-humanist thesis, Anthony Giddens (1982) takes issue with the notion of epistemic blocks or periodisations if this is interpreted as human affairs being determined by unconscious a priori forces human beings are not aware of and can therefore do little to change (once again the tension between structure and human agency, determinism and free will, being played out sociologically and philosophically). Consequently, one might ask, how do we accommodate the notion of freedom of thought and the capacity of human beings for autonomous action, including the efficacy to change given situations, within this Foucauldian framework? It appears there is little room for human agency in this text. Notwithstanding the troublesome nature of such questions raised by Foucault's treatment of structure and the epistemological unconscious of a given era contained in the complex material laid out for us in *The order of things*, the second text for consideration also deals with the theme of discontinuity. This is Foucault's treatment of the transition from public punishments directed at the body to the birth of the prison. Also by doing this we continue to reflect on the relationship between the status of the sciences, knowledge, power, domination and socio-economic relations.

Discipline and punish (Surveiller et punir)

Foucault begins his analysis by describing in graphic detail the execution of Robert-François Damiens in Paris in 1757, in response to his attempt to assassinate King Louis XV. This was an expression of monarchical power under the ancien régime. By contrast the birth of the prison, some decades later, should not be assumed to illustrate the humanisation of punishment according to Enlightenment principles of reason and Comtean progress. Rather the prison – with its timetable for the regulation of bodies, deprivation of liberty, tutelary supervision, programmes that focus on the offender's mind and soul – reflects a new form of Nietzschean will to power. Not so much to punish less but rather to punish better by penetrating more deeply into the individual offender and then outwards from the institution of the prison into the wider social body. Therefore monarchical power, with its assemblages of physical punishments, tortures and executions, is replaced with a form of positive disciplinary power that constitutes different technologies of power and punishment.

Early on (1977, pp 24, 54) Foucault refers to Rusche and Kirchheimer and states they were correct to see torture in relation to existing economic and productive arrangements. Nevertheless Giddens (1982, p 221) suggests that for Foucault it is the prison and asylum, rather than the factory or place of production in Marx, which delineates the modern age (Nietzsche instead of Marx). However, Foucault makes several references to Marx in *Discipline and punish* and it should be reiterated that the late 18th century witnessed the emergence of industrial production contrasted with previous feudal arrangements. This, in turn, produced an expansion of towns and cities on the back of a transition from a medieval to a capitalist mode of production so that 'the economy of illegalities was restructured with the development of capitalist society' (p 87). Consequently it is argued that the birth of the prison, and its expansion in the 19th century, is connected with the problems created by and needs of an industrial society under capitalist arrangements. This was the pressing need to discipline and control those who constituted a threat to the emerging form of social order and vested interests of the few over the many. The prison is said to constitute a new form of power because the institution makes possible the creation of new forms of knowledge of the individual based on close observation. It was also the aim of the reformers, through the institution of the prison, to re-establish the delinquent as an obedient subject, the individual who is subjected to habits, rules and the demands of order (p 128). Accordingly, the power to punish is reconfigured. Additionally the methods which make control of body and mind possible are also found in the disciplinary methods utilised in monasteries, armies, workshops and schools: exercise, training, manipulation by hierarchical power and authority conducive to obedience.

Control over minds and bodies can be illustrated by turning at this point to a more contemporary illustration, but located outside the total institution of the prison, in Wacquant's sociological exploration of the pugilistic arts in *Body and soul*. During his period of study at the University of Chicago in the 1980s Wacquant produced an ethnographic account of boxing that was being practised in a gym not far from the university. When examining the meanings, regimen and ethics of training in this specific art form (in fact Busy Louie acquired first-hand knowledge and experience of boxing), he describes how:

> … the gym functions in the manner of a quasi-total institution that purports to regiment the whole existence of the fighter – his use of time and space, the management of his body, his state of mind, and his most intimate desires. So much so that pugilists often compare working out in the gym to entering the military. (2004, p 56)

This has a Foucauldian resonance. There is even a further reference to the 'monastic devotion' of the boxer (p 60).

Discipline and punish proceeds from what is going on inside the prison to the wider social body, symbolised by the Panopticon. As was mentioned earlier the creation of disciplined, trained and obedient bodies was a necessary requirement for the capitalist industrial machine. It should also be acknowledged that the techniques for examining the individual inside the institution – hierarchical observation and normalising judgement – turns the delinquent into a 'case', the observation of whom becomes an object of knowledge linked to a regime of power. This is the individual rendered measurable and then made amenable to control, classification and eventually normalised. It can also be seen how the prison operates in a realm located beyond legal infraction, the sphere regulated by codified law. In other words, normalising judgements are being made about forms of conduct that are not necessarily in breach of the prevailing legal code. It has therefore been pointed out that numerous judges of morality exist – teachers, doctors, educators, social workers, judges, even probation officers – who operate in spheres which regulate and control behavioural norms (Cousins and Hussain, 1984, p 137) in what is an extended carceral continuum and archipelago.

Towards the end of the book (1977, p 264), Foucault intriguingly argues that the prison, since it inception, has been a 'failure'. What he means is that it does not ostensibly reduce recidivism or diminish the crime rate. By contrast it actively encourages a milieu of delinquency which, at first sight, is the very opposite of the assumed rationale of the prison system. Furthermore the conditions to which inmates are released condemn them to recidivism and adversely affect prisoners' families. Accordingly, one can safely arrive at the conclusion based on numerous criteria that the institution fails, yet it continues to exist, expand and even thrive. Indubitably there is plenty of money for prisons (and imperialistic wars), a relatively expensive mechanism for maintaining law and order. Why should this be the case? Paradoxically, argues Foucault, even though the prison ostensibly fails it is nonetheless *useful*. This is because it produces, as a deliberate political strategy, a specific delinquent class by a deliberate process of criminalisation. In so doing it creates a body of knowledge that is useful for power; it turns the spotlight on one group of fabricated delinquents and thereby directs attention away from other social harms; it justifies the existence of the police; and what seems to be of critical importance, the political construction of a delinquent class separates *crime* from *politics*. Where the last point is concerned this means that crime is constructed as a problem for the criminal, just as poverty can be constructed as a problem for the poor, so that the 'problem' is individualised. Consequently crime becomes detached from the politics of power under capitalist socio-economic arrangements, which diverts attention away from the real source of the problem (see, for example, the analysis of Hall et al, 1978; Simon, 2007). Beirne also advances the intriguing argument that, for Foucault, positivist criminology emerged in France 'as a calculated response to the need for an official and comprehensive discourse which could justify these new strategies of penality', and thus obfuscate the differences between crime and politics (1993, p 68). Furthermore the creation of delinquency divides the working class and turns it against itself and enhances the fear of the prison in working-class communities.

It may be stated that the prison is a failure penologically, yet useful for politically tactical reasons. David Garland raises this point when he says that 'the prison does not control the criminal so much as control the working class by creating the criminal', and this seems to be, for Foucault, the unspoken rationale for its stubborn persistence (1990, p 150). According to the Foucauldian schema it is an institution inextricably associated with the politics of power, discipline and subjugation of recalcitrant populations. Consequently he provides an alternative account of the modern world that resonates with Nietzsche and Weber. Furthermore the Foucauldian thesis is, on the one hand, supported by Cohen's dispersal of discipline thesis (1985), yet, on the other, has been challenged by the analysis of Tony Bottoms (1983).[14] As a retort to the positivist enterprise, Foucault says the following:

> There is not, therefore, a criminal nature, but a play of forces which, according to the class to which individuals belong, will lead them to power or to prison: if born poor, today's magistrates would no doubt be in the convict ships; and the convicts, if they had been well born, would be presiding in the courts and dispensing justice. (1977, pp 288–9)

There is an echo of Foucault in a novel of Eric Arthur Blair (pen name, George Orwell) when we read:

> Fear of the mob is a superstitious fear. It is based on the idea that there is some mysterious, fundamental difference between rich and poor, as though they were two different races, like Negroes and the white man. But in reality there is no such difference. The mass of the rich and poor are differentiated by their incomes and nothing else, and the average millionaire is only the average dishwasher dressed in a new suit. Change places, and handy dandy, which is the justice, which is the thief? (Orwell, 1933, p 107)

Table 2.1 concludes this chapter by summarising bodies of social theory that will later be put to work to explore and explain, in much more detail, the modernised form of probation within the criminal justice system.

Table 2.1: Summarising bodies of social theory

Durkheim	***The division of labour in society*; 'The two laws of penal evolution'; moral education** Crime disturbs society's moral consciousness that elicits a punitive response characterised by passionate outrage, denunciation and vengeance. Law, crime and punishment constitute a visible index of the nature of society, social type and culture, strength of collective conscience, acting as a barometer of social change. Punishment is less concerned with correcting or deterring the offender than reaffirming the moral sensibilities of the law-abiding community, promoting social solidarity and bolstering the collective conscience.
Weber	***Economy and society*; *verstehen*; natural and social sciences; bureaucracy** *Verstehen* is concerned with human understanding, and the meanings human actors attach to their own and others' behaviours. The social science discipline of hermeneutics deals with the complex meanings and interpretations of human action, rather than predictive and invariant laws. Therefore the natural and social sciences inhabit different ontological and epistemological domains, dealing with objects, things and people respectively. Also themes of bureaucracy, managerialism, rationalisation; the image of modernity as an 'iron cage' under industrial capitalism.
Marx	**The Marxist tradition** The base–superstructure metaphor of economic base and dependent non-economic superstructure. The latter includes legal and political institutions, education, family and criminal justice, conditioned by the demands of the productive system which supports the interests of those who own and control the means of production, distribution and exchange. Class-based nature of capitalism; punitive exclusion of surplus populations who, as the subordinate class, constitute a threat to social order under capitalism-neoliberalism.

Foucault	*The order of things; Discipline and punish*
	Epistemological disruptions, radical changes in social unconscious, thinking and institutional practices. Man becomes an 'object' of knowledge for the social sciences, which do not discover the 'truth' of man in his essence, but rather construct forms of knowledge useful for power. Next, from monarchical to disciplinary power and new technologies of punishment, the prison transforms people into objects of knowledge, useful for the politics of power. Post-Enlightenment social order as dystopian Benthamite Panopticon – surveillance, discipline, regulation; the all-seeing gaze of state authorities cast over individuals and families. Normalisation, control of minds and bodies to render docile under industrial capitalism. The separation of crime from politics.

Notes

[1] Beirne (1993) explains how Quetelet and Guerry are the forerunners of the ecology of the crime school that emerged in Chicago in the 1930s. Quetelet contributed to the rise of positivist criminology in that he 'attempted to reveal that the same law–like, mechanical regularity that had been determined to exist in the mechanics of the heavens and in the world of nature also existed in the world of social facts' (Beirne, 1993, p 77).

[2] For additional references on positivism, the natural and social sciences, see Giddens (1978); Garland (1985); Bryant (1985); and Beirne (1993).

[3] For an extended discussion on classical and positivist criminology see Garland (1985); Roshier (1989) remains very helpful.

[4] Merquior (1986, p 38) alludes to Durkheim and Descartes, and suggests Levi–Strauss turned Durkheim on his head in the following way. Durkheimian sociology moved from the mental to the social, from the content of ideas in the mind to the external world, so that the mind mirrored society (Descartes – what is perceived in the mind represents what is outside the mind). But for Levi–Strauss and structuralism the movement is from the social to the mental, from social relations or cultural constructs to intellectual structures.

[5] Durkheim and Merton talked about anomie, but in different ways. Moreover, there are a plethora of sociological and criminological texts that discuss anomie, but probation staff may want to consult Whitehead (2007, p 68f) for an introductory summary of key themes prior to looking at more detailed work.

[6] Additionally the labelling perspective is summarised briefly in Whitehead (2007, p 73).

[7] For additional material on philosophies, theories and *justifications* of punishment, see Bean (1981); Duff and Garland (1994); Hudson (2003); and Easton and Piper (2005). By contrast, when turning to sociological *explanations* of punishment see, for example, Garland (1990); Hudson (2003); and the third edition of Cavadino and Dignan (2002).

[8] For a very helpful paper on Durkheim's theory of penal evolution, see Steven Spitzer (1975).

[9] Radzinowicz and Hood (1990), considering socialist writers towards the end of the 19th century, argue that, for them, law was an instrument which benefited the ruling class. Engels said more about crime than Marx but it is suggested Marx's position was that law benefited property owners; he attacked the bourgeois concept of law and crime. Following Quetelet, crime is a social phenomenon and punishment exists to defend vital interests. He criticised England for its brutal criminal justice system and was more discriminating than Engels in his interpretation of criminal statistics; the criminal is productive and he seems to echo Durkheim that crime is inevitable and beneficial (p 40).

[10] For criticisms of the Marxist tradition see the helpful summaries in Garland (1990, Chapters 4 and 5) and Hudson (2003, Chapter 7).

[11] Post-Kantian philosophy witnessed the attempt to produce a more unified and coherent interpretation of reality. Previously Kant had separated reality into phenomena and noumena, and by doing so imposed limits on knowledge. Subsequently Hegel suggested the purpose of philosophy was to overcome divisions between phenomena and noumena, body and soul, subject and object, finite and infinite, to achieve a more unified approach. Furthermore, for Hegel, the task was to understand reality as a rational process that could be known by the philosopher. By contrast the task of the philosopher for Marx was not so much to understand the world as the unfolding of the absolute/spirit, but rather to change it via social action. The materialism of Marx saw man alienated from his work and socio-economic changes were required to overcome it.

[12] At the end of the second book of the *Essay concerning human understanding*, Locke turns to consider the source of ideas, the relationship between mind and ideas and how knowledge is obtained. He is also aware of problems associated with language. As Copleston explains in volume 5, words can be abused by being used by different people in different senses. Another abuse 'consists in taking words for things and supposing that the structure of reality must correspond to one's way of thinking about it' (Copleston, 1959 [2003], volume 5, p 103). Berkeley also concerned himself with language (Copleston, 1959 [2003], volume 5, p 206). Foucault, in *The order of things*, turns to 'language issues' on several occasions within the context of different epistemes he identifies (episteme understood as a 'positive unconscious' of knowledge; McNay, 1994).

For additional material on the subject of language see the interesting discussion in Belsey (2002) on *Poststructuralism*. Additionally Fairclough takes a challenging position in his book on *New Labour, new language?* (2000), when reflecting on the way in which changing the culture of an organisation depends on changing the language – pertinent for probation developments since 1997. See also Merquior (1986, p 215) on some of the complex issues touching on the use of language.

[13] For some additional help in understanding Foucault see McNay (1994, pp 52–66); Canguilhem's chapter in Gutting (1994, pp 71–91); Merquior (1985, p 56; 1986, p 208); and Piaget (1971, p 128).

[14] See Garland (1990) and Hudson (2003) for a discussion and critique of Foucault's thesis. One should also include Matthews (1999) on Foucault and Weber where it is stated that: 'Foucault's approach is similar to Weber's in a number of ways. Like Weber (1948), Foucault examines in detail how bureaucratic and administrative processes operate within these segregative institutions and how they sustain order and secure compliance. Foucault also focuses on the way in which a bureaucratic institution can become an iron cage which eventually constrains its creators' (p 64). Matthews is here quoting from the Gerth and Mills text (1948).

THREE

Religious, humanitarian and personalist impulses: footprints left by 'the good guys'

Introduction

A developing theme throughout this book is that probation's organisational rationale, situated within the operational dynamics of the modernised criminal justice system sketched out in Chapter 1, has become a site replete with complexity. In other words, it is a multifaceted phenomenon and, because of this, requires an explanatory approach that takes account of various theoretical standpoints. This is why Chapter 2 began to establish the position that it is necessary to summon the excavatory support provided by Durkheim, Weber, Marx and Foucault to facilitate this task. No one approach, represented by any single body of social theory, can adequately capture what can be described as the ontological, epistemological and axiological diversity that currently represents the probation domain. Consequently disparate bodies of social theory are required to foreground complementary but also contradictory layers. Accordingly all of them, in combination, begin to bring into view a clearer image that would immediately become distorted if any one of them was neglected, which will be elucidated further in the next chapter.

Having said that, it is not permissible to remain content, analytically or theoretically, even with the combined weight represented by 'the big guys' of the classical corpus. This is because it is necessary to advance the viewpoint that there has existed, for a considerable period of time, another not insignificant element within probation, the expression of which has influenced the judgements and decisions of the criminal justice system for over 100 years in England and Wales. Not so much a classical social theory as a discernible set of values, a moral sensibility, which has had recourse to the following lexicography: religion, humanitarianism and philanthropy, religious and secular forms of personalism, in addition to social work help, mercy and benevolence. Notwithstanding a politically driven and centrally imposed process of modernisation and cultural change which has dragged probation around the orbit of punishment, personalist impulses have not been eradicated from the operational dynamics of the criminal justice system. In other words, one can plot historically and continue to uncover traces of, in the first decade of the 21st century, footprints left by 'the good guys'. The influence of the good guys may no longer represent a set of dominant impulses for the reason that they have been heavily compromised by the politics of punishment, both in the community and prison. Not that there has ever been a period when they have solely dominated the penal scene, but they are less in evidence now than formerly. It is also possible to suggest that these impulses and sensibilities have indubitably been diluted from *without* (the political impositions discussed in Chapter 1) but also from *within* by organisational representatives who, only two or three decades ago, operated within a very different system of values to the one that currently prevails. In fact it may be suggested that the 'leadership' of probation has allowed itself to be overtaken by the politics of power (and a basic survival instinct), particularly since 1997, when other courses of action were possible, including resistance. All discourses have their day, a perspective that contains some veracity when reflecting on the place and space occupied by social work values within criminal justice during a discrete period of its history. Moreover fashions come and go, as apparently do values and associated narratives within organisations. Accordingly, this chapter draws attention to a religious and humanitarian perspective within the Probation Service, but also the wider context of penal and specifically prison reform. Its longevity needs to be explored. This is a necessary task prior to putting bodies of social theory, personalist impulses and moral sensibilities to work in the next chapter that will conclude the first substantive part of this book.

Some relevant sources

Howard (1777 [1973])	Leeson (1914)
Le Mesurier (1935)	Hinde (1951)
Glover (1956)	Rose (1961)
Clay (1969)	Ignatieff (1978)
Bottoms and McWilliams (1979)	McWilliams (1983, 1985, 1986, 1987)
Garland (1985, 1990)	Rose (1994)

Religious and humanitarian impulses associated with prison reform

Michael Ignatieff (1978), in his nuanced exposition of the penitentiary during the Industrial Revolution (1750–1850), affirms, as of course does Foucault in his graphic overture to *Discipline and punish* (1977), that it was during the 18th century that the system of punishment was predominantly a public spectacle. Moreover, until around 1776 a system of transportation from England to the 13 North American colonies was in operation but, when it abruptly ceased following the War of Independence, certain administrative difficulties were caused for the prevailing system of justice. Subsequently a temporary solution was found in superannuated warships – hulks – prior to the commencement of the second wave of transportation to Botany Bay in Australia after 1787 (Hughes, 1987). In fact this second wave of expulsions continued for a period of 80 years, until the last transport ship left England in 1867. Ignatieff continues the story by reminding us that we had to wait until the 19th century for the system of imprisonment to be firmly embedded within the piecemeal emergence of the criminal justice system. Ignatieff proceeds to develop the analysis by stating that it was during the 19th century that prisons were in the grip of a complex combination of forces. These forces in turn should be located and then disentangled within the wider political, social and economic context of evolving capitalist social relations. Nevertheless one should be reminded that these forces also included measures for reform that can be traced to an earlier period, prior to the 19th century, in the work of John Howard (1726–90), and later Elizabeth Fry (1780–1845). Accordingly, these reforming measures constituted a set of impulses that blended religious and humanitarian elements with political expedience. Therefore not so much a set of alternative impulses that threatened the emerging order of capitalism, or representing a radical challenge to the authority invested in the state, but reforming and humane gestures running alongside class politics, power and the perennial quest for social order. In other words, this can be described as good guy impulses circumscribed and mediated by political imperatives.

According to Ignatieff it is possible to trace a melange of nonconformist religiosity, philanthropy and humanitarianism in the reforming zeal of Howard, who was concerned to improve the physical and mental health of prisoners. It is suggested that Howard's religious sensibilities were not of the order of applying the balm of comfort and warmth to the miscreant's soul, but rather a stern, unyielding and demanding influence, an impulse for reform and human brotherhood, working in conjunction with the discipline and regimentation of the poor in spirit, heart and indubitably pocket. Additionally, within the confines of an 18th- and 19th-century episteme that constructed crime as a disease, a symptom of moral weakness, the offender was categorised as a sinner who required the awakening of conscience by the divine light. Later, when reflecting on the work of Elizabeth Fry, Ignatieff (1978, p 143) draws attention to a spirit of philanthropy, benevolence and a religiosity connected with evangelicalism and quietism (Quaker influences) providing a theological basis for the salvation and moral reform of reclaimable individuals. Fry was not only, as a Christian philanthropist, concerned about the poor conditions she discovered at Newgate, but also about the plight of the homeless. Therefore there is some evidence that can be summoned to advance the view that the penal system in the 18th and 19th centuries and particularly impulses contributing to prison reform had their roots in religion in addition to moral sensibilities manifested in philanthropy and humanitarianism.

In establishing this position one must not lose sight of Ignatieff's sophisticated analysis which he expounds by saying that 'whilst the reformers liked to characterise Prison reform as a neutral philanthropic crusade "above politics", they were, of necessity, drawn into the tactics and strategy of class rule in a time of conflicts' (1978, p 162). In other words, an understanding and analysis of reform must be located within the political parameters of the period in question with its class relations under emerging capitalism; the institutions of prison, workhouse, industrial and reformatory schools; the management and control of the recalcitrant poor constituting a threat to social order; in addition to the inevitable fallout from an economic system conducive to inequality and injustice, particularly for those on the downside of class relations. Nevertheless the importance of Ignatieff's approach is that he accommodates a mélange of impulses into his account of prison reform that takes the reader beyond an account rooted solely in Marxist theory, which we have already considered.[1]

Let me at this point penetrate some of these matters more expansively by referring to R.S.E. Hinde (1951). His little-read and referenced book, *The British penal system 1773–1950*, is more descriptive than theoretical, analytical, or critical, yet I think it contains some material that is worth alluding to within the context of this chapter. Hinde refers to four pieces of legislation during the reign of George III in the 18th century that gave power to the justices of the peace to appoint chaplains to local gaols.[2] In fact Howard discovered chaplains in most county gaols when pursuing his own enquiries (Hinde, 1951, pp 17, 238). It should also be acknowledged when exploring the influence of religion on the penal system during the 18th century that this was the period that experienced the Wesleyan evangelical revival initiated from within the established Church of England. Additionally Hinde draws attention to the work of George Whitfield in Bristol in 1737, then to Abel Dagge who, as the Keeper of Newgate, was converted to Christianity, which animated his spirit in the direction of prison reform. This apparent metanoia led Hinde to state that these 'humanitarian reforms, inspired as they were by deep religious convictions, were also recognised the following year' in the Annual Register of 1761. Consequently, and as indicated earlier, the lives, behaviours and deficits of prisoners could be interpreted within a theological framework as sinners in need of moral reform through the agency of God's saving grace (1951, p 44). It was the same store of metaphysical grace that could kindle the hearts of those who worked with prisoners in the direction of reform. Another example of the latter is Sarah Martin, born in 1791, who stated that 'In the same year (1810) whilst frequently passing the gaol, I felt a strong desire to obtain admission to the prisoners to read scriptures to them, for I thought much of their condition and of their sin before God' (Hinde, 1951, p 71).

It is interesting, before proceeding to other related matters, to pause here so that we can remain with the theme of prison chaplains. Radzinowicz and Hood, at two specific points in their detailed book, *The emergence of penal policy in Victorian and Edwardian England*, turn to consider the work of the chaplain (1990, pp 511, 541–2). It is suggested that they played only a minor role in the 19th-century convict prisons and that governors had the upper hand in terms of influence. Therefore we should be careful not to exaggerate their spiritual influence, or any other form of influence, on prison regimes. In fact it is suggested that chaplains 'seemed to be more like tired functionaries, expected to discharge difficult duties in a hostile environment' (1990, p 541). Initially they were drawn from the Church of England, but from 1864 Roman Catholic priests were appointed. Also Jews and nonconformists were allowed their own religious representatives, in addition to which there were facilities for Hindus. It should also be acknowledged, for the sake of completeness, that the ideological basis of the Victorian era clustered around the salient features of evangelical religion, individualism, laissez-faire liberal economics and post-Benthamite and post-Beccarian utilitarianism (Garland, 1985). Furthermore, towards the end of the 19th century it was the Gladstone Report (Home Office, 1895) that recommended that outside preachers should attend chapel services in prison.

Prior to completing this first section, the situation appertaining to young offenders within the context of personalist impulses and moral sensibilities, notwithstanding the reference to Anthony Platt's research below, should not be overlooked. During the 19th century we can begin to trace the emergence of a separate system of juvenile justice that was manifested in industrial schools for the perishing classes and reformatory schools for the dangerous classes. By the early 20th century the borstal system helped to consolidate these separate provisions, as did the creation of a separate juvenile court established by the 1908 Children Act. Additionally there was further consolidation in the 1933 Children and Young Persons Act that affirmed the welfare principle when working with young offenders. Even though it can be argued that the history of juvenile justice is one of tension between the oscillating demands of care and control, punishment and welfare, justice and treatment, the 1960s stand out as the acme (with hindsight perhaps we should say *aberration*) of the welfare approach. If the 1969 Children and Young Persons Act had been fully implemented, this would have signalled a victory of the welfare approach over one dominated by punishment and custody for young people involved in offending behaviour (Thorpe et al, 1980). However, because of a changing political situation from the summer of 1970, the following decade witnessed a doubling of punitive custody for juveniles; then the 1980s saw a move in the opposite direction; until the 1990s once again witnessed a shift towards punitiveness rather than welfare. There have been, and continue to be, many competing discourses in youth justice as well as adult criminal justice – welfare, justice, managerialism, punishment, authoritarianism. The welfare impulse has not been totally eradicated, but nor has it completely seized the day (Muncie, 2004; Brown, 2005).

Therefore, and by way of summary, if the influence of religion is a factor in analysing and understanding the history of the prison, as well as being associated with reforming impulses after the 1700s in connection with Howard, Fry and many others, it was also a significant factor in the emergence of what was to become the probation system during the 20th century. Writing in 1958 Radzinowicz stated: 'If I were asked what was the most significant contribution made by this country to the new penological theory and practice which struck root in the twentieth century … my answer would be Probation' (1958, Preface). To this we can now turn.

Probation's good guy impulses: orthodoxy tempered with revisionism

With its roots in the 19th-century practices of bail, judicial reprieve and recognisance, and the example of a number of significant individuals including Matthew Davenport Hill and Edward Cox, in addition to what was happening in other countries such as the United States and New Zealand (Leeson, 1914; Rose, 1961; Raynor and Vanstone, 2002), probation work emerged from the Police Court Mission of the Church of England Temperance Society (Whitehead and Statham, 2006; Nellis, 2007). Probation was not conceived as a punishment but rather constituted an alternative to both punishment and imprisonment, containing elements of mercy, advice, assistance, friendship and practical help, mediated through a relationship with a missionary after 1876 and then an appointed officer of the court from 1907/08. Once again, however, we should take great care when analysing the origins of probation. Raynor and Vanstone (2002) argue that it is legitimate to resort to the language of mercy and help when excavating the early history of the probation system within the context of late Victorian philanthropy, evangelical religion and benevolence. Mike Nellis utilises the language of 'humanising justice' when analysing probation history until the early 1970s (2007). Additionally Radzinowicz and Hood state that during the 19th century individual moral reform in conjunction with social amelioration were important features often motivated by 'deep religious convictions, and philanthropic zeal and was thus a true reflection of the dominant ethos of Victorian society' (1990, p 49). Importantly the motivation of the missionaries was a deeply religious one articulated in terms of saving sinners in order to bring them to salvation. Accordingly, the orthodox account is assembled. Nevertheless a necessary injection of revisionism into the explanatory account after 1876 must incorporate the fact that police court missionaries were not extending God's mercy and benevolence to all lost offenders' souls when they appeared before the London Police Courts. The Victorian categories of deserving and undeserving invaded the probation system, and the work of the missionaries orientated towards what is referred to as a middle-class perspective. With this in mind it is interesting to turn to the following empirical corrections.

In an interesting paper by Peter Young (1976), published 100 years after the first appearance of the Police Court Mission, it is first of all acknowledged that reformist impulses in the process of penal developments had been explained by the efficacy of the religious, philanthropic and humanitarian spirit during the 19th century (Young and Ashton, 1956). Nevertheless it was Young's contention that this analysis omitted certain ingredients that he sought to draw attention to in presenting a more rounded sociological analysis of the early history of probation. In other words he was concerned to provide a more nuanced reading of events. Young's main thesis was that towards the end of the 19th century the Probation Service had its roots in the relationship between the classes. In fact this thesis is consistent with a version of social work in that it functioned from within the orbit of the middle class as an attempt to stabilise what was then a rapidly changing social order by extending its largesse towards the working class. Young's position is similar to this. Additionally, however, Young did not see the existence of social work as a mechanism for the liberalisation and democratisation of society, but rather as a means to *drain away* and therefore *neutralise* working-class demands, potential agitation and threats to social order, generated by albeit modified capitalist social relations.

On the one hand, it can be argued that probation work constituted a clear alternative to the Victorian prison system; an alternative to punishment (punishment was in fact suspended and conditional on future behaviour); an act of mercy within a supervisory relationship delivering advice, assistance and friendship. By contrast, after 1907 it functioned as part of a reformed capitalist state; its focus on the individual's soul did not threaten the existing social order; and theological doctrines of salvation and moral reform were conducive to ensuring compliance and order. In other words, Young's analysis was sympathetic to the view that the class position of probation officers, in forming relationships with working-class offenders, was conducive to stabilising the existing social structure under a modified form of capitalism (Stedman Jones, 1971; Garland, 1985). Therefore it had a political dimension and as such constituted more than religious, philanthropic, humanitarian compassion for a specific socio-economically disadvantaged group within society. Probation work was implicated from the beginning in complex class relations, even though Young rejected a class-based conspiracy theory that probation and social work solely existed to promote and maintain ruling class interests. In fact a similar point is advanced when turning to the thesis of Anthony Platt (1977) on young offenders in the United States. The emergence of a separate juvenile justice system in the United States was not an example of humanitarian and liberal developments, argued Platt. Rather, the story he recounted was one of more intrusive supervision, control and the labelling of working-class young people. Consequently political issues, engendered by North American capitalism, were transformed into problems of personal adjustment and, as with Foucault, crime separated from politics. In other words juvenile justice could be understood in terms of malign rather than benign developments.[3]

Even though it is arguably necessary to inject a note of revisionism into the orthodox account, the McWilliams quartet of papers (1983, 1985, 1986, 1987) returned to the view that police court missionaries were possessed of a religious philosophy. The increased power awarded to the justices attendant on the 1879 Summary Jurisdiction Act, then the 1887 Probation of First Offenders Act, enabled the missionaries to inject mercy and leniency into the proceedings of the lower courts. When considering missionary work McWilliams stated that its vision was relatively clear in that it would 'rescue individual drunkards, render them susceptible to the influence of the spirit of God and their souls would be saved' (1983, p 134). After 1876 the magistrates utilised the Police Court Mission on an informal basis to supervise offenders released on recognisance under existing legislation, prior to the legislative creation of the probation system under the terms of the 1907 Probation of Offenders Act. Significantly, argued McWilliams, for a period of 60 years after 1876 the rationale for the Police Court Mission to the courts was the saving of offenders' souls through divine grace (1983, p 138). Subsequently the gradual decline of the missionary spirit after the 1930s, but importantly not its total extinction, was occasioned by the emergence of a more secular and scientific social work discourse as it was applied to the recalcitrant (Whitehead and Statham, 2006).

Cecil Leeson (1914), to whom there are numerous references in the research of McWilliams, had worked as a probation officer in addition to spending a period of two years studying probation systems abroad, mainly in the United States. He referred to probation work in theological terms, as the following illustrates: it is a system for the reclamation and reformation of offenders (p 3) and it is 'essentially constructive and redemptive in character' (p 42). He also made it clear that the probationer required the guidance of a probation officer rather than punishment. Leeson expanded this by saying that it was possible that social and religious agencies could facilitate reclamation, and that the attitude of the officer should be as a 'sensible friend; for the essence of Probation is constructive friendship' (p 114). Before developing the theme under consideration in this chapter it is interesting to allude to a number of additional points raised by Leeson in what is one of the earliest books to have been written on probation in the United Kingdom. First, his work has a contemporary applicability as it stated that probation work was involved in the protection of the community; offending was analysed more at an individual than social level; and the offender's swift return to court was necessary if the probationer breached a court order (which could then rescind the suspension of punishment). Second, and by contrast to those bonds that unite 1907 with the organisation's centenary in 2007, there are marked discontinuities. According to Leeson, probation was about reform and not punishment; an emphasis placed on religious influences; the probation officer was a friend encapsulated in the legislative adage to assist, not a bully or dictator; and the officer must operate with discretion. Therefore there were continuous and discontinuous elements in his account.

If Cecil Leeson's work provides an important resource for understanding probation work during the first few years after 1907, this is complemented by the evidence contained in four Home Office departmental committee reports (1909, 1922, 1936, 1962). These documents, particularly the first three, constitute a rich resource on those impulses under review and contrast markedly with modernising developments since the 1990s. The 1909 Departmental Committee also underlined the rationale of the inchoate probation system as an alternative to punishment – custodial institutions and financial penalties – and that it was suitable for young people as an alternative to the Victorian industrial and reformatory schools. Moreover, the personal influence of the officer was considered an essential component in the realigned system of justice that was taking shape during the early years of the 20th century under a reforming Liberal government. However, the threat of punishment remained for those whose conduct constituted a breach of the court order that would result in a return to the sentencing court. We should remind ourselves that the first probation officers, appointed after 1907, were gleaned from the pool of missionaries that had been accruing since 1876, and by the 1922 report the religious convictions of probation officers remained an essential ingredient in the work. In fact the notion of probation work as a religious vocation was very much in evidence (Home Office, 1922, p 9). Interestingly the second departmental committee report arrived at the conclusion that 'Many qualities were mentioned to us as desirable in a good Probation Officer – sympathy, tact, common sense, firmness, are but a few – but there was general agreement that a keen missionary spirit, based on religious conviction, is essential' (1922, p 13).

By the third and much more detailed report of 1936, part of this document provided a detailed historical survey of the contribution made by former missionaries. These forerunners of the probation system were referred to as examples of a 'humaner spirit' operating within the penal system. Incidentally the document also cited the influences of Howard and Fry during the 18th and 19th centuries. It confirmed that probation officers should avail themselves of religious agencies in their work with offenders (Home Office, 1936, p 64); the probation officer was constructed as a social worker of the courts (p 77); and, to reiterate, the pioneering work of the police court missionaries was given due recognition as follows: 'The example they gave of devotion and self-sacrifice has inspired the work of successive Probation Officers in later years' (1936, p 102). Nevertheless, following the recommendation that the system should evolve into a wholly public service, thus bringing to an end the potential for divided loyalties between the courts and religious associations, religious influences would become attenuated over subsequent decades. Consequently by the 1960s social casework eclipsed theological constructions and justifications for probation practice (Home Office, 1962). However, during a period of change which started to gather force increasingly from the 1960s and 1970s (Whitehead and Statham, 2006), it is appropriate to turn to various academic and practitioner voices that offered support to the impulses and sensibilities which have thematic resonance in this chapter.[4]

Academic and practitioner responses during a period of change

Robert Harris

In two papers produced by Robert Harris (1977, 1980), the argument was advanced that since the mid-1960s probation experienced rapid change and expansion, resulting in the service being drawn increasingly towards the centre of penal policy. Consequently dissonance emerged at three levels that are explained as follows. First, there was moral dissonance, the gap between the justice ideology of society and the welfare ideology of social work. Second, technical dissonance referred to the gap between the task of reducing crime and obvious failure to do so, illustrated by numerous research studies (Brody, 1976). Third, Harris referred to operational dissonance that concerned the complex relationship between care and control that was a distinctive conundrum during the period under review. Therefore one of his central arguments, in response to this predicament, was that the care and control functions within probation work should be distinctly separated. This would result in probation no longer being entrusted to carry out the statutory orders imposed by the courts, which would be the responsibility of a new and separate agency. This would leave the Probation Service to become a court-based social work service:

> ... to provide a highly trained, caring and effective social work service to a disadvantaged section of the community: the offender. It can help him with accommodation, social security, jobs; it can give him counselling with many personal problems; it can teach him social skills; it can help him with marital or family difficulties. (1977, p 436; 1980, pp 180–1)

In the climate of the late 1970s Robert Harris was keen to point out the practical problems involved in implementing such a bifurcated model of probation work, but he was more concerned with its theoretical and ethical efficacy rather than practicability. The lexicography associated with theology may no longer be in evidence, but Harris advocated a distinctive set of axiological impulses within probation work with offenders consistent with personalist sensibilities.

Malcolm Bryant et al

Next, Bryant and other practitioners (1978) *were* concerned with matters of practicability and, after accepting the critique of Harris and also the research which was seriously questioning the efficacy of supervision to reduce re-offending, proposed their two contract model. The primary contract would be made between the court and offender to ensure the latter complied with all the requirements the court imposed. Additionally the subsidiary contract would be established between the probation officer and probationer that would consist in the offer of social work assistance, but at the request of the client and not imposed as treatment. Consequently a failure to comply with the subsidiary contract would not constitute a breach of the primary contract between court and offender. Interestingly the rationale underpinning this approach was that social work help would not be forced onto unwilling clients. Instead a range of welfare services would be made available which could be taken advantage of: counselling, help with family problems, group work, education, welfare rights and employment skills. Bryant et al intended that this approach would encourage clients to deal with their problems, treat them as responsible people and encourage self-determination. The authors also advanced the view that magistrates would have more faith in probation orders if they could determine the length and frequency of reporting under the terms of the primary contract. Accordingly, it addressed some of the criticisms levelled at the Harris thesis, for whereas he argued for a clear separation of care and control, by contrast Bryant et al advocated preserving both care and control but on the basis of redefining their parameters by the way in which both would be delivered and by whom. Therefore probation would become a punishment on the tariff of court disposals according to clear legal requirements, but social work assistance would also be available. It was concluded that, 'In short, offenders would be supervised in the community with opportunities for personal development rather than being "sentenced to social work" as at present' (1978, p 114).

Tony Bottoms and Bill McWilliams

Perhaps the best known and most often cited reconceptualisation of probation practice from the period under discussion is the non-treatment paradigm of Bottoms and McWilliams (1979). These thinkers explicitly stated their purpose as follows:

> We believe there is a need for a new paradigm of Probation practice which is theoretically rigorous; which takes seriously the exposed limitations of the treatment model, but which seeks to redirect the Probation service's traditional aims and values in the new penal and social context. (1979, p 167)

The authors discussed the main elements of practice by claiming that the four basic aims had been and should remain as:

- the provision of appropriate help to offenders
- the statutory supervision of offenders
- diverting appropriate offenders from custodial sentences
- the reduction of crime.

Where the first aim is concerned, Bottoms and McWilliams argued against the medical/treatment model provided by so-called social work experts, understood as something forced onto offenders without proper consultation and which was paternalistically delivered after a one-sided process of assessment and diagnosis. Consequently the word 'help' is an important corrective to treatment, and the rationale of practice based on help is that it faces up to the collapse of the rehabilitative ideal while retaining the values of respect for people and hope for the future. Therefore treatment becomes help; diagnosis becomes shared assessment; a client's dependent need as the basis for social work action becomes a collaboratively defined task as the basis for intervention.

Next, when turning to the second aim, Bottoms and McWilliams were clear that probation officers should accept that probation involved elements of control and surveillance. However, the client should be made aware of the demands of the order consistent with the offences committed. Furthermore, and here is an echo of the Bryant et al model, the court should determine the length and frequency of reporting when clients were made the subject of probation orders. Clients should also be able to accept or reject social work help. The third aim, diverting offenders from custody, could be achieved by social enquiry reports providing social information to facilitate this objective. It is important to keep this aim in mind when we turn to the research findings and changing nature of court documents in Chapter 5. The final aim was concerned to discuss the elusive goal of reducing crime and, consistent with their critique of the treatment model, the authors contended that measures directed primarily at individuals were destined to fail. Because crime was a social problem rather than a consequence of individual pathology, the argument was advanced that it was possible to reduce crime by 'microstructural and socially integrative ameliorations within communities' (p 188). This model, in addition to other contributions being discussed here, must be seen as a response to what was referred to as the collapse of the rehabilitative ideal that had a major impact during the 1970s, precipitating a range of responses.[5]

David Haxby

By the end of the 1970s the Probation Service was, it is reasonable to argue, at a crucial stage of development. Many changes had occurred and more were anticipated, and it was in this situation that David Haxby advanced the argument for the ongoing development of a separate community correctional service (separate, that is, to assimilation within reorganised social services departments, which was a real possibility and which actually occurred in Scotland: McIvor and McNeill, 2007). Haxby's notion of a community correctional service would continue to provide alternatives to custody, it would be involved in crime prevention, it would also have to diversify its one-to-one casework methods by providing group work, and it would remain involved in penal institutions, after-care and hostels. This was a case for a reconceptualised Probation Service that had changed much since the fourth and last departmental committee report of 1962. But what is interesting, notwithstanding change afflicting the service and a corresponding case for change being advanced by Haxby, is the following comment: 'It is my hope that the twentieth century will be able to devise a durable, but rather more flexible and humane, system for dealing with offenders in the community, reflecting a different set of values' (1978, p 299). If Bottoms and McWilliams retained a place for a helping impulse, Haxby wanted to hold on to humane responses.

Peter Raynor

Moving on, it was during the mid-1980s that Peter Raynor (1985) made his contribution to a reconceptualised Probation Service. If rehabilitation via a casework approach had become a redundant ideology, how could one begin to rethink probation? While accepting the critique of Bottoms and McWilliams (1979), Raynor also wanted to retain a philosophy of respect for people, in addition to client responsibility and informed choice, rather than diagnosis and coercion. Therefore Raynor recast probation in terms of a participatory, problem-solving, dispute management model, in which negotiated and agreed outcomes to the problems created by crime were preferred to imposed goals and one-sided procedures. Importantly this approach would enable probation officers to be involved in the criminal justice system that embraced offenders, victims and the community. The aim was not to eliminate crime, which was not feasible, but rather to contribute more to satisfactory ways of living with its consequences. Presciently he warned back in 1985 because the service was being pushed in the direction of more social control, that humane and social work values were important features of probation practice and should remain.

Bill McWilliams

At this point I would like to return to the McWilliams quartet of papers, specifically the final contribution published in 1987. Nearly 10 years after Haxby's book was published Bill McWilliams began his paper by summarising the three main phases of probation work that he had previously analysed. The first phase, from 1876 to the 1930s, contained the theological impulse of saving souls by God's grace. It was the phase of special pleading. The second phase of 'scientific' diagnosis lasted from the 1930s to the 1970s, that is prior to when the collapse of the rehabilitative ideal was fully felt. Then, according to McWilliams, the third phase began in the 1970s that provided the context within which he compiled and completed his quartet during the 1980s. By this time the religious mission was a distant memory as the offender became situated increasingly within a framework of secular government policy. Consequently three main schools of thought were identified: emerging *managerialism*; the radical *Marxist* perspective associated with Walker and Beaumont (1981); and what he referred to as *personalism*. I have previously alluded to the first two, but at this point I need to expand on the doctrine of personalism.

If we approach the rationale of probation practice from the standpoint of a social work, people-orientated profession, then it may be suggested that it is the doctrine of personalism that locates the individual and salience of personal relationships at the centre of theory and practice. It can be postulated that the concept has a long and distinguished history within the Western philosophical tradition and constitutes a corrective to what has become an increasingly scientific, technological, computerised, bureaucratic and therefore impersonal situation for human beings. There is an echo here of the Weberian image of rationalisation associated with the post-Enlightenment modern world as a technicist iron cage from which there is no escape. Accordingly, the personalist ethic emphasises personal and human categories that are set against the drift towards the forces of impersonalism (Mounier, 1952).

Additionally personalism conveys the axiological position that human beings have innate and irreducible meaning and value. Accordingly, the individual is deemed worthy of respect and as a rational being should be treated as an end, rather than used as a means to an end. Nor should a person be approached as an object, thing or 'it' because they are always 'subjects'. In fact within the probation tradition there is an identifiable personalist bibliography: Biestek (1961); Hugman (1977); Millard (1979); Bailey (1980); Stelman (1980); and Raynor (1985). Some of my own work (Whitehead, 2007) is also written from within a personalist-radical tradition that argues the case for probation as a social work organisation in clear opposition to an impersonal, risk-obsessed, politicised, computerised and technicised bureaucracy. It also resists probation officers being reduced to the role of bureaucratic technician by endorsing the notion of therapeutic imagination. Arguably the language of personalism can be seen as the contemporary and secular manifestation of those religious impulses that can be traced to the penal system since the 18th century. In other words, the ethic of personalism encapsulates humanitarianism and social work help directed towards needy people, without a commitment to theological orthodoxy. This chapter contends that probation work within the criminal justice system is not currently, nor has it ever solely consisted of, expressive forms of punishment (Durkheim), class-based justice (Marx), impersonal bureaucratic responses (Weber) or discipline and control (Foucault). This is because evidence exists to support the view that from missionary endeavours to secular social work there have been employees who have been vocationally motivated by the impulse to care, understand, befriend, help and provide humanitarian forms of assistance even to people who offend. Nevertheless, both the religious and secular impulse to understand and care for people in difficulty can be encapsulated within a personalist ethic.

Additional contributions

During the late 1980s I was involved in researching various aspects of probation practice in the North East of England (Whitehead, 1990). On this occasion a total of 11 in-depth interviews were conducted with probation officers in two probation teams. After analysing a number of social enquiry reports where a Probation Order was made by the courts, then later discussed in detail with respondents, content analysis revealed how officers included the following terminology when working with their probationers: help, support, advice and guidance. This was tantamount to providing a predominantly welfare-orientated service to clients, who had a variety of social problems in the areas of accommodation, finance, depression and stress, alcohol and unemployment. In fact this research found that, out of a total of 132 cases that were included in the study, 79.5% were unemployed and 60% had no educational qualifications. A few years later research undertaken with young offenders, by Lancaster University academics, found widespread disadvantage among probation clients. Specifically 64% were unemployed and there was evidence of impoverished educational experiences (Stewart et al, 1994).

Returning to some of the findings of my own research in the 1980s, when discussing underpinning and sustaining ideologies with respondents these were articulated as advise, assist and befriend; care and help; and a social work service which was utilised to pursue the goal of rehabilitation. Punishment hardly featured at all, which is understandable because this was before *punishment in the community* started to take hold of the organisation. I summarised part of the findings of this study, worth repeating in the modernised context, by saying that:

> In essence, whilst Probation Officers are engaged in a diverse range of practices, which are sustained, at times, by conflicting ideologies and with an eclectic approach to methods, *the unifying thread weaving its way through all the paradoxes and dilemmas is a commitment to a personalist philosophy concerned with the meeting of human need.* Probation work, for these respondents, is primarily about a social work service to the disadvantaged and not about social control or social action. (Whitehead, 1990, p 152; emphasis added)

During the same decade Fielding (1984) interviewed 50 probation officers and found that empathy and support were important attitudes towards Probation Service clients.

Conclusion

Alongside the introduction to and exploration of bodies of social theory in Chapter 2, this chapter establishes the point that religious beliefs, personalist impulses and moral sensibilities have been woven into the textures of the penal system and particularly the Probation Service throughout its 100 years of history. To some extent they remain part of the contemporary service, receiving some support from the literature associated with NOMS, but there are other contradictory pressures very much in evidence that were alluded to in the first chapter. The main elements of Chapter 3 can be summarised as follows, in Table 3.1.

Table 3.1: Summarising the personalist perspective

Personalism	A series of overlapping personalist impulses and moral sensibilities associated with evangelical religion. Humanitarian values, altruism and benevolence; advise, assist and befriend the probationer from 1907. Alternatives to custody and punishment; care and compassion, tolerance and social work assistance; understanding, support and help. The importance of establishing personal relationships between probation officers and people who offend.

After introducing bodies of social theory in Chapter 2 ('the big guys'), and now spending some time with 'the good guys' of the criminal justice system, Chapter 4 begins to put these theories and personalist impulses to work in order to explore and explain more fully what the modernised and culturally transformed Probation Service has become.

Notes

[1] The chapter on imprisonment by Rod Morgan (1997) considers how 18th-century penal reformers were motivated by a blend of religion and humanitarianism. By contrast Roger Matthews (1999) marshals his evidence in such a way to provide a more critical account of penal history. In other words, not so much a story of enlightened reform that attenuated punishment, but rather a different form of punishment, which echoes Foucault's analysis. Additionally, on John Howard, and then Elizabeth Fry, Matthews states that these two in addition to other 'evangelically-minded reformers, wanted Prisons to operate as healthy and efficient institutions' (1999, p 7). Therefore a number of factors are relevant when theorising the prison. Finally it is of interest to refer to Copleston's analysis (1966 [2003], volume 8). When assessing the work of Jeremy Bentham and the doctrine of utilitarianism, he supports the view that in the movement for social reform during the 19th century humanitarian influences, sometimes rooted in Christian beliefs, played a significant role.

[2] During the 1700s Hinde (1951) confirmed that justices of the peace had the power to appoint chaplains to gaols and that Howard found chaplains in most county gaols (pp 17, 238). Moreover, relevant 18th-century legislation is as follows: 13 Geo III, c 58. This was amended later by 22 Geo III, c 64; 55 Geo III, c 48; 58 Geo III, c 32.

[3] The Garland thesis (1985) should be alluded to. One must not overlook the wider context of *change* towards the end of the 19th century, and how these changes precipitated a *crisis* in relation to the role of the state in socio-economic matters – from laissez-faire to more state intervention – including the most effective means to manage, contain and control the recalcitrant poor, some of whom were offenders. There were many *responses*, at social and penal levels, to these changes and crises, one of which was social work and the beginnings of probation in 1907. Consequently mercy and benevolence melded with a changing political framework that could employ probation work in the service of a new approach to controlling and exercising discipline over offenders on behalf of a modified capitalist state. Altruism and political expedience were therefore held together in a realigned class-based politics during the early years of the 20th century. The idea of religion as ideology that, in Marxist terms, masks the true function of the criminal justice system which fundamentally addresses the politics of power rather than overt humanitarian benevolence.

[4] It should be acknowledged, for the sake of completeness, that B.B. Gilbert (1966) spent some time addressing those humanitarian agencies in Victorian society that were concerned with the souls of individuals. Next Le Mesurier, writing during the 1930s

(1935), included material on the religious influences of the missionaries. Young and Ashton discussed the salience of religion in their excavation of social work in the 18th and 19th centuries. In fact it was stated that in 'some quarters there existed a belief that if only the poor could be persuaded to read their Bible all would be well' (1956, p 31). Furthermore, and intriguingly, Elizabeth Glover's book on *Probation and re-education* (1956) contains a chapter on faith, indicating that the religious impulse remained a feature of the work some 70 years after the first missionary was appointed. Nevertheless it is possible to express care and concern for people without being committed to a specific religious orientation, which can be described as a secular form of personalism.

[5] Reform and rehabilitation are ideas with a long association within the prison and probation systems. For Mathiesen (2006), rehabilitation in prison conveyed the notion of a return to law-abidingness. Furthermore Garland argues that it played a prominent role in the 20th-century penal welfare system. In fact it was the 'hegemonic, organising principle' (2001, p 35) whose acme can be found during the 1950s and 1960s, supported by an inclusive welfare state. However, the rehabilitative ideal has taken a battering since the 1970s and its decline is one of Garland's indices of change in *The culture of control* (2001).

FOUR

Social theory and organisational complexity: putting theories and impulses to work

Introduction

The purpose of this chapter is to put to work the theoretical tools established in Chapter 2 ('the big guys'), in addition to the personalist impulses and sensibilities discussed in Chapter 3 ('the good guys'), with a view to explaining what *probation has become*. I have already discussed the way in which probation studies have been approached over the years from the descriptive and sequential, to various ideologies that cover discrete historical periods, then finally the possibility of applying social theories to account for the becoming of probation by its centenary year (1907–2007). Arguably it is this third approach which is the most fruitful when trying to account for organisational complexity and multifacetedness, predominantly a consequence of modernising convulsions associated with New Labour reforms since 1997. In fact it is worth repeating that modernisation has been at the heart of the change agenda within the public sector (Cabinet Office, 1999), and where probation is concerned is associated with the following features: the heightened attention afforded to punishment talk and responses; organisational restructuring associated with the creation of a nationalised service in 2001 followed by NOMS in 2003/04; de-professionalisation on the back of computerisation, bureaucratisation and the creation of a target-audit culture; the launch of accredited programmes; stringent enforcement practices; and new community sentences provided by the 2003 Criminal Justice Act. I begin the following exploration by revisiting but also developing the theoretical framework established by Durkheim, Weber, Marx and Foucault, prior to exploring a remaining vestige of the personalist perspective with the good guys.

Organisational and political knee-jerk reactions

When former Prime Minister, Tony Blair, was resident at Chequers during the Easter of 2000, there is evidence he allowed his political imagination to wander, which culminated in the following memorandum:

> On crime, we need to highlight tough measures.... We should think now of an initiative, e.g. locking up street muggers; something tough

with immediate bite which sends a message through the system. Maybe the driving licence penalty for young offenders. But this should be done soon and I, personally, should be associated with it. (Quoted in Windlesham, 2001, pp 275–6)

At first sight it may appear less than straightforward to juxtapose Durkheimian sociological insights with probation work even though, as we saw earlier, Durkheim directly addressed issues of crime and punishment in *The division of labour in society*, 'The two laws of penal evolution' and, to some extent, *Moral education*. Nevertheless it is possible to suggest that part of the Durkheimian corpus draws attention to certain identifiable features that contribute to an exploration of what probation has become. Accordingly, over recent years the Probation Service has fallen under the spell of a more intrusive and politically driven penal policy, one feature of which is the rise of expressive forms of action, including punishment, with its heightened emotional tone. We should remind ourselves of how Lucia Zedner succinctly summarised the Durkheimian position by saying that the function of punishment is less concerned to control crime than it is to be a vehicle for expressing outrage when a crime is committed, with a view to reaffirming the social value transgressed. In other words, the subject of punishment is not primarily the offender, but rather the powerful message being communicated throughout the whole social body in response to crime events (2004, p 77).

Continuing in this vein, David Garland (2001) propounds that the late-modern crime complex (the one which has emerged since the 1970s mainly in the United States and the United Kingdom) has responded to the predicament posed by an increased sense of insecurity and risk, including rising crime, in three main ways: adaptation, denial and acting out. In fact contemporary crime control policies operate at two distinct levels: an instrumental means-to-an-end directed at offenders and an expressive-emotional end-in-itself communicating a cogent message throughout the social body. The latter, resonating with retribution, condemnation and denunciation, has emerged as a salient feature of populist penal politics which, in turn, ineluctably draws probation staff into a cultural trajectory affecting thinking, feelings and individual/organisational behavioural repertoires when responding to people who offend. Additionally this expressive tone is repeatedly fed by a rich diet of injudicious reportage in media outlets, a veritable surfeit of sensationalist headlines responding to the phenomenon of crime that in turn drives government policies in a punitive direction. Even government ministers are not averse to passionate knee-jerk reactions exemplified by their emotional rhetoric rather than providing a dispassionate analysis of personal and social problems, of what lies beneath the latest ephemeral event or media-driven headline. *In fact they comment on the public bad and good – a comment for every human occurrence!*

Within a chapter utilising bodies of social theory as well as being empirically based, it is possible to hint at Durkheimian features within probation practice illustrative more of expressivism and acting out. First, and to set the scene, one of Garland's indices of penological change, which has disrupted penal-welfarism[1] and which prevailed for most of the 20th century, is expressive justice, reflecting a heightened emotional tone (2001) if not a vestige of vindictive populism (Reiner, 2007a). It may be suggested that acting out, manifesting the display of sovereign power, is a response that resonates with the war against crime touched on earlier.[2]

Second, George Mair et al's research (2007) on the 2003 Criminal Justice Act found problems with, for example, the Suspended Sentence Order, which implicates probation in up-tariffing offenders, thus making sentencing more punitive, which is a point acknowledged by Lord Carter's report on the state of prisons (2007, p 51). In other words, this new sentence, which has been available since 2005, is used as an alternative to community rather than custodial sentences, and probation reports prepared for sentencers seem to be contributing to this upward custodial trend for which there is some empirical support. Consequently during April/May 2008 the Ministry of Justice invested an additional £40 million into probation to cover the period 2008/09. This cash injection was allocated to facilitate community rather than short custodial sentences, in addition to improving compliance with community orders and licences to reduce the need to initiate breach and recall proceedings that have also fuelled custodial inflation. Significantly the share of this allocation in one specific probation area precipitated a business plan for the period 2008/09, which specified how the money would be spent. It is recorded that some of this additional funding would be used to reduce proposals for custodial sentences in court reports because it was found that the Teesside Probation Service proposed custody in a high percentage of pre-sentence reports (PSRs) at 5.2%. Significantly this percentage figure is much higher than the national average of 2.7%, and constitutes the fourth highest in the country. This is the same local criminal justice system which had its problems overusing custody during the 1980s compared to the national scene, specifically for young people (Whitehead and Macmillan, 1985), and it is as though each new criminal and youth justice generation needs to be reminded of this in order to avoid perpetuating previous avoidable errors.

Third, inappropriate recommendations in breach reports prepared by probation can have serious consequences for offenders.[3] Again the Carter review of prisons (2007) found that the number recalled to prison for breaching licence conditions increased from 150 in January 1995 to 5,300 in August 2007. The number in prison for breaching (failing to comply with) a community court order increased from 180 in January 1995 to 1,200 in August 2007. In turn these factors are swelling the prison population. It may therefore be extrapolated that a review of recommendations contained specifically in breach reports for magistrates' courts is required because they can be prepared by probation service officers (PSOs) rather than professionally trained and qualified probation officers (although there are also problems with PSRs, which *must* be prepared by qualified staff, as we have just seen). Mark Oldfield (2008) stated that in 2002 there were 4,083 PSOs rising to 7,247 in 2006, a 77% increase. In other words, qualified probation officers comprise only 47% of probation staff (Haines and Morgan, 2007, p 187). This could be a significant factor worthy of critical scrutiny within a context where enforcement has received intrusive political attention if not encouragement since 1997. This means that unqualified members of staff are very much involved in the writing of breach reports (as well as the delivery of accredited programmes), without much attention being given to the consequences for practice outcomes of the former specifically. Furthermore it is important for the criminal justice system to differentiate between sanctions available for breaching probation rules that do not involve committing new offences, and re-offending while subject to a community order. This is because the sanctions for the former should arguably be less punitive than the latter because the levels of seriousness are not the same. Yet both have been subjected to the same punitively emotive discourse.

Fourth, it should be recorded how initial proposals by government on breach of community orders prior to the 2003 Criminal Justice Act included a mandatory prison sentence for a second unacceptable failure to comply. Moreover there was even an attempt to withdraw state benefits from offenders for a reported failure to comply *even before* a finding of guilt was established by a court by testing out the evidence.[4] It has therefore been stated that, with hindsight, it is difficult to see how government ministers and their advisers failed to appreciate that the imposition of punitive sanctions before establishing a finding of fact by due process of law not only undermined a fundamental precept of justice, but also amounted to being punished twice (Windlesham, 2003, p 275). This amounted to putting political and punitive imperatives before the claims of justice, individual circumstances and the evidence. In fact what other reasons could there have been for the introduction of the benefit sanction experiment from 2001 to 2009, which allowed a proportion of state benefit to be withdrawn for up to four weeks from an unemployed offender? It is tantamount to an additional punitive tax on the poor with its questionable morality and efficacy to reduce further offending. The same question can be posed when thinking about pursuing a US-style policy of zero tolerance, the three strikes legislation contained in the 1997 Crime (Sentences) Act and the language of *war against crime* (see Simon, 2007, on the war against crime in the United States). These illustrations, it may be suggested, are constitutive of organisational and political responses at a visceral level that taps into a primitive emotional urge in the face of wrongdoing. Such responses communicate a powerful message via government and the courts throughout the whole social body. In fact such measures present a 'symbolic spectacle of reassurance' directed at the law–abiding majority (Pratt, 2007, p 30).

Consequently the application of a Durkheimian theoretical framework to these developments suggests probation may be more involved in emotionally expressive practices rather than adhering to dispassionate professional and organisational logics designed to explain and control crime, provide help and support and prevent the damaging effects of custody. Accordingly, the organisation allows itself to become captured by the prevailing cultural zeitgeist of punishment for its own sake, doing what is expedient rather than what is morally right, a veritable conduit for the rich and sometimes disturbing symbolism of gesture politics at the expense of certain sections of the community. This represents the dilution of its historic mission as an alternative both to punishment and custody enshrined within the probation ideal (Whitehead, 2007). Indubitably the Probation Service is constantly under considerable pressure to demonstrate credibility with politicians, courts and the wider public by resorting to punitive gestures in response to complex human problems within neoliberal regimes (Harvey, 2005; Wacquant, 2008). Nevertheless emotive knee-jerk reactions operate more at the level of political expedience, as in breach policy and the benefit sanction, than doing what could be deemed to be penologically effective, rational, helpful or even evidence-based. Jock Young (2007, p 40) discusses the expressivity of crime displacing its instrumentality. This is complemented by organisational expressivism fuelled by the politics of outrage and punitive vengeance largely directed against some of the most vulnerable people within society.

It can be argued that the growing involvement of probation in the political web of punishment is manifested in a much greater preoccupation with risk and harm, public protection, punishing and controlling offenders via tougher and demanding community sentences, and stricter enforcement arrangements. Consequently it is a retributive penal agenda, fuelled by punitive populism, which has shifted the rationale of probation from caring control to punitive control (Burnett et al, 2007). Moreover, and to repeat, all four tiers of the NOMS offender management model incorporate some measure of punishment. Therefore the shift from advice, assistance and befriending, to enforcement, rehabilitation and public protection, facilitates the message that crime is a key indicator of a deep-seated malaise within society and that the punitive response contributes to reinstituting a sometimes fragile social order. Whether it reforms or deters the offender is not really the issue but rather the powerful message communicated throughout the whole social body from politicians and on through the media, courts and the Probation Service. Within this process offenders become expendable subjects within a process resonating with Durkheimian themes where punishment is used to bolster the law-abiding through targeted expressions of outrage and vengeance. The system may no longer involve itself in hanging and whipping, but there is evidence of a punitive drift associated with New Labour after 1997 and before that with the Conservatives after 1979. The dominant message is that something is being done about crime, but at what cost for the future cohesion and stability of the social body? By engaging at this level probation is doing more harm than good.

Relentless march of the bureaucratic technicians into the 'iron cage'

It has already been suggested that selective Weberian themes have an appealing cachet when excavating what probation has become within the modernised criminal justice system. It is worth repeating that *verstehen* draws attention to an understanding of the individual as the primary unit of sociological analysis, which challenges the contemporary preoccupation with bureaucratically managing aggregates of potential risk through numerically based computer systems (Young,

1999; Whitehead, 2007). Then, second, there is the category of bureaucracy itself, and the main elements recorded in Weber's *Economy and society* can be reprised as follows: a specialised division of labour with its hierarchical chain of command; the actions of officials which operate within the parameters of rules and regulations leave little room for individual autonomy, initiative and discretion; appointments to office are based on merit; a clear distinction between public and private life; and a uniformity of organisation replete with documents, files and the knowledge of technical experts. Additionally Weber advanced the view that a major feature of the modern capitalist world was the trend towards rationalisation. This conveys the meaning that it was planned, technical, calculable, measurable and efficient. However, this could be at the expense of human feeling and as such could be described as the disenchantment of the world (MacRae, 1987, p 86; Turner, 1996, p 62). Bureaucracy may well be the most technically efficient form of domination in a modern, capitalist, industrial society, but it comes at the cost of a personalist ethic that will be highlighted in the following analysis.

As the probation system and its initial theological mission evolved into secular complexity within an expanding organisation by the 1960s, managerial tendencies began to make their mark (McWilliams, 1987, 1992; Whitehead and Statham, 2006). However, it is necessary, I think, initially to differentiate *managerialism* from *bureaucracy* as analytical categories because the two are not necessarily synonymous. This is because managerialism can be a positive, creative and arguably necessary construct within complex organisations that purport to work with people who have offended, even within those committed to the principle of *verstehen*. In other words, management can be a creative force that can be utilised to empower staff to work in such a manner that it is committed to understanding and helping individuals with their needs and problems. Indubitably there is nothing to prevent managerial structures from supporting and complementing such an organisational configuration. By contrast it can be argued that creative management is different from, and can even slide into, bureaucratic inertia and it is the latter that is often portrayed pejoratively. This is because bureaucratic systems and structures, rules and regulations, impersonal procedures and processes, can be put before, almost as ends in themselves, human–professional relationships and the initial purpose of the organisation. Therefore these two approaches should be disentangled from each other, and we need Weber to remind us that the development of bureaucratic power should be prevented from controlling rather than serving the organisation and its values.

On the back of the collapse of the rehabilitative ideal and accompanying social work rationality, which supported professional training to establish requisite people skills – building relationships, engaging with individuals and probation officers exercising autonomy and discretion when formulating judgements and making decisions about people – the new rationality of the period since 1997 has been orientated towards the efficient containment and control of risky populations. Consequently the language supplied by new public management[5] has transformed the professional probation officer with the potential for exercising therapeutic imagination into a functioning bureaucratic technician accompanied by the relentless pursuit of economy, efficiency and effectiveness; achieving value for money; chasing politically imposed objectives and targets; and the auditing of tasks in a more routinised environment. In fact a public service organisation has been modernised and culturally transformed into a *business* controlled not so much by professionals from within the organisation, but by civil servants and government officials since it was centralised and nationalised in 2001.

The work of Colin Leys (2003) develops the point that the Blair governments after 1997 accepted and continued to build on the legacy of the Thatcher–Major era. This was the era of pro-business, privatisation and an increasingly marketised public sector that operated as a business in conditions of economic freedoms complemented by a strong centralised state. What the Conservatives initiated during the 1980s, New Labour continued after 1997 with its audits, league tables and targets, which undermined professionalism and trust by the 'we know best' approach of central government (O'Neil, 2002). Accordingly, within the Probation Service the creation of a business-like and market-driven operating environment has transformed a people-orientated service into one of commodities and products that can be competed for in the marketplace by public, private and voluntary agencies according to the principles of contestability. Even though such developments could raise standards of performance within the criminal justice system, on the other hand, bureaucratisation with its emphasis on technical and calculative features may well attenuate the pursuit of social and criminal justice that has been part of probation's remit over a number of years. In fact John Pratt says that the 'scientific' assessment of risk, and accompanying panoply of actuarialism, helps to inject legitimacy into the concept of dangerousness. Moreover it allows bureaucratic organisations to avoid 'the moral consequences of their policies by relying on statistical computations rather than human judgements' (2007, p 134). Consequently it keeps people at a distance; prevents meaningful engagement with the individual person as the primary unit of analysis within the context of social work relationships; and 'fixes' the category of risk conducive to managing people but not necessarily understanding human actions. Within this analytical context serious questions should be posed concerning the time probation staff, including social workers, actually spend engaging with their clients compared to sitting in front of computer screens in order to maintain the structures of accountability within bureaucratically controlled public service organisations. The answer to this question could, I suspect, be revealing but also disquieting for a number of organisations.

Additionally it can be argued that a number of these bureaucratic elements, associated with the appearance of NOMS in 2003/04, can be slotted into a Weberian bureaucratic framework. In other words, the modernised business-orientated and commercially driven organisation has become more *calculable*, a target culture emphasising quantification and measurement; *efficient*, pursuing maximum outputs for minimum inputs; *predictable*, the imposition of a blanket of national standards to curtail local variations; and *controlling uncertainty*, reducing staff autonomy, discretion and scope for individual judgements and decisions. In fact while the provision of help and support remain part of the NOMS structure, one of the sustained criticisms is that case management, currently termed 'offender management', has been perceived as a direct threat to the work of practitioners with offenders. This is because of the additional time needed to undertake bureaucratic tasks and also because of an increased emphasis on referring probationers to other services. It can be said that reliance on the time-consuming computerised OASys, in addition to the offender management model located at the heart of NOMS, exacerbates these trends (Mair et al, 2006).

At this point it is interesting to turn to the insights of Michael Barber (2007), who was head of the Prime Minister's Delivery Unit from 2001 to 2005, and who was directly involved in public service reform. The book he compiled, based on his first-hand experiences, is devoted to the mechanics of 'deliverology' with its strategies, planning, objectives, targets, delivery maps, delivery chains, trajectories, stocktakes and league tables.[6] Intriguingly Barber informs the reader that not everyone in the public services likes league tables, but extraordinarily 'I love them' (2007, p 96). There is a touch of the obsessive and even oppressive about this self-congratulatory text, and the way in which it justifies the expanding net of central government control by resorting to incomprehensible government-speak infected with jargonistic flourishes.

Furthermore there is a frantic atmosphere of desperation surrounding the narrative, in addition to which there are some delicious examples of Birtspeak, a feature located within the *Private Eye* satirical publication. This functions as a variant of Orwellian newspeak which, in *Nineteen Eighty-Four*, was the English tongue ordained by the Party. One example appeared in a June 2008 issue of *Private Eye*, when a BBC trust report on the BBC website stated: 'Overall, we believe that bbc.co.uk performs very well against all these drivers.... Quality metrics demonstrate that approval and other perceptions of bbc.co.uk are high'. With this illustration of Birtspeak before us we can see that it has also invaded NOMS, because in the document on corporate performance responsibilities of March 2008 we read that *corporate HR* provides HR transactional services; *capability and capacity* ensures effective talent and succession management; *finance and commercial* leads zero-based reviews; *strategic planning and performance* provides change and portfolio management and a project and programme management (PPM) centre of excellence in addition to delivering cross-cutting corporate change programmes; *communications* (is this an example of a sense of humour pervading NOMS?) maintains the departmental stakeholder map; and, finally, which I must confess is my favourite contribution, *research and analysis* leads the Ministry of Justice horizon scanning and blue sky thinking. It also incubates new strategy and policy issues. Moreover, located within the NOMS offender management model (2006) we stumble across the language of 'brokerage' and how 'each offender's period of engagement is a project'. Therefore what does this language mean for those within the Probation Service whose job it is to work with people who offend within the context of human–professional relationships and often in difficult circumstances? It should be stated clearly that much of this constitutes meaningless jargon, gibberish located at the heart of a vast bureaucracy. It obfuscates more than elucidates the professional task, convoluted Birtspeak that mires the organisation in vacuous inexplicability.

Arguably the current bureaucratic form of organisation has inflicted a heavy price on local area services and working environments for probation staff. Most staff join the Probation Service (and other people-orientated professions such as social work) to engage and work with people labelled offenders and value the autonomy to be creative and exercise imagination in what is demanding work in order to make a difference. Nevertheless they currently find themselves in a politically dominated and centrally controlled organisational landscape with its authoritarian top-down mechanisms of power and control; bureaucratic management rather than charismatic leadership; cogs in an all-enveloping NOMS machine; a marketised and computerised working environment endorsing contestability; and relentlessly pursuing numerical targets in a much more routinised organisational culture which has attenuated the human dimension. These developments are not unique to probation but exist throughout the whole of the public sector, including the health service (Crawshaw et al, 2002).

The iron cage of Weberian bureaucracy, which in turn has diluted the notion of *verstehen*, offers a theoretical framework to account for what probation has become in contrast to, for example, a personalist philosophy situating the individual and efficacy of personal relationships at the centre of theory and practice. Probation was once an integral component of the personal and professionalised social services, but it has become a politically dominated and predominantly office-based bureaucracy in a business-orientated environment. Since 1997, particularly after the creation of the National Probation Service in 2001 that was quickly followed by the emergence of NOMS after 2003, the bureaucratisation of probation and other public sector services has been in full spate. For those who remain committed to operating within a social-democratic criminology, and who are supportive of an individualising tradition of *verstehen*, this is professional anathema. In fact it constitutes a distorted operational rationale for probation that should primarily focus on understanding the individual and the possible meanings attached to behaviours, as the fundamental starting point for formulating judgements, making decisions and protecting the public. This level of meaning and understanding cannot be separated from wider social and economic structures, family, education, employment opportunities, the effects of neoliberalism, deprivation and poverty and inequalities. Consequently this leads on to the next section.

Punishment of insecure populations under neoliberalism

It was made clear in Chapter 2 that there is a discernible Marxist criminological tradition that is relevant for an exploration of crime and punishment, one of the latest distillations being the work of my colleague Mark Cowling (2008). This is a body of theory that explicates the view that economic change is a necessary condition of social change that, in turn, has implications for the approach taken towards understanding crime and punishment (McLellan, 1986, p 41). Moreover Lucia Zedner makes reference to the enduring nature of Marxist analysis because it establishes a framework for thinking about punishment as a government strategy bound up with power relations, economic struggle and ensuing social conflicts (2004, p 80). At the heart of this approach is the base–superstructure metaphor, translated as the fundamentally important economic base and dependent non-economic superstructure. And as commented on earlier when reviewing Rusche and Kirchheimer, systems of economic production discover punishments that correspond to productive relationships connected to the supply and demand of labour (1939 [1968], p 5). Therefore there is more to crime and punishment than a simple crime and punishment relationship. Rather, the system of penality is involved in promoting the interests of the rich over the poor, the powerful over the weak, the few over the many, with a view to ordering and controlling surplus populations under specific economic conditions. Additionally a significant text when thinking about the Probation Service within this theoretical framework has already been mapped out by Walker and Beaumont (1981). My task in this section is to move around within this Marxist framework with a view to exploring the latest manifestation of capitalism in the guise of neoliberalism, and its implied implications for offenders within the modernised and culturally transformed probation and criminal justice system.

In *Punishment and welfare* (1985), then later *The culture of control* (2001), two texts enriched by an exposition of numerous sociological theories in *Punishment and modern society* (1990), David Garland advances a theory of historical change which has implications for penal policy and the operational functioning of criminal justice. Beginning in the 1985 text with an analysis of late-Victorian penality, underpinned by an ideology including individualism and a laissez-faire minimalist state, he proceeded to give an account of the emergence of the penal-welfare state which took shape during the early years of the 20th century under a reforming Liberal government (1906–14). When looking at the system of penality during the late-Victorian period, then the very different contours of penal welfare from the early 1900s to the 1970s, finally concluding with the most recent period which has taken shape since the 1970s, Garland argued that the institutions of criminal justice had their own internal dynamics and could develop according to their own professional logics, values and institutional responsibilities. However, it should never be forgotten that penality was also a *state-directed practice* that was directly implicated in the management of disorderly behaviours, whose practices were shaped by wider social movements located within the constraints of macro-social structures. Accordingly, the Garland thesis drew on Marxist concepts of base and superstructure, yet without being obsessively devoted to this one theoretical position. In other words he borrowed material from Durkheim, Weber, Foucault, as well as Marx, in the explication of how penal policies emerged, developed and changed over time.

In the 2001 text he stated that it was not possible to explore or explain contemporary crime control strategies in isolation from wider macro-level political, social-economic and cultural variables. Therefore a central argument being advanced was that the late-modern crime complex was not solely a response to rising crime rates – which have been falling in the United States and the United Kingdom over recent years (Wacquant, 2009). Rather it was an adaptive response to late-modern conditions with its preoccupation with crime and associated insecurities, the declining efficacy of rehabilitation and a less generous attitude towards an inclusivist social welfare state. Consequently there was a strategic 'fit' between penal arrangements, the shape of the criminal justice system and macro-structural factors, ideology, hegemony, class relations and the powers arrogated by the state. The conditions of existence and surface of emergence for the late-modern criminal justice system, which included the *modernised and culturally transformed Probation Service*, was the 'risky, insecure character of today's social and economic relations' (Garland, 2001, p 194) concerned as it was with risk, harm, dangerous predators, appropriate mechanisms of control, maintaining order and, of course, public protection. The roots for all this lay deep within the socio-economic dislocations of the 1970s since when probation has struggled to find a coherent voice consistent with its original mission. At this point we need to look at some of these issues in a little more detail by turning initially to the captivating analysis found in the work of Eric Hobsbawm.

From the 'golden age' of post-war Keynesian economic management, full employment, rising living standards during the 1950s and 1960s and the welfare state, to the 'crisis decades' after the tumult of the 1973 oil crisis when the world lost its bearings and 'slid into instability" (Hobsbawm, 1994, p 404; see also Clarke, 2004); by utilising this comparative perspective Hobsbawm delineated the features of the 'crisis decades' by alluding to the massive rise in unemployment during the 1980s; the reappearance of homeless paupers on the streets of relatively wealthy countries; growing social and economic inequality manifested in extremes of wealth and poverty; and the supporting role played by the conservative economic doctrines of Hayek and Friedman, who advocated allowing the invisible hand of Adam Smith to replace Keynesian economic interventionism. It was during the 1980s under Margaret Thatcher, ably supported by the intellect of Keith Joseph and the right-wing political predilections of Ronald Reagan in the United States, that neoliberalism was endorsed. Additionally academic cogency was provided in the United Kingdom by the Institute of Economic Affairs that began in 1955, the Centre for Policy Studies (1974) and the Adam Smith Institute (1976). The following themes are resonant of the neoliberal coda: expecting individuals to be responsible for their own lives and destinies; the strong rule of law – directed mainly towards the bottom of the social pile; free markets and individual freedoms operating within a strong centralised (and penal) state; privatisation; competition between individuals and organisations seen as a virtue; and the 3Es of economy, efficiency and effectiveness, including value for money (see Wacquant, 2009, for a detailed analysis of neoliberal effects). Importantly within neoliberal cultures the failures of individuals are more likely to be blamed on individuals themselves, rather than society and its prevailing economic arrangements conducive to inequality and differential opportunity. In fact Harvey says that from the 1970s, but particularly after the Conservative election victory in 1979, neoliberalism was a political project to 're-establish the conditions of capital accumulation and to restore the power of economic elites' (2005, p 19), which involved the pursuit and maintenance of profit for the few at the expense of Fordist industrial solidarity for the many. Unfortunately neoliberalism shed jobs much faster than it could create them. Free markets and competition put the maximisation of profits before jobs and social security for all. Furthermore during the 1980s the trade unions were reduced to a weakened state and rendered unable to resist these developments affecting their members, particularly after the miners' strike in England and Wales. But such developments have come at a cost in terms of reduced social security, anomie, the breakdown of informal social controls within communities and the accompanying rise of anti-social behaviour (Harvey, 2005, p 80). For Wacquant, neoliberal doctrine constitutes 'a *transnational political project* aiming to remake the nexus of market, state, and citizenship from above' (2009, p 306, emphasis in original). In the brave neo-Darwinian world created by neoliberalism the fittest survive and the most vulnerable, if they resort to offending, will receive a dose of punishment to bring them back into line with the prevailing orthodoxy. *This is the prevailing context for probation practice.*

Jock Young (1999, 2007) contributes to this analysis by pointing to the many cultural changes during the 1960s, followed by the economic dislocations of the 1970s that exacerbated relative deprivation among the poorer sections of the community in the United States and the United Kingdom. Moreover, the same economic anxieties, among the better-off, fostered a sense of growing intolerance for those below them on the social ladder, which had the capacity to fuel punitive impulses. When people feel threatened they can lash out and fight back against the *essentialised other* who gets blamed for the prevailing ills of society (from offenders to trade unions, welfare scroungers and immigrants). On this very point Katz cogently states that by 'mistaking socially constructed categories for natural distinctions, we reinforce inequality and stigmatise even those we set out to help' (1989, p 5). Therefore the argument is advanced that crime, insecurity and punishment do not have their roots in some essential or positivistic differences between those who offend and those who do not (see again the provocative quotations from Orwell and Foucault at the end of Chapter 2), but are associated largely with the dislocations of labour markets, wider structural processes engendered by the neoliberal economic musculature. Furthermore late-modern conditions have culminated in mass migration, flexible labour, the breakdown of communities, more fluid reference points and a prevailing miasma of instability, insecurity and the dizzying effects of vertigo (Young, 1999, 2007; Reiner, 2007a). Philippe Bourgois (2003), in his ethnographic research located within East Harlem, talked about crime and drugs as manifestations of economic dislocations since the 1970s. While he drew attention to human agency, he also pointed to the effects of structural factors (family, school, employment and the economy) on human behaviours that conduced to vulnerability and relative deprivation, including marginalisation. Importantly these features are unquestionably associated with the punitive turn.

Furthermore Loïc Wacquant, in his disquieting book *Urban outcasts* (2008), combined empirical research, sociological theory and detailed materialist analysis of the post-Fordist situation mainly in America and France. He also alluded to other countries including England and Wales. It can be argued that the modernisation of the Probation Service and the wider public sector has been taking place alongside the modernisation of advanced economies in the West, which includes the phenomenon of capitalist rationalisation. The result of this restructuring is that the Keynesian-Fordist era of cyclical poverty within working-class communities has assumed a more permanent form, 'fixated upon neighbourhoods of relegation enshrouded in a sulphurous aura, within which social isolation and alienation feed upon each other as the chasm between those consigned there and the broader society deepens' (2008, p 261). It is within this new terrain that the criminal justice system has been expanding, and will continue to expand, in response to the inevitable casualties produced by these conditions. Accordingly, poverty and associated vulnerabilities are being criminalised by an exclusionary and increasingly punitive response, rather than pursuing policies of amelioration through maintaining an inclusionary social welfare state.

Over recent years we have therefore seen the creation of a vast carceral network in the United States, and expanding community and custodial criminal justice system in England and Wales. Parenti, reflecting on the same set of issues, explored the adverse effects of neoliberalism and its implications for criminal justice responses. He argued that the criminal justice estate specifically in the United States, with particular reference to the prison, was a rational strategy for responding to the fallout from the restructuring of capitalism (1999, p 169). He proceeded to suggest that the main function of the prison was to 'terrorise the poor, warehouse social dynamite and social wreckage, and, as Foucault argued, reproduce apolitical forms of criminal deviance' (1999, p 169; see also Reiman, 1998). Further evidence for such links can be found in the persuasive comparative material produced by Cavadino and Dignan (2006). In this text they explore the relationship between different political economies and their penal systems located in 12 countries. Consequently the thesis was stated that while they did not support a crude form of economic determinism, nevertheless neoliberalism, with its potential for egoism, markets, competition, individualism and the decline of the social, was associated with more crime and punishment. This finding was confirmed by Reiner (2007b, p 373) who, after reviewing much relevant empirical evidence, confirmed the links between economic factors, type of political economy, crime and punishment. Accordingly, this evidence helps to demonstrate that neoliberalism, as distinct from social-democratic political economies, tends to have a *dark heart* that embraces serious crimes and cruel punishments.

During the course of their book that was written during the early 1980s, Walker and Beaumont arrived at the point when they gloomily argued that a fundamental conclusion of their analysis was that probation staff were paid to undertake a specific job on behalf of the state which was a role generally supportive of capitalism (1981, p 160). It is my contention that this is not the only job probation officers are engaged in but it can be argued that modernisation, located within a material framework of neoliberalism and new public management, has channelled the organisation in a particular direction and to adopt a different posture. Therefore to what extent has the Probation Service abandoned its ideals and values that were rooted in anti-punishment and anti-custody? Has the nature of probation work itself (as opposed to the positions adopted by NAPO) abandoned its campaigning role on behalf of the most vulnerable and disadvantaged people who can end up trapped within the criminal justice system, which is where they initially come into contact with staff from the Service? To what extent are probation reports for the criminal courts increasingly blaming the individual offender, rather than analysing in detail the risks and violence being imposed from 'above' by a state-sponsored economic theory? In other words, the state has been involved (I am thinking here of Britain and the United States) in inflicting military violence in Iraq and in the process many thousands of innocents have been killed. Similarly the state has increasingly been involved in inflicting penal violence against sections of the community in its media–driven war against the criminal *other*, the victims of neoliberal socio-economic policies with its 'asymmetrical effects of power' (Simon, 2007, p 14). Therefore if New Labour after 1997 in its warm embrace of neoliberal economics abandoned its traditional constituency by continuing the policies of previous Conservative governments in order to seize power and ensure electoral success whatever the cost in terms of human wreckage, is it not the case that probation has abandoned its traditional constituency among the poor and vulnerable in order to ensure its survival regardless of the cost to its pre-modern ideals, values and organisational integrity? If this is the case, to what extent have the forces of modernisation diluted the moral responsibilities of the Probation Service to convey the lives of clients, to tell their stories, to magistrates and judges who have a duty to make informed sentencing decisions based on all relevant information? Some of these points will be explored empirically in greater detail in Chapter 5.

Disciplinary normalisation

Within the Marxist tradition, prison-based punishments, including probation reconfigured as a punishment in the community, were the blunt tools of state power and repression directed largely against the urban poor. When revisiting some of the work of Michel Foucault (1977), he appeared more concerned with what was occurring within institutions under capitalist social relations, and how power was being exercised (Hudson, 2003, p 134). Before developing this point it should be explained that the next and last substantive subsection of this chapter will return to a progressively humanitarian reading of probation. Similarly the argument can be restated that there is a progressively utopian reading of broader historical developments since the 18th-century Enlightenment that endorses the positive march of human reason and progress. These developments are encapsulated within the institutions of liberal democracy, the notion of individual rights, the social contract, as well as the contributions made by the emerging social sciences.

By contrast Foucault presents the reader, as discussed in some detail in Chapter 2, with a dystopian discourse of post-Enlightenment events, an anti-Enlightenment and anti-reason analysis. This leads us into the dark shadows where lurks a Nietzschean will to power, which is oppressive, disciplinary regulation and subjection at the hands of the state. Moreover the social-human sciences constitute new forms of knowledge constructed within power relations under specific socio-economic conditions, namely industrial capitalism. In other words, rather than the social sciences emerging in the 19th century as a direct response to the human subject conceptualised as the sole origin of meaning (McNay, 1994), it can be reiterated that this is illusory because the human subject is instead a by-product of discursive formations linked to the politics of power and demand for order, not so much *discovering* or *describing* man as he is in himself, in his essential being, but rather *producing* and *constructing* by systems of words and numbers for overt political purposes. Accordingly, one should wise up and always look for the structures of domination behind the language and numbers generated by the social sciences, political processes and organisational functions.

Features of probation work can also be located within a dystopian realm at odds with, for example, those humanitarian impulses that we will return to shortly. Accordingly, the probation officer works with individuals and families within a framework of disciplinary regulation and normalisation, as the eyes and ears of the regulatory state. A very early review of the inchoate system talked about the provision of help and moral reformation (elements of the orthodox perspective). Nevertheless there is always lurking in the background the sanction of the penal law and 'the knowledge that the probation officer is the eye of the magistrate' (Home Office, 1909, para 13). In fact the foundation legislation, the 1907 Probation of Offenders Act, enabled the probation officer to exercise 'a much stronger hold over the offender than the recognizance that was previously the rule' under the police court missionaries (Home Office, 1909, para 13). This perspective reverberates much later in the Morison Report in acknowledging that while probation officers were concerned with the well-being of individual offenders, they were also the agents of a system concerned with the protection of society on behalf of the state (Home Office, 1962, p 23).

Located in a place and space beyond the commission of the offence, the officer of the court, formerly the probation officer but now the rebuilt and more muscular offender manager, who keeps the magistrates informed of offenders, casts a disciplinary and normalising gaze over all aspects of the offender's life. This includes thoughts and feelings, levels of insight and awareness, how the commodity of time is being utilised, behavioural repertoires, recreational interests, friends and associates, hopes and aspirations, employment prospects and so on. Nothing should be beyond the all-seeing penetrating gaze of the state that is exercised through the court and dispersed through its probation officials. If punishment under the ancien régime could destroy the body of Damiens (Foucault, 1977) it was the prison, and later probation, which could retrain and discipline minds and bodies with a view to reconstructing offenders into compliant and useful citizens. The point has been made at various places earlier that probation was initially configured as an alternative to punishment and imprisonment. Moreover Garland adds to the discussion by saying that it was the task of probation officers, and the agents of numerous after-care societies, to produce the same reformative effect as the borstal system which came into existence during the same decade as probation. To achieve this effect a variety of means could be adopted from detailed surveillance, controls exercised over associations and various interventions in the offender's family life in addition to the importance of personal influence or perhaps even religious conversion (1985, p 25). Similarly Roger Matthews says that probation was basically a welfare sanction that attempted to normalise behaviours under a form of continuous supervision and surveillance (1999, p 23).

Within this Foucauldian theoretical framework it can be suggested for illustrative purposes that, since the late 1990s, accredited programmes attached to supervisory orders (for example 'Think First') have operated as mechanisms to inscribe *normal* thinking, problem solving and social skills into the genome of offenders. Accordingly, probation and its accompanying suite of programmes do not so much address adverse socio-economic factors engendered by neoliberalism as one of the explanatory contexts of offending, as engage in cognitive restructuring to inculcate new behavioural drills conducive to docility regardless of the prevailing social circumstances, a form of equine dressage which joins the notions of 'taming, enskilling, and inuring' (Wacquant, 2009, p 106). On this very point Stanley Cohen, when reflecting on the 19th century, stated that the reform of prisoners, in addition to the instruction of schoolchildren, confinement of the insane and the supervision of the worker, became 'projects of docility related to the new political and economic order. Hospitals, schools, clinics, asylums, charities, military academies become part of the panoptic world' (1985, p 26). Consequently, returning to the present, offenders are provided with the requisite skills over the course of a few months by participating in the Think First programme, inducing *cultural capital* (Bourgois, 2003) to foster compliance with what are often unpropitious personal and social circumstances. By doing so they become cognitively tooled up to negotiate structures of inequality, disadvantage and the threat of prison exclusion if offending persists. On the one hand, the teaching of such skills can be deemed to be a positive attempt to do offenders some good – surely a touch of cognitive reprogramming cannot do any harm! On the other hand, the same skills are teaching, with a view to establishing, discipline, self-management and self-control, largely within the poor and vulnerable living daily with burdensome social problems. Life is unimaginably difficult, the future is bleak and there are lots of risks out there, *but at least we have acquired the skills to handle it, to negotiate around it!* This could be the position offenders find themselves in at the end of such a programme that means well – new thoughts conducive to orderly controls over minds and bodies – but could change very little those macro-factors requiring fundamental alteration (Beynon et al, 1994).

Additionally Foucault's *Discipline and punish* (1977) proceeds from what is going on inside the prison, outwards into the social body, symbolised by Bentham's Panopticon. As mentioned earlier, the creation of disciplined, trained and obedient bodies was a necessary requirement for the capitalist-industrial machine. It should also be acknowledged that the techniques for examining the individual inside the institution – hierarchical observation and normalising judgement – turn the delinquent into a 'case', the observation of whom becomes an object of knowledge linked to a regime of power. Offender managers may well be involved in the provision of much needed help and advice to offenders, but they are also involved with other institutions in processes of disciplinary regulation and normalisation on behalf of a more authoritarian state. Nevertheless we should not overlook the ongoing provision of assistance within a supportive supervisory environment, which is why we need to turn our attention at last to the good guys again.

Last remains of the good guys

The emergence of the probation system a century ago, based on an orthodox more than revisionist reading of its entry into the penal system (Raynor and Vanstone, 2002; cf Young, 1976), was associated with positive initiatives under a reforming Liberal government. Following in the footsteps of 18th-century Enlightenment reformers imbued with the quality of reason, probation has been constructed as a progressive, humanitarian, altruistic innovation, and an outbreak of benevolence in opposition to the contours of what was a harsh Victorian penality. In fact Nellis cogently analyses how the appearance of probation exemplified the humanisation of justice (2007). Accordingly, it constituted an alternative to punishment and incarceration with its philosophy of advice, assistance and friendship, mediated by supervisory oversight in the community. It was also marked by religious endeavour in that the Church of England Temperance Society had been providing the inchoate system with police court missionaries since 1876, in addition to which religious organisations facilitated the probation task (McWilliams, 1983; Garland, 1985). The dynamic of religion was also significant within penal reform long before the missionary forerunners of probation officers appeared on the late Victorian scene (for example in the work of John Howard and Elizabeth Fry: Hinde, 1951; Young and Ashton, 1956), as we saw in Chapter 3.

If we peer through this benign lens of modified penal sensibilities underpinned by evangelical theology a number of features hove into view that, traditionally, have been associated with probation. Some of these features can be enumerated as working with individuals who offend within the context of humane relationships; understanding, mercy and help; offenders as ends in themselves rather than means to an end; respect for people and the irreducible worth of human beings; a concern not only for behavioural repertoires (*what* people do) but also an empathic and ineffable *feel* for who they are which takes cognisance of holistic personal and social needs. Accordingly, such features represent a distinctive axiological orientation that the organisation of probation has brought to the complex workings of the criminal justice system during the 20th century within the warp and woof of care and control, punishment and welfare, justice and treatment. Even though the analysis of crime is indubitably complex because of incompatible theoretical perspectives, when it comes to responding to people who offend there is a body of work that argues for the retention of humanistic values and approaches alongside the advocates of harsher forms of punishment.

Notwithstanding major changes affecting probation since the policy-driven 1980s, its dalliance with punishment in the community from the early 1990s, and particularly the politics of modernisation since 1997 (Nellis, 1999), humanitarian and personalist impulses may have been attenuated but indubitably not eradicated. Of course it is difficult to quantify the existence of such impulses within the culturally transformed probation domain. Nevertheless they continue to attract support from other criminal justice organisations illustrated by research undertaken with a number of solicitors (Whitehead, 2007) in addition to the research findings that will be presented in the next chapter. Furthermore it is important to acknowledge that the effective practice agenda which evolved during the 1990s gives some credence to a personalist axiology in support of working with offenders (Raynor, 2002; Chui and Nellis, 2003; Gelsthorpe and Morgan, 2007), and NOMS continues to resort to the language of support and help to address the underlying causes of poor behaviour such as inadequate accommodation, lack of educational and employment opportunities, financial problems and drug and alcohol addictions (Ministry of Justice, 2008b). In fact the NOMS strategic business plan for the period 2009–11 endorses values of equality and diversity, and states that offenders should be treated with respect and decency (Ministry of Justice and NOMS, 2009). To reiterate, probation may have been reconstructed by a narrative of punishment in the community, and experience periodic bouts of modernising transformations, but it is encouraged to promote helping strategies to facilitate rehabilitation. Furthermore academic research invites us to proceed beyond, for example, bureaucratic systems and procedures, to acknowledge the efficacy of humane and engaging social work relationships. In fact it is the quality of the relationship between the kind of person the probation worker is and the offender that constitutes a key ingredient of therapeutic success rather than over-reliance on theories, methods and organisational constructs (Smith, 2006). Similar points have been made by Raynor and Vanstone (2002, p 115) when they comment that indications from Australian research by Trotter suggest that probation officers who have received social work training engage more effectively with the 'what works' agenda than those who come from other backgrounds.

During 2005/06 a number of retired probation staff were interviewed after a request was made in *NAPO News* and contact made via the Edridge Fund. These interviews were subsequently published in *Changing lives* (NAPO, 2007). Importantly interviews were provided from probation careers spanning six decades, beginning remarkably in the 1940s. Some of the voices heard, which constitute a rich oral history, reflect personalist impulses and sensibilities. It is recorded for posterity that probation was something other than a punishment. Even though the organisation established boundaries, engendered responsibility in offenders, sought to bring about positive change and exercised authority on behalf of the state, nevertheless 'I think Probation reflected the great strength of having an alternative to punishment in our society, because punishment is a dead end' (p 60). Another retired officer joined the service in 1966 and stated 'I think Probation bothered about people … I advised, assisted and befriended and brought about change' (p 34). Someone else said that we gave social work help and 'I advised, assisted and befriended, and I gave them a lot of befriending' (p 50). Yet another commented that 'The biggest tragedy was taking away advise, assist and befriend' from the philosophy of probation (p 68). Additional voices can be heard saying: 'I cared about the client' (p 47) and probation offered someone to talk to, a relationship, care and showing an interest in the person who offends (p 48). Another probation officer trained in 1969 was an active member of the Probation Officers' Christian Union (p 62) that reinforces the long-standing religious association with probation work. Additionally the importance of relationships is underlined (p 63) when we hear that 'I wanted to be in an organisation that was caring' (p 67). Consequently it could be understood as a vocation more than just another job.

Also included in this oral history is a lament for what probation work has become: over-managed, bureaucratic, de-professionalised, with the appearance of National Standards and accompanying loss of autonomy and discretion, in addition to the emergence and debilitating effects of a target culture. Two further quotations are worth including. First:

> For me, I think the sense of a disciplined independence in using personal discretion. Essentially it was professionalism and not tick boxes. It was forming a judgement, expressing a view, but within a framework of understanding in which you placed the material you had, and then put forward a view about what was the most positive way of dealing with the person given all the circumstances. (p 59)

This is a former probation officer articulating his understanding of the pre-modernised service. Second, and crucially, Rod Morgan states that over recent years: '*The service was cast adrift in a sea of structural uncertainty, incoherent management-speak, ideologically-driven poor leadership and political vacillation*' (p 93; emphasis added because this captures some of the key modernising changes which have occurred).

Therefore it is possible to argue that the above establishes the point that combinations of religious beliefs, personalist impulses and moral sensibilities have been tightly woven into the undulating textures of the Probation Service throughout its history. This continues into the present in the form of, for example, the Probation Service Christian Fellowship that is concerned to express Christian care and concern within the structures of the criminal justice system. There are other organisations also worth noting: Social Workers Christian Fellowship,

Evangelical Alliance, Lawyers Christian Fellowship and the Churches Criminal Justice Forum. There is also a Prison Fellowship that leads neatly on to the next point. During the preparation of this book I made contact with the Chaplain General of HMPS, Reverend William Noblett, who provided the following information. In 2008 it was confirmed by letter that chaplaincy arrangements in the 130 public sector prisons comprise multi-faith teams. These teams are made up of employed, fee-paid (sessional) and voluntary chaplains who represent the faiths and denominations of inmates at each prison in England and Wales, which embraces Anglican, Roman Catholic, Free Church (for example Methodist), Hindu, Jewish, Muslim and Sikh. At the time of writing it was made clear that statistics were held on employed chaplains, a mixture of full- and part-time posts, and totalled 334 staff, giving an equivalent of 268 full-time posts. However, and importantly, the prison system has a further 700 chaplains who work part time or sessionally. In addition to the public sector prisons there are a further 11 in the private sector. Where the latter are concerned chaplains are employed by the respective private company, which means that the Chaplain General is not required to maintain any official statistics.

Furthermore, since the creation of NOMS in 2003/04 the work and potential contribution of faith communities (as part of the third sector) within the criminal justice system has been acknowledged and encouraged by central government. Beginning with the Communities and Local Government document on *Working together* in 2004 (Home Office, 2004c), there are a number of examples supporting this development that can be cited as follows. A document published by NOMS (2005) on *Reducing re-offending* made it clear that the government was keen to involve the community in achieving its strategic objectives for reducing re-offending, resettling offenders on release from prison and rehabilitation. Accordingly, faith communities were expected to play their part in this initiative that reached beyond the statutory organisations comprising the criminal justice system. Next, in a speech to the Prison Reform Trust on 19 September 2005 – 'Where next for penal policy?' – Charles Clarke, Home Secretary, referred to the support which could be provided by the voluntary and faith sectors, specifically in the form of *community chaplaincies*. This was also mentioned in the rebalancing document (Home Office, 2006b), where it was additionally stated at paragraph 3.23 that reducing crime and re-offending 'should be everyone's business'. Subsequently a Cabinet Office and HM Treasury document (2007) reinforced the message that central government wanted to strengthen consultation with the third sector, which was deemed to have an important role in the transformation of public services. By November 2007 NOMS published a consultation document on *Believing We Can: Promoting the contribution faith-based organisations can make to reducing adult and youth re-offending* (NOMS, 2007a). In this document it was noted that faith-based organisations currently provided 6,000 volunteers, contributing 16,300 hours every four weeks within the prison estate. Finally it should be acknowledged that the 2007 Offender Management Act provides the legislative basis for contestability within NOMS. This means that the public, private and voluntary/third sectors can compete for the business to provide offender services. This policy was given further support by the Ministry of Justice (2008c), which wants to see a thriving third sector, which includes religious communities, as part of the criminal justice system.

From a much wider perspective, it is interesting to note that a combination of Christian-democratic communitarianism which can be described as a tolerant form of Christianity, in addition to humane paternalism and libertarian social democracy, created the conditions for a form of penality more lenient than in most Nordic countries (Cavadino and Dignan, 2006, p 115, when they were talking about the situation in the Netherlands). Consequently in the fullness of time it will be important to theorise and critically analyse some of these third sector developments. For example are faith communities going to become a challenging presence within the criminal justice system, thus providing resistance to the punitive and exclusionary drift? Or, alternatively, are they being encouraged to get involved to provide legitimacy for the punitive policies of central government but also to reduce costs when the Ministry of Justice has to save £1 billion by 2011? Nevertheless at this point the primary point to establish is that the widest possible interpretation of personalism conveys a set of ideas, a framework of thought and a distinctive set of dispositions and values. These attitudes and values should affect the judgements and decisions of the criminal justice domain of those who endorse them, and they have a considerable history.

Conclusion

Bodies of social theory, in addition to acknowledging a remaining vestige of religious and humanitarian impulses, combine to offer an approach to excavating probation and criminal justice that has some analytical merit. One hundred years ago it was possible to make sense of the emergence of probation by recourse to an orthodox and revisionist perspective. The former is associated with religious and philanthropic features encapsulated in the now redundant and politically unacceptable message to advise, assist and befriend. The latter constructs probation as a state-directed enterprise to discipline, control and normalise the recalcitrant in a class-divided society in such a way to obfuscate the links between crime and politics. Now that the organisation has arrived at and proceeded beyond its centenary year in 2007, a combination of philanthropy and Foucauldian discipline is analytically inadequate. It is therefore necessary to put additional theories to work associated with Durkheim, Weber and Marx. None of the theoretical keys introduced in Chapter 2 and put to work in this chapter adequately explain, in isolation from each other, what the Probation Service has become. Instead it should be argued that all five perspectives are required to capture some of the complex undulations of what is now a multifaceted organisation, operating at different levels, against the background of New Labour's modernising tendencies and accompanying cultural transformations. Accordingly, offender managers can operate as the good guys of the criminal justice system who represent a distinctive set of values rooted in personalist ethics, albeit attenuated by the punitive upsurge. But they could also be involved in expressive knee-jerk reactions consistent with a heightened emotional notation (Durkheim); function as bureaucratic technicians within the NOMS structure (Weber); punish and sometimes exclude (as a conduit to prison) the recalcitrant residuum (Marxist); and operate as disciplinary regulators and normalisers, the eyes and ears of the courts and an increasingly centralised and authoritarian state (Foucault).

If recourse to these disparate perspectives has any analytical cogency when exploring the development of probation during the modernising period since 1997, it may be concluded that a state of confusion has erupted because of the lack of a coherent organisational rationale. This is because probation has become a theoretically contested site, ideologically diffuse, primarily reconstructed to conform to a political image consistent with New Labour's view of the world of order and disorder. In other words, modernisation has created a system of criminal justice and probation institution with multiple identities. This multiplicity has not enriched but instead coarsened organisational responses because of the way in which it has bureaucratised, punitised and depersonalised problems rooted within a market-driven society under neoliberal arrangements.

Nevertheless if the above suggests a nuanced and textured methodological approach is required to elucidate what the National Probation Service has evolved into, the same theories and impulses can be put to work to critique and explore future developments concerning what the essence of the organisation should in fact be – to which I will turn in the final chapter. If this chapter, which concludes the four chapters comprising the first substantive part of the book, has focused on exploring *what probation has become*, the next empirically research-based chapter will look at *what it ought to be* from the standpoint of numerous respondents within one local criminal justice system. But first, a summary of the main elements of this chapter is presented in Table 4.1, as follows.

Table 4.1: Summarising putting theories to work

Organisational and political knee-jerk reactions	Probation less concerned to control crime than to express outrage to bolster the law-abiding. Penal populism, sensational media reporting, injudicious political and criminal justice knee-jerk reactions. Acting out and displays of sovereign power through enforcement; inappropriate custodial recommendations in reports for magistrates and judges; benefit sanction 2001–09; and war against crime as a symbolic spectacle.
Relentless march of the bureaucratic technicians	From facilitative management to bureaucratic inertia. From the individual offender as the primary unit of analysis, to controlling aggregates of risk via the diminution of therapeutic imagination, autonomy, discretion, initiative, amounting to a de-professionalised workforce. More emphasis on new public management, 3Es, value for money, procedures, processes and systems, than on engaging with people. National Standards, business audits, targets, computers, NOMS and marketisation, contestability, not forgetting the new language of jargonistic and Orwellian Birtspeak.
Punishment of insecure populations under neoliberalism	Probation as part of the government's punitive strategy directed against the poor. Neoliberalism produces casualties from among the most economically vulnerable, so that in a neo-Darwinian socio-economic system only the fittest survive. The criminal justice system, with its reconfigured Probation Service, is a response to the fallout that follows the pursuit of neoliberalism via increased punishment and exclusion. Blame attached to individual failings, rather than social and economic 'violence' inflicted from above. But offenders can be victims too.
Disciplinary normalisation	The offender manager casts a disciplinary and normalising gaze over offenders, as the eyes and ears of the regulatory state that employs them. Deviant populations must have their minds and bodies retrained to establish compliant citizenship. Accredited programmes, such as Think First, induce normal thinking through social and problem-solving skills conducive to docile behavioural drills. Probation and wider criminal justice system are essential components in a Benthamite Panoptic society.
Last remains of 'the good guys'	Religion, personalist impulses and moral sensibilities combine to work with offenders within the context of engaging social work relationships. Provision of support and help for personal and social problems rather than punishment. A distinctive set of attitudes and values that promote respect for people and treat them as ends not means. Helping strategies to promote rehabilitation remain a feature of NOMS discourse.

Notes

[1] In the first chapter of *The culture of control* (2001), Garland explores the contours of the penal–welfare system that had been in operation from the early 1900s to the 1970s, since when certain 'indices of change' can be identified:

- decline of the rehabilitative ideal
- re-emergence of expressive punitive sanctions
- changes in the tone of crime policy
- return of the victim
- public protection
- politicisation of penal policy

- reinvention of the prison
- transformation of criminological thought
- expanding the infrastructure of crime prevention and community safety
- commercialisation of crime control
- a new managerialism
- a perpetual sense of crisis.

[2] The war against crime resorts to emotive language that has become crystallised in a powerful political and media image. It resembles the war that is constantly being waged on dirt and germs by household products to maintain cleanliness.

[3] An explanation of breach reports is required. At various points this book makes it clear that procedures and practices concerning breach and the enforcement of community orders have become more stringent. When the courts impose a community sentence, offenders are expected to comply by maintaining regular contact with their offender manager. If they fail to do so the offender manager has a duty to return the offender to the original sentencing court, either by summons or warrant, where action will be taken. Either the order will be allowed to continue with an onerous requirement imposed (following the 2003 Criminal Justice Act); or the order will be revoked and the offender re-sentenced for the original offence, which could result in imprisonment.

[4] This point is linked to the previous note because offenders who breach their community order, and who are unemployed, and therefore in receipt of state benefit, can have a proportion of their benefit withdrawn for up to four weeks. For more information on the benefit sanction see Whitehead and Statham (2006, p 201); also Windlesham (2001, 2003). For a wider discussion on the politics of withdrawing state benefits see the discussion in Rodger (2008, p 86). Additionally it is important to clarify that the benefit sanction experiment, which operated in four areas of the country – Derbyshire, Hertfordshire, West Midlands and Teesside – came to an ignominious end in 2009 after eight years.

[5] The phenomenon of new public management has been dealt with at length previously (Whitehead, 2007, p 34).

[6] The public sector remains in the grip of numerous targets and it is difficult to know who is responsible for this development since 1997 – Tony Blair as Prime Minister or Gordon Brown as Chancellor? Therefore it is very interesting to hear what Barber has to say on this subject when it is stated: 'Blair himself sometimes appeared politically ambivalent about targets. He worried they would generate unnecessary bureaucracy. He always favoured fewer rather than more targets, and rightly worried that the system would take them too literally and hit the target but miss the point' (Barber, 2007, p 81). Perhaps this helps to resolve the query.

FIVE

Researching modernisation and cultural change in probation: views of solicitors, clerks, magistrates, barristers and judges

Introduction: practitioner research in probation

By the mid-1980s I was several years into working as a probation officer at 'Northtown' within a rapidly changing organisation (Haxby, 1978). The election of a Conservative government in 1979 signalled a discernible shift of direction for criminal justice in England and Wales, from an ostensibly rehabilitative discourse towards a more punitive, law and order tone. Paradoxically events circa 1983/84 culminated in a statement of national objectives and priorities – SNOP (Home Office, 1984) – which encouraged probation to pursue a policy of alternatives to custody. Consequently the theme of alternatives to custody became emblematic during the 1980s, which culminated in the 1991 Criminal Justice Act and its advocacy of punishment in the community to enhance the credibility of community sentences to magistrates and judges.

Within this situation I pursued empirical research between 1985 and 1989 as a practitioner-researcher (Whitehead, 1990). My main aim was to determine whether the Probation Order was being used as an alternative to custody in the post-SNOP political and local service organisational context. I used various methods: a quantitative recording schedule to collect numerical data on Probation Orders being proposed by probation officers in their reports on offenders, and then subsequently imposed by courts; and a qualitative semi-structured interview schedule and additional unstructured interviews to pursue relevant topics in greater depth. Data were collected on the rationale of probation, court sentencing practices, probation ideologies and methods of working with offenders. Individual and focus group interviews comprising probation staff, magistrates, judges, recorders and court clerks were conducted among 69 respondents.

Arguably during the 1980s there was a tangible sense of unity between government and probation at the point both pursued alternatives to custody. Additionally one can recall a land of opportunity for the practitioner-researcher to initiate and undertake research activities in the 56 probation areas. In fact once it was decided to research an issue of penological concern, the process was supported by staff at 'Northtown'. Governance arrangements enabled Chief

Probation Officers (CPOs) to grant permission to aspiring practitioner-researchers, without Home Office approval, if potential benefits were justified. Importantly the CPO office was imbued with the requisite autonomy and accompanying authority to make such decisions at local level. Once permission was secured then access to data and respondents proceeded uneventfully within circumstances where research was perceived as a valued activity, particularly if it contributed to effective practice outcomes. Additionally it should be acknowledged that Durham University provided oversight that added academic legitimacy to the research. These findings engender an air of nostalgia for what was a very different probation culture.

Notwithstanding a changing political and criminal justice context during the 1980s, it is important to summarise that local probation areas maintained room for manoeuvre facilitated by flexible governance arrangements; politicians and probation were united in pursuing alternatives to custody; opportunities existed for practitioner-researchers; local support endowed the practitioner-researcher role with legitimacy; the service was interested in research findings which enhanced effectiveness; and there were few issues surrounding access to respondents and data collection. I recall isolated pockets of resistance but they were not insurmountable in pursuit of definable objectives.

Further research after 20 years: 2006–07

During the summer of 2006 I returned to undertake research within the same probation area, but this time in a markedly different political climate that had noticeably transformed organisational dynamics. I was now employed as a part-time probation officer in a team servicing magistrates' and crown courts, in addition to teaching part time at a nearby university. Significantly, since 1997 New Labour had embarked on a mission to modernise the public sector, including criminal justice. This politically inspired process culminated in the nationalisation and centralisation of probation areas in 2001, one of the effects being the attenuation of local autonomy. Moreover, the imposition of new governance arrangements transformed the role of CPO, by government diktat, into a chief officer as a centrally appointed civil servant. Arguably this reconfiguration adversely affected operational relationships between senior managers and other grades of staff (Whitehead and Statham, 2006). One effect was the creation of less propitious circumstances for individual practitioner-researcher initiatives within local probation areas. Research activity exists, but it is strategically controlled by the Ministry of Justice.

Therefore I would advance the view that political, cultural and organisational reconfigurations since 2001 (Whitehead, 2007) transformed governance arrangements affecting the work of senior managers, and the fact that not all senior managers have worked as probation practitioners raises questions about their level of experience, knowledge and insight into practice issues and related questions of occupational legitimacy. Importantly the imposition of a political orthodoxy which actively promotes a 'can do' culture in the public sector predominantly means *just get on with the job* specified by central government, rather than engage in critical scrutiny via research.

Accordingly, these were some of the dynamics by 2006 when I formulated my research into the nature and effects of modernisation and accompanying cultural changes at 'Northtown'. I was particularly interested in this theme because of first-hand experience of the cultural effects on probation since 1997, but especially since 2001 while continuing to work within the organisation. I also surmised it would be difficult to obtain permission from senior managers to pursue my research interests, particularly if this involved interviewing probation staff. Nevertheless anticipated obstacles within probation inspired innovation, as I was encouraged to turn my research gaze from *inside* to *outside* the organisation, to solicitors, court clerks, magistrates, barristers and judges. The theme of modernisation remained intact, but the research angle was fortuitously transformed.

Before discussing matters in greater detail it should be acknowledged that some of the features just alluded to, indicative of a new set of operational dynamics confronting the practitioner-researcher, were manifested during the summer of 2007. The data collection stage was well under way when my immediate probation line manager informed me, sotto voce, that senior managers were asking questions about my research activities. But because the process of research with respondents was being undertaken during lunch breaks at the 'Northtown' courts, and quite often interviewing on days when employed by the university, it became unnecessary to satisfy their curiosity. This defensive posturing in response to research activities – reframed as 'snooping around' – did not prevail in the culture of the 1980s.

Operational framework for current research

After 10 years of New Labour's modernising agenda, in addition to the approach of probation's centenary (1907–2007), the decision was taken to research some of the meanings and implications attached to the related themes of modernisation and cultural change in the Probation Service. Formulating a proposal should not be limited to specifying *what* the researcher wants to do, it also benefits from reflections on *why*. Therefore the experience of working as a probation officer since 1981, periodically as participant-observer/ethnographer, confronted me with a series of profound cultural effects associated with the politics of modernisation that were worth exploring and explaining.

Next, after consulting with university colleagues, it was decided to select quantitative and qualitative methodologies to collect data on perceptions and understandings of modernisation and cultural change in probation from the standpoint of chosen respondents. The quantitative element comprised two tick boxes that facilitated the collection of numerical data on two specific areas and were administered during the course of the interviews. Where the first tick box is concerned, respondents were invited to consider a total of eight statements illustrative of cultural change in probation. They were asked about the cultural changes they were aware of and then requested to tick the boxes that corresponded with their experiences. For example: 'Are you aware of a change of emphasis within probation from advise, assist and befriend to punishment in the community?'. These results are assimilated in Tables 5.1 and 5.2 below.

When turning to the second tick box, this was used to cast some light on their understandings of probation work after considering a set of 14 statements. Accordingly if they associated probation work, for example, with a social work ethos or, by contrast, with an organisation which exists to provide a robust, tough, punitive approach to offenders – or possibly even both – again they were asked to tick the appropriate box or boxes which corresponded with their views. There was no limit to the number of boxes they were allowed to tick and these results are contained in Tables 5.3 and 5.4. The form of words which comprise the second tick box were constructed carefully in an attempt to represent contrasting value categories (for example values of tolerance, care, compassion and decency, contrasted with a robust, tough and punitive approach to offenders). These contrasts can be said to represent some of the competing impulses, sensibilities and conflicting rationalities within modernised criminal justice.

The qualitative research instrument was a semi-structured interview schedule that posed the same questions to all respondents, in addition to providing opportunities to pursue points of interest in greater depth to yield rich bodies of data. The interviews were taped and some areas of interest pursued were: the rationale of probation work; tensions between achieving government targets and pursuing justice for individual offenders; punitisation of reports prepared by the Probation Service which included recommendations for custody; the personal and social circumstances of offenders; and contestability which opens up offender services to competition between the public, private and voluntary sectors within NOMS. Therefore I concur with Newburn's assessment that some of the most useful research involves combining qualitative and quantitative methodologies (2007, p 899). A combination of personal knowledge of probation and criminal justice accrued since 1979, assistance by university library staff and utilising Google Scholar confirmed there is a paucity of published research on modernisation in the criminal justice domain. Accordingly, it was particularly difficult to track down publications related to solicitors and court clerks, which hopefully makes the current project innovative. By contrast there is a vast literature on magistrates, barristers and judges.[1]

Indubitably employment as a probation officer over many years (from 1979 to November 2007) cultivated important contacts with different criminal justice professions. Accordingly, to progress the research, I initially approached as many 'Northtown' magistrates' solicitors as I could on the court landing during the summer of 2006 when still working as a part-time probation officer. Preliminary explorations revealed that 36 solicitors appeared regularly before the justices to represent their clients. Subsequently when data collection began in September 2006, 31 out of 36 made themselves available for interview. Significantly it was made clear that unless they had worked with me, thus establishing professional trust built up over a period of time, interviews would probably not have occurred. In other words, a letter sent to a solicitor's firm by an unknown practitioner-researcher may not have received a favourable reply. Consequently my professional status as a probation officer opened doors into spheres of research activity, and most solicitors were enthusiastic as well as intrigued about participating when asked to do so. Consent was generously provided in writing and interviews were completed by December 2006.[2]

When expanding the research to court clerks and magistrates it was necessary to obtain permission from the clerk to the justices with whom I discussed the interview schedule and clarified that interviews could last up to 45 minutes. Permission was quickly obtained which facilitated 22 out of a total contingent of 30 clerks, in addition to 20 magistrates responding to the invitation to be interviewed between February and July 2007. There are over 300 magistrates at 'Northtown' and time constraints could only accommodate 20 of them. However, it became manageable for 101 magistrates to complete the two quantitative tick boxes that could take up to 15 minutes to complete before they went into court at 10am. It should be added that only one magistrate declined to be interviewed because of a reluctance to be submitted to tape, notwithstanding assurances of confidentiality.

It is worth acknowledging that this research does not claim scientific rigor in terms of being nationally representative, nor could parity be achieved between groups of respondents, because I did not have complete control over how many would agree to be interviewed. Therefore the findings below are simply the result of what became possible during the time allocated. Most of my time as a practitioner-researcher was spent at the magistrates' courts. Consequently I made a virtue out of necessity by completing interviews with solicitors, clerks and magistrates, before approaching crown court barristers and judges who were based in a different location. There are identifiable issues of time management when working as a practitioner-researcher, particularly when combining part-time probation work with university teaching. Nevertheless it was possible to be creative when undertaking this research to ensure completion between late summer 2006 and autumn 2007.

It is also worth reflecting on differential experiences at magistrates' court compared to the crown court, which were not anticipated. The different phases of the research process proceeded smoothly with solicitors, clerks and magistrates. By contrast, when approaching barristers at 'Northtown' Crown Court, a central issue which emerged was not so much securing permission to undertake the research but rather creating space to conduct interviews. Friday is the busiest sentencing day when barristers attend court en masse. Consequently demands associated with defending clients were such that 45-minute research interviews were untenable. Moreover, after approaching the resident judge, professional proprieties would have been breached if I had conducted interviews with 'the brothers', even after guaranteeing confidentiality. However, again reaping virtue from necessity, 20 barristers and 10 judges agreed to complete the two quantitative tick box documents. In the circumstances of prevailing political sensibilities, including time constraints, I could not have expected any more from the higher court. Either tick box data or nothing at all was the decision I had to make. The former was gratefully accepted even though this imposed limitations on my initial data collection expectations that will become clearer later.

Because the research was conducted with the support of a local university the proposal was scrutinised by the ethics committee that raised no ethical issues. However, as an *insider* who had established working relationships with respondents from different organisations, I could have been charged with using them to put academic research before sensibilities prevailing within the Probation Service. Additionally the epistemological privileges inherent within the practitioner-researcher role could benefit some organisations within the criminal justice system at the expense of others. Therefore there could be a price to pay for knowledge.[3] At this juncture I turn to the quantitative data gleaned from the respondents by utilising the two tick boxes, briefly embellished by a handful of qualitative contributions when some of the respondents made unsolicited comments on the tick box forms as they were completing them. The first two tables focus on the theme of modernisation and cultural change.

Modernisation and cultural change

Rigorous enforcement procedures

If offenders do not comply with the requirements of court orders by, for example, absenting themselves from appointments with probation without valid reasons, they can expect to be returned to court in enforcement proceedings. Under the terms of the 1995 edition of National Standards, offenders would receive two final

Table 5.1: Evidence of modernisation and cultural change at 'Northtown' Magistrates' Court

	Defence solicitors (*n*=31)	Clerks (*n*=22)	Magistrates (*n*=101)
	Number (%)	Number (%)	Number (%)
Rigorous enforcement	21 (67.7)	18 (81.8)	44 (43.6)
From advise, assist and befriend to punishment in the community	20 (64.5)	19 (86.4)	49 (48.5)
Target-driven organisation	18 (58.1)	13 (59.1)	49 (48.5)
From social work help to a law enforcement agency	17 (54.8)	10 (45.5)	34 (33.7)
Focus on managing the risk of re-offending and harm	17 (54.8)	18 (81.8)	72 (71.3)
Public protection	14 (45.2)	11 (50.0)	45 (44.6)
Benefit sanction	11 (35.5)	19 (86.4)	50 (49.5)
More concerned with victims than offenders	6 (19.4)	4 (18.2)	14 (13.9)

warnings before the probation officer proceeded to intention to breach, which resulted in a return to court after a third failure to cooperate with the requirements of supervision. However, by the 2000–02 version of National Standards this was reduced to one final warning followed by intention to breach at the second absence – from three to two strikes then back to court, which remains the legal position. Additionally the 2003 Criminal Justice Act introduced the practice of more onerous requirements as the sanction for breach if the sentencing court allowed the Community Order to continue, thus eliminating the more liberal regime contained under the 1991 Act which allowed for discretionary verbal warnings (a ticking off could suffice).

Therefore there has been a tightening up of procedures, corresponding to a diminution of probation officer and court discretion and flexibility, which is one of many factors currently contributing to the seemingly inexorable rise in the prison population. To repeat the review of prisons undertaken by Carter and published in December 2007, this states that the number of people in prison for breaching an order of the court (this does not include recalls on licence, which constitutes another area of difficulty) increased from 180 in 1995 to 1,200 by August 2007. Consequently a number of respondents were aware of these changes, as the first variable of Table 5.1 makes clear – 67.7% of solicitors, 81.8% of clerks and 43.6% of magistrates. One court clerk deduced that probation was no longer a "benevolent organisation…. For example in the breach courts there are extremely tight rules about non-compliance and there is no discretion and that seems to be a backward step".

From advise, assist and befriend to punishment in the community

Section 4 of the 1907 Probation of Offenders Act stated that one duty of the probation officer was to advise, assist and befriend the probationer at a time when the Probation Order constituted an alternative to punishment and custody within the remains of the Victorian prison system. By contrast, from the mid-1980s and culminating in the 1991 Criminal Justice Act, the organisation was reconfigured as a punishment in the community. Accordingly the duty to advise, assist and befriend was deleted from the legislation. This was part of the government's strategy to make community sentences more credible to magistrates and judges because of growing concerns over a steadily escalating prison population, including worrying future predictions which are currently being fulfilled (Windlesham, 1993). From advise, assist and befriend to punishment in the community constitutes a significant cultural shift, which 64.5% of solicitors, 86.4% of clerks and 48.5% of magistrates were aware of. One magistrate said that the:

> "… shift to punishment I think was mainly as a result of the public perception that we were too soft on offenders and so that came down to harsher management of offenders and you had to set aside whatever they had experienced in their life and some young people

were particularly damaged and it was as if they had to take total responsibility for whatever happened. I'm not altogether accepting of that myself. We have to take heed of what life experiences are given to some people."

Alternatively another magistrate stated that, "I feel the word befriend is inappropriate; it belongs in the voluntary sector". Furthermore a district judge commented that there has been "a move away from advise, assist and befriend culture, which is where I came into probation 25–30 years ago, to managing risk, managing harm, both to the offender and those offended against, and public protection".

Target-driven organisation

The development of managerial objectives in probation can be traced to the early 1980s, followed by the introduction of a regime of numerical targets from the 1990s that expanded after 1997. It is clear that the introduction of a target-driven agenda is an integral component of a central government strategy for enhancing performance levels within organisations and demonstrating greater accountability. It should also be acknowledged that NOMS operates within this auditable framework, indicative that probation has acquired the accoutrements of a quantitative business mentality ill at ease with a professional culture that exercises discretion. On this very point Tim Newburn has recently stated that 'the setting of explicit targets and performance indicators enables the auditing of efficiency and effectiveness' (2007, p 553) within a more business-orientated environment (for a fuller discussion of these developments and their implications within the public sector, see Whitehead, 2007).

Similar proportions of the respondents were aware of a cultural shift towards targets, as Table 5.1 reveals – 58.1% of solicitors, 59.1% of clerks and 48.5% of magistrates. It is interesting to note that one of the clerks stated that, "Unfortunately all organisations have statistics and sometimes it is better for things to take slightly longer to be done properly rather than thinking that we have to get things done to reach targets. I think that's in our organisation as well". Moreover, the chair of 'Northtown' Bench asserted that:

> "I feel that the Probation Service should not be a target-driven organisation. Having attended a NOMS conference with ministers, both myself and many of the magistrates and judges attending were shocked by what we heard that you are going to be given targets for: the number of drink drive courses, the number of various other courses that you can provide are going to be target driven. We expressed concern about what happens when you have reached your target and there is no more money for others and if you haven't reached your target for those orders are probation reports going to be, as it were, influenced by this and perhaps recommend that we adopt a sentence

for some of the targets you haven't reached in order to meet those targets? So certainly my understanding is that the judiciary are not happy about a target-driven probation service and personally I am not."

Another magistrate said, "I think it's becoming increasingly target driven and I think that is very frustrating for magistrates but we live in a target-driven society, I guess, and we're all very concerned with ticking the boxes". This issue will be taken up in more detail later.

From social work help to a law enforcement agency

For decades probation was conceptualised as part of the helping professions in the inclusivist post-war welfare state and probation officers were defined as the social workers of the criminal justice system (Home Office, 1962). In fact probation officers were trained social workers who were in a position to address complex personal and social problems associated with the diverse repertoires of offending behaviour. However, there has been a discernible shift towards a law enforcement rationale which means that the implementation and enforcement of criminal laws (including organisational procedures such as achieving central government targets) have taken precedence over pursuing a deeper understanding of those factors which are deemed to be associated with and underlying presenting behaviours, then fully explaining them to magistrates and judges. Moreover, within a more neoliberal political and neoclassical criminological context greater emphasis is being placed on *what* offenders have done – their rational choices – including future risks, rather than carefully exploring, interpreting and explaining *why*. It should also be acknowledged that changes that are currently being made to the nature, form and content of probation reports are suggestive of this cultural shift, which will be explored later in this chapter.

Nevertheless this is not to suggest that all aspects of the 'old' or pre-modernised service could always withstand critical scrutiny, and that the new wine of modernisation is indubitably corked. It should be acknowledged, lest we allow our minds to distort events by romanticising the past, that previous research revealed that probation officers could propose custody inappropriately, made decisions which drew people deeper into the criminal justice system and failed to take seriously incidents of domestic violence (Bean, 1976; Bottoms and McWilliams, 1979; Cohen, 1985). Some of these points can be expanded by turning to Steven Box (1987), who concluded that probation officers contributed to a rising prison population by recommending tougher sentences in their reports to maintain credibility with sentencers (second-guessing the magistrates). He also stated that some officers considered a number of offenders unsuitable for their professional help, which culminated in a shift up-tariff if community sentences were deemed inappropriate. Additionally, by moving down-tariff to find clientele to maintain sufficient numbers being supervised in the community, probation officers unwittingly expanded the net of social control by advocating supervision for those who previously would have been dealt with by a financial penalty or conditional discharge. These problems, supported by the doctrine of unintended consequences, have a perennial character (Carter, 2007). Therefore a sense of balance is required when attempting to explain modernising developments during the last decade, just as much as historical accuracy is needed when excavating periods which belong to the pre-modern and the complex outcomes attached to a social work rationality. From Table 5.1, 54.8% of solicitors, 45.5% of clerks and 33.7% of magistrates acknowledged the shift from social work help to a law enforcement agency.

Focus on managing the risk of re-offending and harm, including public protection

These two variables capture another cultural shift both in probation work and criminological thinking, from a rationality of understanding and help with personal and social problems, to managing, containing, controlling and allocating offenders to various categories of risk. The language of risk is associated with re-offending and harm, and to protect the public from both is the primary task of probation. This time Table 5.1 presents data on more marked differential responses by solicitors, clerks and magistrates, particularly in relation to risk – 54.8%, 81.8%, 71.3% respectively. One clerk embellished the tick box by saying that, "Yes the focus is now on managing the risk of re-offending and harm".

Benefit sanction

This refers to the withdrawal of a proportion of state benefits from selected offenders who do not comply with community orders but in four designated areas only, including 'Northtown' (but see note 4 at the end of Chapter 4). This provision is contained under Sections 62–66 of the 2000 Child Support, Pensions and Social Security Act and has been construed as an extra punishment against the unemployed offender imposed by New Labour (Kennedy, 2005, p 245; see also the discussion in Windlesham, 2001). It is important to state that this measure does not apply to those offenders who are in work, which clearly discriminates against the unemployed. Accordingly this measure constitutes an example of a more punitive and authoritarian state bringing the unemployed offender to heel with which probation has inadvertently colluded by its involvement in the process.

More court clerks (86.4%) are aware of this cultural shift than solicitors (35.5%) and magistrates (49.5%), mainly because the former are involved in explaining the provision to offenders in court. In fact one of the clerks offered the following, perhaps surprising. observation when she commented that the:

> "Benefit sanction, not a lot to be said; it's there as a punishment but I'm sure it does create problems. The defendants are put under a huge amount of strain. These are the people who do not have a lot of income

in any event and if they have their benefits stopped it just seems to be an invitation to go and commit further crimes, but that's just a personal view."

In marked contrast a magistrate said that, "I personally think that has been a huge step forward. I think the thought of actually losing their benefit has got to be a good sanction to have because you can clearly say 'do it again and we're going to reduce a lot of your dole'. That gets people's attention and is one of the few ways it will hit people".

More concerned with victims than offenders

Lastly respondents were asked to consider if they thought the Probation Service had become more concerned with victims than offenders. This was included in the research due to the fact that victim issues have had a raised profile over recent years (Garland, 2001; Home Office, 2005; Newburn, 2007, ch 17). However, the vast majority of these respondents were not aware that probation services were more concerned with victims than offenders – 19.4% of solicitors, 18.2% of clerks and 13.9% of magistrates. It should be noted that other organisations exist which seek to respond to the needs of victims, even though probation continues to make a distinctive contribution in this area of work because it has its own victim liaison officers. But within the context of discussing this theme one of the clerks volunteered the following construction on the approach to victims by saying that, "I don't think perhaps the magistrates look at the issue of the offender being a victim but there must be clear circumstances where they are".

Therefore when perusing the data collected on all eight variables in Table 5.1, there is some evidence to suggest that these solicitors, clerks and magistrates are differentially aware of cultural change in probation over recent years and have different perspectives on what has occurred. Now let me turn to a more limited data set from 'Northtown' Crown Court (see Table 5.2).

Table 5.2: Evidence of modernisation and cultural change at 'Northtown' Crown Court

	Barristers (n=20)	Judges (n=10)
	Number (%)	Number (%)
Rigorous enforcement	8 (40)	7 (70)
From advise, assist and befriend to punishment in the community	9 (45)	8 (80)
Target-driven organisation	9 (45)	2 (20)
From social work help to a law enforcement agency	4 (20)	5 (50)
Focus on managing the risk of re-offending and harm	13 (65)	9 (90)
Public protection	16 (80)	9 (90)
Benefit sanction	6 (30)	2 (20)
More concerned with victims than offenders	5 (25)	1 (10)

It was always my intention to include a crown court perspective as part of this research. However, after completing the quantitative and qualitative data collection stage at 'Northtown' Magistrates' Court, it became evident that data sets gleaned from barristers and judges would not include interview material. As mentioned earlier the particular logistics at the higher court made it difficult to reach for the tape recorder to interview barristers and judges, in addition to which one could not escape from observing the prevailing political and organisational proprieties. Nor did I want to damage working relationships between the judiciary and probation. Consequently the choice was between quantitative tick box data or nothing at all. In settling for the former it should be reiterated that obvious limitations were placed on the amount of data that could be collected.

Therefore, when turning to the quantitative data collected from the 20 barristers and 10 judges on their awareness of cultural changes, the following may be cautiously observed. The analytical point underlying Table 5.1 on the 'Northtown' Magistrates' Court data sets can be tentatively extended by elucidating that there are differential responses when comparing the two sets of respondents at 'Northtown' Crown Court in Table 5.2. The largest percentage difference is the shift from advise, assist and befriend to punishment in the community (45% of barristers and 80% of judges). By contrast the closest they come to agreement was on public protection (80% of barristers and 90% of judges). The percentages were relatively low for target-driven organisation (45% of barristers and 20% of judges) and benefit sanction (30% of barristers and again 20% of judges). The caveat that should be introduced at this point is that it is unwise to engage in speculation and force unwarranted extrapolation from such limited data, particularly when it was not possible to probe what may lie behind the responses. Nevertheless there is some insight into some of the many cultural shifts that have occurred. At this point I turn from cultural change to respondents' understandings of probation (see Table 5.3).

Understandings of probation

This is a more interesting and significant data set compared with Tables 5.1 and 5.2. By initially detaching the first column of data presented in rank order on solicitors, the point can be established (this applies to all three groups but in different ways) that not all 31 respondents define their understandings of probation in exactly the same way. This is what I would have expected anyway when interviewing a group of independent and strong-minded professionals. Nevertheless, a high proportion of solicitors clarified their perception of probation in terms of an organisation which brings an understanding of *why* people offend into the criminal justice system (96.8%); awareness of an offender's personal and social circumstances (93.6%); promotion of criminal and social justice through the provision of information contained in court reports (90.3%); an organisation with a set of identifiable values rooted in tolerance, care, compassion and decency (80.7%); in addition to advise, assist and befriend (77.4%), which is no longer a legislative requirement. Therefore notwithstanding differential responses among the 31 solicitors in relation to all

Table 5.3: Understandings of probation at 'Northtown' Magistrates' Court

	Solicitors (n=31)	Clerks (n=22)	Magistrates (n=101)
	Number (%)	Number (%)	Number (%)
Understand why people offend	30 (96.8)	19 (86.4)	77 (76.2)
Awareness of offenders' personal and social circumstances	29 (93.6)	20 (90.9)	75 (74.3)
Promote criminal and social justice through court reports	28 (90.3)	20 (90.9)	85 (84.2)
Values of tolerance, care, compassion and decency	25 (80.7)	13 (59.1)	44 (43.6)
Advise, assist and befriend	24 (77.4)	14 (63.6)	36 (35.7)
Empathy	20 (64.5)	8 (36.4)	25 (24.8)
Deliver punishment in the community	18 (58.1)	18 (81.8)	81 (80.2)
Manage, contain and control	18 (58.1)	15 (68.2)	71 (70.3)
Social work ethos	17 (54.8)	6 (27.3)	23 (22.8)
Keep out of custody	14 (45.2)	7 (31.8)	39 (38.6)
Public protection	13 (41.9)	11 (50.0)	57 (56.4)
Rigorously enforce orders	7 (22.6)	17 (77.3)	66 (65.3)
Robust, tough and punitive approach	1 (3.2)	4 (18.2)	33 (32.7)
Victim support	0 (0.0)	1 (4.5)	31 (30.7)

14 variables, it can be argued that these data reveal a discernible, albeit qualified, professional perspective in that some features are more important than others when it comes to how they think about and understand the role of probation within the criminal justice system, about what they want to see from probation.

When turning to compare percentage data across the three groups of respondents, which is more revealing than looking at each group in isolation, there are points of similarity between them, specifically in relation to the following variables: understanding why people offend; awareness of an offender's personal and social circumstances which implies putting behaviour into a holistic context; promoting criminal and social justice; and, interestingly, keeping people out of custody (lower percentages but similarities of response at 45.2%, 31.8%, 38.6% for solicitors, clerks and magistrates respectively). However, there are a number of contrasting responses in relation to: certain values associated with probation; advise, assist and befriend; empathy; whether probation should be a punishment in the community; social work ethos; rigorous enforcement; and a robust, tough and punitive approach to people who offend. These contrasting perspectives provide an insight into different operational philosophies at work within the criminal justice system and differential roles being undertaken, including criminological approaches to offenders and perhaps political allegiances.

The social work ethos variable is worth accentuating because traditionally probation was involved in helping offenders with their personal and social problems, as opposed to delivering overt forms of punishment towards those classified as failures for not playing by the rules. In other words, offenders themselves could be constructed as the victims of an unjust and unequal capitalist socio-economic system, thus necessitating a broad explanatory context within which to analyse and explain certain forms of offending behaviour. This was probation with a radical edge and campaigning voice which constitutes a challenging perspective towards those cultural shifts which have occurred over recent years (Walker and Beaumont, 1981). Nevertheless, the language of social work should not be used solely to convey the view that it is always associated with benign outcomes. Social work impulses can have both positive and negative effects and, where the latter is concerned, can suffer from the doctrine of unintended consequences, as the aforementioned research by Box (1987) indicates.

The politics of modernisation and associated cultural transformations, as Chapter 1 made clear, has placed more emphasis on punitive and custodial responses, bureaucratic targets, reclassifying offenders as statistical units of risk (low, medium, high, very high), managing risk rather than holistically understanding the past, rigorous enforcement practices with onerous requirements and generally tougher attitudes towards offenders. Yet *despite* or *precisely because of* these changes, the complex dialectics of the modernised criminal justice system among these respondents in 'Northtown' retains a place and definable space for a probation organisation associated with a set of more benign rather than punitive impulses. Arguably such an understanding of probation belongs more to its pre-modernised manifestation (pre-1980s). Accordingly some of these respondents revealed that a number of pre-modernised elements have not been completely eradicated from their thinking and responses. This finding, I think, is particularly pertinent when considering the nature of probation developments within the NOMS structure, particularly if a number of public, private and voluntary agencies displace probation during the next few years from its monopoly position, a direct outcome of contestability. When reflecting on the punitive turn taken by probation within the criminal justice system it is interesting to hear the disquiet of two magistrates expressed as follows. First, "the sentence that the court passes is intended as a punishment. I would not have thought that it was the aims of probation to be punitive". Second, "The punitive approach to offenders seems to me to conjure up probation staff themselves being punitive and I don't see them as doing other than delivering the punishment the court has advised, so I didn't tick it for that reason". These data suggest that solicitors, court clerks and magistrates at 'Northtown' Magistrates' Court were involved in a complex conversation with probation because of modernising developments within the criminal justice system over recent years. Now let me turn again to 'Northtown' Crown Court (see Table 5.4).

When thinking about the more limited data set on how barristers and judges express their understandings of what features should define probation, the

Table 5.4: Understandings of probation at 'Northtown' Crown Court

	Barristers (n=20)	Judges (n=10)
	Number (%)	Number (%)
Understand why people offend	16 (80)	7 (70)
Awareness of offenders' personal and social circumstances	16 (80)	7 (70)
Promote criminal and social justice through court reports	19 (90)	10 (100)
Values of tolerance, care, compassion and decency	9 (40)	5 (50)
Advise, assist and befriend	7 (35)	5 (50)
Empathy	6 (30)	3 (30)
Deliver punishment in the community	9 (45)	8 (80)
Manage, contain and control	8 (40)	8 (80)
Social work ethos	5 (25)	3 (30)
Keep out of custody	6 (30)	3 (30)
Public protection	12 (60)	6 (60)
Rigorously enforce orders	11 (55)	4 (40)
Robust, tough and punitive approach	1 (5)	3 (30)
Victim support	2 (10)	1 (10)

following tentative observations can be made. A proportion of respondents understand that probation should deliver the politically modernised features of punishment in the community (45% of barristers and 80% of judges); and manage, contain and control offenders (40% of barristers and 80% of judges). These constitute differential responses not without interest. The proportions are identical for public protection, at 60%. This leaves 55% of barristers and 40% of judges saying that probation should rigorously enforce orders of the court; but intriguingly only 5% of barristers and 30% of judges agree that probation should be associated with a robust, tough and punitive approach, which of course challenges recent modernising drifts and cultural shifts.

By contrast it is interesting to observe the relatively high percentages set alongside the following variables and correspondingly high agreement between barristers and judges: probation officers should understand why people offend (80% and 70%); there should be an awareness of offenders' personal and social circumstances (again 80% and 70%); and the promotion of criminal and social justice through court reports (90% barristers but all 10 judges ticked this box). Furthermore, even though the percentages are less for the following – the values of tolerance, care, compassion and decency; advise, assist and befriend; empathy; social work ethos; and keeping offenders out of custody – nevertheless, a proportion of respondents continue to associate probation with a pre-modernised vocabulary in addition to modernised reconstructions. We must be cautious when interpreting these data because, having been denied opportunities to interview respondents, detailed explanations and qualifications could not be sought. Nevertheless these preliminary findings, based on the completion of the quantitative tick boxes, are of some interest when considering changes to the criminal justice system since 1997. Even though these respondents could not be interviewed it is worth noting that, rather unexpectedly, six barristers added a number of unsolicited hand-written comments when handing in their responses to the tick boxes. Let us hear them articulate a veritable mixed bag of views at this juncture. First is a positive endorsement: "The Probation Service's value to the criminal justice system is inestimable". Second:

> "I often find that a pre-sentence report is written in negative terms because the defendant appears to deny or minimise some aspect of the offence, even where this has been agreed between prosecution and defence. Sometimes it's obvious the PSR author has taken a dim view of the defendant or the offence. I think this occasional lack of objectivity is regrettable."

On the subject of targets, another barrister stated that probation reports were "More reliant on tick box computer programmes than experienced judgement. OASys seems to dictate the outcome even though it is focused on static factors". Arguably this comment echoes John Pratt talking about actuarialism when he states, 'It allows bureaucratic organisations to avoid the moral consequences of their policies by relying on statistical computations rather than human judgements' (2007, pp 134–5). Fourth we hear that "I would like to see even more rigorous enforcement of breaches". Penultimately, the:

> "Pace of change is unprecedented.... Your budget-savvy managers have spotted an opportunity to deskill the service. Thus we have hard working officers (who may not be too well trained/experienced) cranking out FDRs in a mechanistic fashion which have no place for the nuances a well-qualified practitioner might have about a client and the problems he poses."

Finally, and this is a powerful assessment:

> "The Probation Service has changed beyond recognition over the course of the last 10 years. The shift of the Probation Service has left the criminal justice system unbalanced. There is too much emphasis on punishment, and a void where there should be an agency dedicated to values of befriending and assisting."

In summary we have an endorsement, expression of frustration, two laments, support for enforcement and a concern about the nature of cultural change. Therefore, after presenting quantitative data, occasionally embellished with a mèlange of explanatory and qualifying comments, the next substantive section focuses on interviews with court clerks and magistrates at 'Northtown' on a number of pertinent themes (see note 2 at the end of the chapter). But first I begin with a brief profile of the respondents (see Table 5.5).

Profile of respondents

Court clerks

Gender

My aim was to provide a balance between male and female respondents. This was achieved to a limited degree as five male and 17 female clerks made themselves available for interview.

Table 5.5: Age of court clerks

Age	Number	%
30–39	7	31.8
40–49	11	50.0
50–59	4	18.2
Total	22	100.0

Note: The average age of these 22 clerks is 43.5 years.

Ethnicity

Even though there were a handful of clerks from a minority ethnic background working at 'Northtown', all my respondents were White British. Again this was not planned but emerged as a result of those who were willing to be interviewed. I think that nothing negative should be read into the fact that no clerks from a minority ethnic group presented themselves for interview; this was nothing more than a coincidence.

Length of service

The average number of years the respondents had been employed as a court clerk was 17.4 years. Consequently it can be deduced that they were experienced at their work, in addition to which they were ideally placed to comment on changes to probation over recent years.

Table 5.6: Number of years working as a court clerk

Years	Number	%
1–9	3	13.6
10–19	10	45.5
20–29	8	36.4
30–39	1	4.5
Total	22	100.0

Magistrates

Gender

There were 13 male and seven female respondents.

Ethnicity

All respondents identified themselves as White British, but one of the magistrates did not want to be pigeonholed into any ethnic category. By the summer of 2007 there were over 30,000 magistrates in England and Wales, 7% of whom were from minority ethnic backgrounds.[4]

Length of service

The average number of years the respondents had been working as a magistrate was 17.3 years, almost identical to the 22 clerks. Again the point can be made that they were experienced magistrates and therefore well placed to comment on probation changes during the period covered in this book.

Table 5.7: Age of magistrates

Age	Number	%
40–49	3	15.0
50–59	6	30.0
60–69	11	55.0
Total	20	100.0

Note: The average age of these 20 magistrates is 58.7 years.

Table 5.8: Number of years working as a magistrate

Years	Number	%
1–9	3	15.0
10–19	11	55.0
20–29	5	25.0
30–39	1	5.0
Total	20	100.0

Purpose of probation

The literature produced by the erstwhile Home Office, but since May 2007 by the newly created Ministry of Justice, promotes an image of the National Probation Service as a law enforcement agency that, since 2003/04, has been incorporated into NOMS. With its 21,000 staff located in 42 areas throughout England and Wales, subdivided into 10 regions, its primary goals are articulated as follows:

• Public protection
• Reduction of offending
• Punishing offenders in the community
• Ensuring offenders are aware of the effects of crime on victims
• Rehabilitation.

This is a list that resonates with the purposes of sentencing located in the 2003 Criminal Justice Act. A high proportion of staff are female even though the vast majority of offenders are male. The Probation Service has approximately 246,360 offenders under various forms of supervision, made up of 149,280 under a court order in the community and a further 97,080 being supervised pre- or post-release from custodial facilities (Ministry of Justice, 2008c). It also prepares in the region of 250,000 reports annually for the magistrates' and crown courts, a subject that will be explored in more detail shortly.

When turning to the views of respondents, it is interesting to note the tone they struck when explaining how they understood the purpose of probation. After more than a decade of modernising reforms, including the punitisation of probation work (since the 1991 Criminal Justice Act reconfigured the Probation Service as a punishment in the community), the key word used by 10 clerks and four magistrates was 'rehabilitation'. The concept of rehabilitation has a long association with the prison system and means a return to a state of law-abidingness (Mathiesen, 2006, p 27). It is also one of several sentencing aims in the 2003 Criminal Justice Act, and an ideology traditionally embedded within probation mediated through a constructive relationship between offender and officer. One clerk explained by stating that in the long term the purpose of probation "I guess ... is for the rehabilitation of offenders in essence", a view complemented by illustrative comments from a further two magistrates: "I think it's to help the rehabilitation of offenders to a better life basically. It is to help them, families and courts"; "Well my view of the Probation Service is to support, rehabilitate where necessary and if appropriate punish".

Of course this is not the only level of understanding, already indicated by the quantitative data sets above and acknowledged by the magistrate just cited. During interviews with clerks, as well as a number of references to rehabilitation, other voices stated: being "an essential service for the courts"; "helping people if they had problems"; it is something *other than* custody; "to carry out court orders"; "assist and educate them"; as well as its modernised association with punitive impulses. The tone set by magistrates was captured in the following responses: a dual role which involved a responsibility in the courts but also towards offenders; to prevent re-offending; the provision of support to and supervision of offenders to deal with their problems; *as* rather than *for* punishment; and public protection and monitoring. Therefore I was presented, quantitatively and qualitatively, with a multifaceted discourse, a multiplicity of voices, utilising concepts of varying philosophical origin to attach different meanings to the purpose of the organisation 10 years after New Labour became responsible for criminal justice. This suggests that for clerks and magistrates, probation was not solely or even predominantly conceptualised in terms of a punitive stance towards people who offended. Rather there was a rehabilitatively positive, supportive, helping and as such anti-punitive discourse at work. Nevertheless when summarising these responses it can be advanced that respondents were engaged in a complex dialogue with the Probation Service in the sense that there were different voices clamouring to be heard.

Purpose of probation reports

In the first of four papers on the history of changing ideas in probation, Bill McWilliams (1983) suggested that it was difficult to say exactly when police court missionaries became involved in making enquiries on offenders before sentence. Nevertheless, it was probably around the 1887 Probation of First Offenders Act. Subsequently paragraph 36 of the departmental committee report on the 1907 Probation of Offenders Act (Home Office, 1909) recorded that the first probation officers were undertaking preliminary enquiries for magistrates. Additionally, it is 'obviously an advantage to the Probation Officer to know all the circumstances relating to the offence' (para 37). In one of the earliest books ever written on the inchoate probation system in England and Wales, already cited above, Cecil Leeson confirmed that probation officers were involved in making enquiries for courts to determine suitable cases for probation supervision (1914, p 67). Such enquiries were conducted by taking note of the offender's character, domestic circumstances, education and employment, associates and habits. Arguably this was during a period when offending behaviour was constructed by a narrative of character defects and moral weakness, rather than theorising the possibility of a behavioural response to problems generated by the political economy. Furthermore, by the 1930s comprehensive advice was being issued on the preparation of written reports for the courts (Le Mesurier, 1935).

By the rehabilitative and welfare-orientated 1950s (Home Office, 1959), followed by Streatfield (Home Office, 1961), part of the latter document was concerned with selecting the most effective form of treatment for offenders appearing before the courts. The probation system had by this stage evolved beyond its theological phase (1876–1930s) to a more secular, professional and 'scientific' expression, associated with a personalised medical-treatment model of corrections. It should also be acknowledged that the Streatfield Report resulted in a burgeoning of reports for courts (Bottoms and McWilliams, 1986; Bottoms and Stelman, 1988). Moving on, there are copious references to the importance of probation reports in Haxby (1978, p 136) and by the 1980s, when some 200,000 were being prepared annually, the social enquiry report, as it was then called, was potentially an instrument for diverting offenders from custody in the post-rehabilitative era (Home Office, 1984). The 1991 Criminal Justice Act transformed the social enquiry report into the PSR in a more justice- than treatment-orientated criminal justice system (Whitehead and Statham, 2006). Therefore, notwithstanding the different epistemological, political and cultural frameworks within which information has been processed and reports prepared since the 1880s – theological, welfare, treatment, rehabilitative, justice and then punishment in the community – it is clear that they have constituted a central feature of probation practice for over 100 years.

Currently section 158 of the 2003 Criminal Justice Act provides the legal basis and rationale for the preparation of reports. Accordingly, a report is prepared 'with a view to assisting the courts in determining the most suitable method of dealing with an offender' (s 158). Furthermore, section 160 of the Act refers to *other* reports, which means that in addition to the comprehensively written PSR, other formats are possible. Several years ago the probation officer working in the criminal courts could be asked by magistrates and judges to deliver a *stand-down report* if this was appropriate. In such circumstances a case was stood down by the courts (between 30 minutes to one hour) to enable probation to conduct a brief interview before delivering verbal feedback to bring matters to an expedited sentencing conclusion. More recently this practice metamorphosed into the *specific sentence report* that involved the preparation of a briefly written document, which in turn has been further refined into the fast delivery reporet (FDR). Therefore it is currently possible for the Probation Service to be involved in the preparation of three different report formats.

First, the comprehensively written PSR, structured by the computerised OASys and National Standards, is normally prepared within an adjournment period of 15 working days, but 10 days if the offender is remanded in custody. The adjournment period enables probation to conduct interviews at the office and/or home of the defendant, in addition to making relevant investigations and verifying information. This is a detailed report because it is written by taking cognisance of the following OASys headings: offending information; analysis of the offences; accommodation status and history; education, training and employability; financial management and income; relationships; lifestyle and associates; drug, alcohol and other addictions; emotional well-being; and thinking and behaviour including the offender's attitudes. Furthermore the author has a duty to consider risk of re-offending and harm prior to making a sentencing proposal for the magistrates' and crown courts to consider.

Second, an FDR should ideally be completed on the day requested by the courts, certainly within five working days. In other words, interviewing and writing the document, normally by the court duty officer, should be completed within a couple of hours. This format, unlike the full report, is structured differently by utilising a series of tick boxes to expedite the presentation of collected data. However, scope remains to include explanatory written text to expand on tick box data if required. This type of report, by definition briefer than the full report, also takes cognisance of the same OASys headings alluded to above, but without the necessity to undertake a computerised and time-consuming OASys assessment. Rather the offender group reconviction scale (OGRS) is applied in addition to the OASys risk of harm screening.

Finally, it remains possible for probation to be invited to prepare, or even initiate, a verbal report (its lineage is the former stand-down report) to expedite the sentencing function of the courts even further. After a brief interview with the person who has offended, probation delivers verbal rather than written feedback to sentencers.

Further clarification is provided by Probation Circular 12/2007 (NOMS, 2007b), when it is stated that the standard delivery full report, fast delivery and oral format, are all PSRs. In fact the three formats are deemed to be of equal standing. It is also made clear that courts must be given the information they need in order to reach a sentencing decision that begins to raise a number of pertinent issues. One of these, emerging from the 2003 Criminal Justice Act and Circular, concerns who determines the amount of information required to facilitate a sentencing decision. For example, is the Probation Service the recognised lead authority or is the decision made after taking soundings from the dramatis personae within the magistrates' courts – court clerks as legal advisers, defence solicitors and magistrates themselves perhaps? Another inescapable issue touches on the differential distribution of power within the organisational composition of local criminal justice systems with their different ideologies, organisational dynamics and discrete agendas being pursued. Insights into these differential perspectives are expressed in Tables 5.1–5.4 above. In other words, probation officers, clerks, magistrates and solicitors have their own views on and approaches to offenders and offending which shape the information considered necessary and the uses to which it will be put. There will be those who are motivated by the arguments for efficiency, and others who are concerned to promote criminal and social justice without recourse to cost. Accordingly such issues begin to raise potential difficulties associated with the selection of report formats, what is considered to be relevant information and evaluations of justice that will now be explored in more detail by resorting to empirical findings.

A preliminary discussion with court clerks on their understanding of the purpose of reports revealed documents which assist the courts to arrive at a sentencing decision, clearly stated by one respondent: "To assist the courts in deciding what sentence they should reach". This echoes the rationale articulated at section 158 of the 2003 Criminal Justice Act. Importantly nine clerks juxtaposed the term 'background information' with the production and rationale of reports, expanded on by one who said that, "when you get a report that has lots of information, with a strongly reasoned conclusion, that does carry a lot of weight with the magistrates". Another said that it was to give "a fuller picture of the defendant, their personal background, their offending background". Therefore prior to arriving at a sentencing decision, relevant background information should be presented to the courts by probation.

When exploring the purpose of reports with magistrates the responses provided were: to be as objective as possible and to steer a course between defence and prosecution; to provide information on backgrounds and circumstances; and to inform decision making. Moreover, "There's always a story to tell … and I think that it is important that we hear about social backgrounds, family and what is going on in their life and to me the PSRs and FDRs are of great importance before we go to sentencing". Another stated, "To give us greater insights into the offender and to give us recommendations as to community penalties". Also, "It helps us to put the individual into context, where they've come from and why they might have done what they have done". Therefore for nine magistrates, as well as nine court clerks, the provision of information on offenders' backgrounds and circumstances remained an important probation function. In other words, information about the person (who you are) as well as the offence (what you have done) was required. It could be argued that for both sets of respondents, there was a distinct logic to the provision of information on offences and offenders;

for clerks it facilitated informed advice to courts and for magistrates it facilitated the sentencing process.

Expanding on the term 'background information', Neil Hutton, albeit within a different context, makes the point that research utilising focus groups and deliberative polling has revealed that the public may not be as punitive as survey data indicate. In fact, when people are given individual cases to deal with and provided with relevant background information about the criminal justice system, 'and allowed to engage in dialogue with each other' (2008, p 205), they are less punitive but more rational and constructive about sentencing matters. The Probation Service at 'Northtown' used to participate in sentencing exercises with clerks and magistrates that utilised probation reports containing background information on individual offenders they proceeded to sentence in mock exercises. Similar exercises occur at court open days when members of the public can observe role-plays of a sentencing court in operation. However, it is becoming increasingly less likely that courts will receive detailed background information on *all* offenders because of the prevailing emphasis on fast delivery and oral reports. This is an issue that requires careful exploration because of the implications for criminal and social justice that may be little understood because of the current emphasis on saving money.

Fast delivery reports and the 40% rule

When narrowing the focus of enquiry to incorporate the elevated status increasingly arrogated to fast delivery and oral reports, it should be acknowledged that until 2006/07 the target for FDRs was 40% of all reports being prepared in magistrates' courts. The figure of 40% remained in force but became part of a service-level agreement (SLA) between the 10 NOMS regions and local services, rather than a specific target, when the research was undertaken. Consequently it was important to turn to this subject with respondents during interview. In other words, if the full report appeared destined to be restricted to more serious offenders, were there any implications or even concerns if current policy was pushing probation and the courts towards the production of shorter format reports?

First, it should be clarified that there were 12 positive responses from clerks and 11 from magistrates, which means that these respondents did not anticipate problems with an SLA of 40%. Consequently a selection of positive responses from the 12 clerks revealed: "I would certainly like to see a greater number of FDRs used rather than the full report. I think there are several issues with a full report – length, time, defendants not attending court, failure to attend appointments, the backlog is ultimately there". This senior clerk also gave support for the oral report to quicken the process of bringing cases to a sentencing conclusion. Another stated, "The FDR is very good but it is not easy to read and I think there are a lot of tick boxes which mean very little. I think what we have found with an oral report is often much better because it sticks to the point of what the magistrates need to hear; not the tick boxes as I don't think they are very relevant and the magistrates don't find them easy to read". Next, "The aim of the FDR I would say is speedy justice, which is something I believe in because I do think that delay isn't good. I do think the faster you deal with things the better". "The number of cases that are going to need an in-depth enquiry that's proportionate to what we are actually going to do I think are quite slim." "Well I personally agree with having FDRs in the majority of cases because I do not think in most cases that there is any need to adjourn for a full report."

When turning to responses from some of the 11 magistrates we hear that, "I don't in principle have a problem with that [achieving 40% FDRs] provided that the key issues are drawn out within the time available and we are aware of all the important things that in sentencing we need to have". It is also stated that if the FDR was not appropriate then the safeguard of a full report existed. This is an important caveat when discussing the provision of information to the courts. "I think when I have had an FDR it has been quite frequently just as good if not better than the PSR. I don't know whether it focuses the mind but the experience of them has been very positive." FDRs and orals were helpful at saving time and money, which was a benefit for the courts, and "I certainly think there are lots of occasions when a full report is requested when it is not necessary", as one magistrate responded. This magistrate, because of her position on the local bench, was acutely aware of the financial constraints pressing on Her Majesty's Courts Service. Another magistrate commented that, "I don't see that it is any different from the full report; it just means that it is delivered faster and perhaps gets to the point rather more quickly". Therefore a number of respondents were in favour of the shorter format reports.

By contrast eight clerks and six magistrates raised some concerns with the FDR format in the following terms, beginning with the clerks: "I think that they are only scratching the surface with FDRs". The 40% implication was that "you might not get the full picture … you could be missing a problem in the person's history that needs addressing". Missing information, scratching the surface, rushed, concerns about tick boxes linked to chasing targets – "Personally I don't like the FDRs, they are not easy to read. Too many ticky boxes like a magazine quiz … well I wouldn't mind an FDR like a shortened version of a full report, set out in proper paragraphs. The FDR is not user-friendly". Additionally:

> "I think it's to get work done more quickly really. FDRs aren't terribly fascinating to read; in fact I often skip the ticked boxes and look at the written information. I don't think the full picture is going to come out. I think it is just a way of moving the work along quickly and everybody meeting targets in terms of speed."

Corresponding comments of concern from magistrates included: "I am not a great believer in targets because I think it has got to be case-driven rather than target-driven". In other words, the assessed needs of the individual offender should come first. Other comments were:

"Everybody is very concerned to deal with cases as quickly as possible and from the victim's point of view, which is important, there should be minimal delay. The problem I foresee with increasing the number of FDRs is that you will perhaps fail to spot the people who need more specialised disposals than they would do so if they had the opportunity to prepare a full PSR."

This could be a pertinent point because of the increasing number of unqualified staff involved in writing FDRs. Moving on, the 40% could result in probation "rushing through things and I think a full report gives us a better understanding of the person". Moreover:

"Because of the timescale, when we got full PSRs it was a lot easier if we wanted to come back on a case (due to the operation of the magistrates' rota). FDRs make that more difficult and therefore I think that the defendants see more magistrates involved in their eventual penalty and I think the problem is you lose continuity of people who are eventually going to decide your punishment."

"I'm a great fan of the FDR and even greater fan of oral reports … but yes I think you miss an awful lot." Lastly, two clerks were reluctant to express a view on this subject and in the circumstances I deduced it would be unhelpful to press the respondents further; three magistrates' comments were also difficult to categorise. Therefore, in addition to some respondents concurring with the direction of travel towards the production of shorter format reports, by contrast we also heard a number of voices expressing concern.

Achieving business efficiency or justice? New public management and morality

Penetrating even more deeply into the subject of reports for the sentencing function of the court led to a discussion surrounding whether the criminal justice system was currently putting the goals of efficiency before notions of criminal and social justice (Cook, 2006). In other words, the new public management agenda imposed on the public sector, which emphasises the 3Es (economy, efficiency and effectiveness) and value for money, was also being applied to reports and the emphasis on the fast delivery format was a pertinent example (Whitehead and Statham, 2006; Whitehead, 2007, p 34). In fact the contemporary context which contextualised the discussion with clerks and magistrates can be outlined by paying attention to the following factors which are applying discernible pressures to create specific outcomes consistent with business efficiency.

Spend less money on reports

In a speech delivered at HM Wormwood Scrubs on 7 November 2006 the then Home Secretary stated that too much money was going on the writing of reports and not enough on practical help (Reid, 2006, para 14). It may be surmised that one of the reasons for this was the introduction of the computerised OASys in 2001, since when it has been taking longer to prepare a full PSR – a workload weighting of 6.5 hours (formerly 8 hours) compared to 1.5 hours for an FDR. This is because in addition to interviewing and writing time, numerous items of collected data must be entered into the computer (Mair et al, 2006; Whitehead, 2007, p 28).

However, during the summer of 2009 the latest version of eOASys was released (4.3.1). It has introduced the concept of *layered assessments* so that the type and tier of the offender determines the amount of detail required. In other words, for the less serious and risky offender, assessment demands will be reduced because the strain placed on eOASys will be less. On the one hand, this adds weight to some of my concerns that a paucity of information militates against understanding; on the other hand, staff time could be freed up to engage more fully with people who offend, which could in turn rehabilitate the category of understanding.

The triple 'S' agenda

The simple, speedy, summary justice initiative (Home Office, 2006c) that began to influence the practices of magistrates' courts towards the end of 2007 was an attempt by government to introduce a more efficient modus operandi. In fact this initiative was consistent with the principles of new public management committed to the 3Es and value for money. This agenda signalled a much greater emphasis on dealing with cases expeditiously, thus reducing the average number of hearings before a case was dealt with from five/six to an expectation of one in guilty pleas. In pursuing this objective the logical implication was a preference for fast delivery and oral formats, rather than a full report adjourned for three weeks. The triple 'S' agenda may well achieve simple, speedy and summary justice (whatever this means), but is this the same as social justice for people who offend (Roberts and McMahon, 2007)? The Ministry of Justice endorsed the triple 'S' agenda at the Magistrates' Association Annual General Meeting on 17/18 November 2008, and we should remind ourselves that the magistrates' courts deal with approximately 95% of all criminal cases.

Service-level agreement (SLA)

As a consequence of the emergence of NOMS since 2004, there was a Service Level Agreement between the 10 regions and local area services that 40% of all reports should be fast delivery. Additionally, in a document published by the Ministry of Justice – *Value for money, delivery agreement* (Ministry of Justice, 2008e)

– it was stated that the ratio of fast to standard court reports should be improved. This was taken a step further in Probation Circular 06/2009, which reinforced that the FDR was becoming the default document in magistrates' courts by raising the SLA from 40% to 70% (National Probation Service, 2009). It can therefore be extrapolated that the preparation of reports is weighted increasingly towards briefer formats. It should be pointed out that even though there is a predilection for the FDR, in certain circumstances an adjournment for three weeks to prepare a full report could well be the judgement of probation staff, even when the court has asked for a brief document. This is an important safeguard. Additionally it should be noted that the business plan of the Teesside area service (Teesside Probation Service, 2008), for example, specified that for 2008/09 the SLA indicative values were £318 for a full report and £79 for a fast delivery. Therefore, on the grounds of business efficiency alone the latter is a more attractive product than the former.

Offender Management Bill and Act

It is pertinent to allude to the debate in the House of Commons (2007) on the Offender Management Bill. On this occasion it was clarified by the Home Secretary that within the NOMS structure the preparation of reports, in addition to the supervision of offenders and breach proceedings, would remain a probation task within the public sector. However, and tellingly, this state of affairs was guaranteed to last for three years when, because of contestability, the preparation of reports could become the responsibility of another organisation, perhaps in the private sector. If this is a vision of future developments beyond the next general election in 2010, then the historical association of the Probation Service providing a range of information to the courts could be coming to an end.

Therefore questions can be posed, issues raised and concerns expressed within the operational dynamics of the criminal justice system that are relevant to the changing nature of information being provided to sentencers, ostensibly driven by cost. To reiterate, one of the main areas of contention is the potential conflict between the legitimate goal of ensuring efficiency when allocating taxpayers' money to criminal justice, and pursuing ideals of criminal and social justice. Of course these two objectives are not inherently incompatible but in certain circumstances they could be. Furthermore, even though the aforementioned Probation Circular states that the three report formats are of *equal standing* as a basis for justifying sentencing decisions, it is difficult to support the position that they are of equal standing in terms of content. In other words, the full standard delivery report provides much more text-based information on offenders' background circumstances, thus providing a comprehensive basis for sentencing, compared to fast delivery (tick box-driven) and oral formats.

It may be suggested that there will be occasions when probation formulates the judgement, then advises the court, that it is appropriate to prepare a fast delivery or verbal report. Certain cases, of an uncomplicated nature, lend themselves to briefer formats without diluting the pursuit of justice, of doing what is deemed to be morally right for the offender, victim and sentencing outcome. Nevertheless there will be occasions when a full report is required in the interests of justice. Consequently the complex task of sentencing involves more than routinely and proportionately matching offence seriousness with sentencing bands contained in the 2003 Criminal Justice Act; complying with an SLA to achieve 70% FDRs; and making decisions motivated primarily to achieve efficiency savings. This is because sentencing is a moral issue existing alongside and informing its technical and legal requirements, which means thinking carefully about the right thing to do for each individual having regard to *all* the circumstances. This, in turn, has implications for the selection of report formats and requisite judgements about an offender's culpability that is beginning to change, as Table 5.9 illustrates.

Table 5.9: Criminal reports written by the Probation Service at magistrates' courts from Quarter 4, 2006 to Quarter 4, 2007, England and Wales

	Q4 2006	Q1 2007	Q2 2007	Q3 2007	Q4 2007	% change Q4 2007
SDRs	24,737	25,618	24,249	23,584	21,787	−12
FDRs	10,833	12,183	12,492	12,957	12,506	+15
Oral	2,585	3,278	3,401	4,011	5,197	+101

These data, gleaned from the Ministry of Justice probation statistics, disclose interesting comparisons between a 12% reduction in the full standard delivery over the course of a year, but a 15% increase in fast delivery and 101% increase in oral reports. In fact a perusal of *Probation statistics quarterly brief* (Ministry of Justice, 2008d) since the beginning of 2007 reveals a clear shift in the fall of the standard PSR, and corresponding rise in FDRs and orals (see for example Ministry of Justice, 2009).

My research found that 12 clerks and six magistrates indicated that they were concerned the current system was putting efficiency before the demands of justice. Some of these 12 clerks can be heard saying that, "It does sometimes seem that way. I think tick box formats can always give that impression, that the answers are too narrow"."Yes it appears that way. It may be that offenders who have had an FDR prepared on them are given the most appropriate order for them; it may be coincidental; but there may be the risk that with a short format report information has been missed." "I suppose you could see it like that, yes, because it comes across as a computerised tick box, not particularly about the individual." "Yes definitely. And for the victims, the whole thing gets lost in the urge to get work done quickly."

Moreover the six magistrates expressed similar concerns that efficiency was being put before justice, but the replies appeared more nuanced. One stated that FDRs were clearly about efficiency and others embellished:

> "I don't know; it's always a worry if the FDR is done fast and we don't get all the relevant information or whether it's just that we ticked the box but there might be more to add in that box. But when I've had an FDR we have usually been able to sentence through it."

> "I mean for the vast majority FDRs are the way to go and I think they do have sufficient information to make me feel that I can make a decision. I just worry, and there's a little bit of tension in me, that I might be missing something and that probation might miss something that I need to know."

> "Oh gosh, possibly, but I don't know that I have any evidence to be able to back that up, but I think just a gut response to the question would be yes, I do think so … I feel that there is less personal information on FDRs…. Whereas obviously a more text-based standard delivery report is more flexible and there's an awful lot more that seems to go into that, but I do understand that it takes longer to produce."

Alternatively nine clerks expressed less concern about the potential conflict between efficiency and justice and a selection of comments included initial concerns expressed that this was justice on the cheap because of the tick box format. However, "I think I am of the opinion that the way the justice system is being run, justice being seen to be done and delivered in a very short period of time, it is helpful". This does not necessarily compromise justice and it all depends on how well they are written. The public has a right to expect speedy justice and again written information contained in a full report will mitigate concerns. "I think it does still aim to achieve justice, but I think a lot of it is about speed." Finally, one clerk did not express a coherent view on the matter. When turning to the 10 magistrates who expressed fewer concerns, it was stated:

> "I can see the problems that there could be, but from my perspective I feel that defendants should be dealt with as quickly as possible and I sometimes feel that adjournments for three weeks for a full report is too long and is causing them more anxiety and problems. Whereas if it can be done efficiently and without prejudice to the defendant as an FDR, I feel that is much better for the defendant and also for the courts."

Initially yes, but not now, because "My view is that FDRs seem to be providing the kind of service that I am happy with". "I'm not sure that the FDR does actually make that a more difficult thing to achieve. I think we are still getting enough information and we are still ending up with a recommendation, so that we can sentence on the report." But concerns were expressed about the tick boxes. There were tensions but if probation staff were around to elaborate on the FDR in court, "then I don't think justice will suffer at the hands of targets". "Yes but I understand that we rely on the Probation Service to come back and tell us it is inappropriate for an FDR, so you would hope that the Probation Service would still do that and request a full report." The remaining four magistrates' responses were that one was ambiguous about the nature of our discussion; another simply restated the problems with tick boxes; the next did not really answer; nor did the last. Therefore there is a mixed picture in that 12 clerks and six magistrates indicated concerns; by contrast nine clerks and 10 magistrates expressed fewer concerns with some of these recent developments in probation.

Punitisation of reports

This became a specific concern at 'Northtown', illustrated by repeating the following statement which surfaced during the course of this research and which we have already encountered: "Teesside Probation Service proposes custody in a high percentage of PSRs – 5.2%. This is far higher than the national average of 2.7% and is the fourth highest in the country at proposing custody" (Teesside Probation Service, 2008). Moreover, and to reiterate, the context for the qualitative interviews during the period 2006–07 with representatives from criminal justice agencies working alongside the Probation Service was the cultural shift towards punishment. Therefore I wanted to understand if respondents perceived that probation reports had become more punitive. Interestingly, but not surprisingly given the above statement in the business plan, 14 clerks and nine magistrates said they perceived what could be described as the punitisation of reports. Illustrative comments from clerks are as follows. As to whether probation officers were more willing to accept no alternative to custody in certain cases: "Yes definitely and obviously it must be a general feeling as I have it commented to me as well, by magistrates, they have observed that", and "There was a time when probation never recommended prison, but now they do and that's after legislation stated that is what they are for, to recommend a penalty rather than just recommend a probation sentence." One clerk also felt that reports are now more realistic because they can recommend custody: "Yes but I don't altogether think that is a bad thing."

Similarly some of the nine magistrates said, "Yes I think it is because of a change of emphasis of the Probation Service, that you are no longer seen as advise, assist and befriend; you are now seen as recommending what is the correct punishment for society, for that offender", which would result in proposals for custody. "Yes things have changed; Probation Service is more credible compared to previously when recommendations could be unrealistic." Even though some magistrates may not be aware of more recommendations for custody, one magistrate commented that "community sentences with requirements are more punitive and harder". "Historically there always used to be laughter that a report would never ever say custody was appropriate for a person. That does actually happen nowadays, so more punitive, more honest." "That has definitely been a big climate change", from not recommending custody to doing so, and "I think reports are more credible because of that". Finally, proposals for custody were "a good thing" because of the injection of realism.

By contrast the following comment was typical of the seven 'No' responses from clerks:"Haven't noticed that; it's very rare that you come across a recommendation for custody". Additionally eight magistrates perceived reports had not become more punitive:"No it's very, very rare that you actually recommend custody and I can understand why. I mean custody doesn't work anyway, well I don't think it does". Furthermore:

> "At one time you would never ever see a custodial sentence recommended. I know I think only on one occasion have I actually seen it in the recent past, so although I know they are making those recommendations now, I wouldn't say, from my experience, that there are a lot of them coming in."

This was not the case in the reports another magistrate had been reading, which is no bad thing because "we have to look forward to where we can be looking towards rehabilitation rather than a sentence of custody".

When theorising the reasons for such differential responses among respondents, it needs to be made clear that there are 14 courts within the 'Northtown' Magistrates' Court building, which sit during the morning session (10am to 1pm) and then during the afternoon (from 2.15pm until the business of the day is completed, which could be between 5 and 6pm). Furthermore clerks and magistrates are part of a court rota system, with the result that even though all 14 courts could be sitting during the course of each day, probation reports will not find their way into all of them. In fact during the course of the research there was a designated court during the afternoon session for dealing with all those cases that had been adjourned for a report. Accordingly only one clerk and three magistrates, out of 20 clerks and 60 magistrates on duty during the course of one specific afternoon, would be reading reports. Additionally some reports will be less punitive than others. In saying this it is also possible that, during the course of each day at 'Northtown', probation reports could also find their way into other courts, notwithstanding designated afternoon courts. Consequently it can be surmised that there is differential exposure to reports among magistrates and clerks that can account for these variable findings. But after allowing for court dynamics and contingencies, I draw the conclusion that something is going on which is discernibly different to previous years. This is supported by official statistics that have generated concerns and called for remedial action prior to receiving a share of the additional £40 million allocated to probation. Finally, one clerk was unsure and the remaining three magistrates did not specifically address the issue under consideration.

Verstehen and the art of probation

One area of practice explored with clerks and magistrates was: are probation reports demonstrating *less understanding* of offenders' personal and social circumstances? The somewhat slippery but important notion of understanding is arguably the distinctive and defining contribution of probation work to the criminal justice system, primarily through the medium of court reports. In other words, before judgements are formulated and sentencing decisions made about offending episodes, relevant factors should be collected and pondered by an organisation trained to interpret the vagaries of human conduct. In fact the qualities at one time looked for within probation officers were described as 'flexibility of mind and a capacity for listening to and understanding others' (Jarvis, 1974, p 268). This, of course, is a complex task, but complexity should not preclude engagement with an issue associated with the pursuit of criminal and social justice (Whitehead, 2007). Having said that, the modernised context is hardly conducive to facilitating a framework of understanding because of the interpretative limits imposed by the tenets of neoclassical criminology (Garland, 2001); those discernible shifts in the rationale of probation outlined in the opening chapter; a much greater emphasis placed on individual responsibility associated with a punitive culture engendered by neoliberalism and new public management; and a politics of condemnation rather than understanding which has been a feature of criminal justice policy since 1997 and before that. Additionally, Garland and Sparks have insightfully stated that:

> The posture of 'understanding' the offender was always a demanding and difficult attitude, more readily attained by Liberal elites unaffected by crime or else by professional groups who make their living out of it. This posture increasingly gives way to that of *condemning* criminals and demanding that they be punished and controlled. (2000, p 17, emphasis in original)

Understanding is an important variable for probation work, but it is under pressure, as the following illustrates.

The bigger picture

As considered in Chapter 4, the Keynesian post-war settlement enabled the political establishment to intervene in socio-economic matters with a view to mediating between the competing interests of capital and labour, promoting inclusivity and solidarity through a social-democratic welfare state (Garland, 2001; Cavadino and Dignan, 2006). When this began to break down under the weight of economic turbulence during the 1970s, the resultant rise of neoliberalism had implications for criminal justice. Neoliberalism has reconstructed a grand narrative of individual responsibility, competition, private sector over public sector solutions, coupled with new public management (Leys, 2003), in addition to explaining offending as neoclassical rational choice (Young, 1999, 2007; Garland, 2001; Harvey, 2005; Wacquant, 2008, 2009). This narrative vies with an alternative analysis located within the political economy of crime exemplified by Bonger's criminology (1916). The Chicago School (Smith, 1988) and Robert Merton (1968) located problems people experienced within the social structure. Additionally Taylor et al (1973), Hall et al (1978) and Ian Taylor (1997) argued that capitalism was criminogenic, which demands a fully social theory of deviance reaching beyond individual responsibility, culpability and punishment. This holistic sociological analysis, which is intellectually opposed to a reductionism looking no further than blaming the offender (Reiner, 2006), reveals how macro–economic factors are associated with crime due to the 'extent and impact of unemployment, poverty and inequality following the collapse of the post-war Keynesian, welfare state compromise, and the social tsunami of neo-liberalism' (Reiner, 2007a, p 164). Similar points are advanced in Harvey's analysis (2005, p 80), and the Cabinet Office document (PMSU, 2006) acknowledged the relationship between adverse economic conditions and fluctuations in crime.

This body of macro-theorising is relevant for probation practice because the process of sentencing, to which it has contributed for over a century, proceeds according to parameters established by legislation and National Standards which take account of numerous variables. Some of these variables, touched on earlier, draw attention to offence seriousness, previous convictions, aggravating and mitigating factors, which of course are incorporated within OASys. It is the principle of offender mitigation specifically which should draw the courts into reflecting on the personal histories and wider social circumstances of individuals appearing before them, historically brought to their attention by information contained within a full *social enquiry* report. This constitutes a challenge to reach beyond the offence (*what* has the offender done?), notions of individual responsibility and rational choice, to consider behavioural repertoires associated with, and perhaps sometimes a rational response to, adverse socio-economic factors. On a daily basis the Probation Service, and other court personnel, are confronted with people from adverse social backgrounds, with educational and employment disadvantages, differential life chances, relative deprivation and associated alcohol and drugs problems. Such matters are well documented in the literature and constitute the staple ingredients of probation practice (Walker and Beaumont, 1981; Stewart and Stewart, 1993; Stewart et al, 1994).

If the principle is reaffirmed that decision making ought to take account of the social circumstances of offenders, and that the pursuit of criminal and social justice should be informed by this dynamic, then it is possible to conclude that the weight currently being placed on fast delivery and oral reports may not always be conducive to just and right outcomes. This is because of the danger of superficially skirting over salient background information that should be brought to the courts' attention by probation staff within a full report. It is not possible to reduce complex human behaviours to tick box formats completed within a couple of hours by hard-pressed and unqualified probation staff. Sometimes the stories of people's lives require careful analysis and diligent recounting. Therefore, to return to our question, are reports demonstrating less understanding of the lives of offenders? It is interesting to observe that according to nine clerks, probation reports are demonstrating *less understanding* of offenders. There is a concern that tick boxes entail less background information and "less feeling for how the person has ended up where they are". "On the old style full PSRs I would say no I haven't noticed that, but maybe a little on the FDRs, yes." "I think the full PSR still looks at the offender as well as the offence, but again I think that's possibly a problem with the FDRs, they don't look at the personal circumstances of the offender so much." Other voices were commenting that there had been good reports recently but the FDR could not get into the issues as well as a full report. There were issues with the FDR format in that they provided little time for the offender to open up to probation staff. One clerk said that, "There used to be a very strong emphasis towards the individual, explanations for offending and underlying problems with the offender's circumstances. It has changed to a degree; they are looking more at the offence". Only two magistrates said reports were demonstrating *less understanding*: "The full PSR, done properly, does cover the ground that the social enquiry report used to, but yes, by and large, there is less of that and more emphasis on offence analysis". "Not in an SDR [standard delivery report], but I think in an FDR…. Going back to the FDR, there is the danger that there could be issues with the individual concerned that don't come to light so the longer you take, the longer time you have to prepare the report."

By contrast 10 clerks and 14 magistrates indicated that reports were certainly not compromising on the principle of understanding. Illustrative comments from clerks were:

> "I think that depends on the author of the report. Some reports we have had have been excellent where they have really looked at the offender's personal circumstances and how they can be helped. Other reports you sometimes feel that they have picked bits, set phrases that they think fit that person."

Additionally, "I don't think they have changed that much in that respect". Reports still looked at background issues and were not demonstrating less understanding. When hearing from magistrates it was said that, first:

> "I don't think so; I think that is one baby that we haven't thrown out with the bath water. I think we still have a considerable amount of understanding of social deprivation, of social problems, that lead to offending and I don't think that we have necessarily thrown that out when we lean more to punishment or enforceability. I think we still have that but it is more measured and tempered with public protection issues."

Second, "Overall I would say the vast majority of reports that we get are full of detail. They seem to have become extended to what they were". Next:

> "I have to be perfectly honest, the reports that I have had lately have been excellent and there's been a fine balance between how their lifestyle has got them to where they are and what the offence is. So it's a fine balance and I think it is important that we do know some of the deeper structure of people's lives."

Fourth, "I still think you have a very similar level of understanding of the offender's personal and social circumstances. I think reports have got better". Finally, another said:

> "I think it is more balanced than it used to be. I think the digging, the antecedent history, more importantly the social background perhaps, used to be the major part of some reports and now we are getting a more balanced report about what they have done; why they did it; and even what should be done about it."

Nevertheless one magistrate stated somewhat exceptionally: "certainly the opposite. I find it more for the offender than punishment now. Personally I don't think that some reports tally with the offence or their behaviour". In the last analysis three clerks did not expatiate and one of the four magistrates who found it difficult to express a clear view stated, it was "difficult to make a judgement" on this matter.

It can be argued that the analytical category of human understanding pursued within the context of writing court reports is associated with the exercise of discretion, differential treatment and responses. It is possible for the exercise of discretion to produce malign outcomes, illustrated by questionable sentencing practices (Freiberg and Gelb, 2008). By contrast it can be construed as a positive factor when exercised in adverse social circumstances. For example Hudson argues for a form of discretion that facilitates leniency in sentencing practices because of poverty. Similarly Tonry alludes to social adversity mitigation that would provide sentencers with the licence to have regard to the 'particular difficulties faced by impoverished, unemployed, and otherwise disadvantaged offenders' (quoted in Zedner, 2004, p 192; also Cook, 2006; Roberts and McMahon, 2007). Indubitably this is a contentious issue, both professionally and politically, in circumstances where there has been a profound cultural shift of emphasis towards the law-abiding majority rather than focusing on the needs of offenders. Exercising discretion can be seen as making excuses and condoning offending, but it is also informed by the principle of understanding that can establish a basis for advancing arguments for greater leniency. There are great problems reconciling these competing interests, but it can be argued that probation work has a moral duty to operate within a framework of understanding, and to exercise discretion, if it wants to make a serious contribution to criminal and social justice. Will the development of NOMS erode the principles under discussion in this section? With this question in mind I want to turn to NOMS again by specifically addressing the important subject of contestability.

NOMS and contestability

Court clerks

Table 5.10: Clerks' understanding of NOMS

	Number	%
No understanding	11	50.0
Some understanding	9	40.9
Clearer understanding	2	9.1
Total	22	100.0

When exploring the level of awareness and understanding court clerks had of NOMS, it became clear that 11 had no understanding of the new organisational structure which has brought prisons and probation closer together or potential implications; a further nine disclosed some understanding; and two were very much clearer. When hearing from the 11 clerks who had no understanding of NOMS, typical yet surprising comments were: "Never heard of it"; "No idea. I don't know what NOMS is"; "I don't think I know a great deal about it; it's not something that we are involved in". Next, for those nine who expressed some understanding, we hear: "The new name for probation"; "I don't know, probably the governing body of the Probation Service"; "I assumed that was a fancy umbrella name for the whole of the Probation Service. I've heard of it, yes, but it's never really registered to be honest"; "It's the Probation Service. That's my understanding of it; it's just a new name for it". Finally, there were two clerks with a clearer understanding, as follows:

> "My understanding is that it's a service in its own right and comprises the Probation Service and the Prison Service. I'm not sure if anyone else is involved but it's to manage offenders both in the community and in prison and following release and it's therefore both those agencies combined in effect."

> "It's a service that incorporates probation, the Prison Service, others, and basically it is a service that joins up and manages someone from the time they are sentenced to the time that they finish their sentence. A joined-up service if you like, including one or two different agencies."

Furthermore I thought it would be interesting to find out if any of the 22 court clerks had heard of contestability. The findings are not without interest, as Table 5.11 suggests.

Given that NOMS, with its commitment to contestability, will have radical implications for the delivery of offender services over the next few years, it is surprising that only one clerk was familiar with the term: "Yes, it's another word for competition".

Table 5.11: Clerks and contestability

	Number	%
Yes	1	4.5
No	21	95.5
Total	22	100.0

Magistrates

When turning to the 20 magistrates it was discovered that 12 of them expressed no understanding of this significant development, but that four had some understanding and, as one of them stated, it was "another name for probation". By contrast the remaining four were clearer that the term covered probation and prison services and, as one clarified:

Table 5.12: Magistrates' understanding of NOMS

	Number	%
No understanding	12	60.0
Some understanding	4	20.0
Clearer understanding	4	20.0
Total	20	100.0

> "My understanding is that it has been created within the Home Office, three or four years ago now, to bring together probation and prison services and principally with a need for I think the phrase is end-to-end offender management. It has also created a regional structure in order to do so."

Again, when turning to whether magistrates had heard of contestability, the following findings are surprising, as show in Table 5.13.

From Table 5.13 we can see that four magistrates said they had heard of contestability (compared to only one court clerk), one of whom acknowledged that it meant work that could be provided by another body or services. The one I have located in the qualified category said that "I've heard of it, but I'm not quite sure what it entails". The remaining 15 said they

Table 5.13: Magistrates and contestability

	Number	%
Yes	4	20.0
No	15	75.0
Qualified	1	5.0
Total	20	100.0

had not heard of contestability. In fact one of these 15 proceeded to comment that, "If it's actually a buzz word it's not quite clicking". Another commented incorrectly that, "Well, yes, where someone is not happy with a report, or an action within court, they have the right to contest. Is this right?". Again it is surprising but also concerning that there is such a lack of awareness of NOMS and the implications of contestability for probation and the operation of the courts. As I proceed towards the end of this research-based chapter, I want to include some final material that emerged from talking to the respondents about how they see the future of the Probation Service. First, clerks should be able to speak for themselves.

Last word on the future of probation from the clerks

It was acknowledged during the course of these interviews that even though the future largely depended on political decisions outside of the interviewees' control, there were concerns regarding the rationale of targets, in addition to the considerable pressure on probation. Because of these pressures one of the clerks stated that probation should be split, "so that you've got on one side the more traditional approach and then one that is more punitive and monitoring of the more serious offenders". This clerk was unaware that her suggestion echoed, to some degree, the thesis of Robert Harris (1980) alluded to in a previous chapter. Other voices heard, which embellished on these concerns, were:

> "I will have to be slightly negative and say that I can see services being led down the path that is controlled by financial constraints and by the need to meet targets which I don't think the Probation Service and the criminal justice system as a whole is all about. It's the same with the clerks, we are very much pushed not to grant adjournments, not to do this, not to allow that, whereas in reality in the interests of justice you should be allowing it and you should be doing x, y and z. We are criticised at meetings when we don't meet our targets and it also has funding implications if we don't meet our targets and I suspect the Probation Services are probably under the same pressures. Really I think that the probation team that work at the courts are extremely helpful, really pleasant, excellent at their job despite the fact that they are put under a lot of pressure and the majority of the reports that are written are really good and I don't have any problems with the Probation Service at all, I think they are very helpful."

This is an extremely revealing comment from a court clerk who has been working at 'Northtown' for over 20 years. Next we hear that:

> "I think if you continue to go down the road of increased government interference, the justice system both in terms of the courts, particularly lower courts such as magistrates' and a body like the Probation Service,

will lose its independence and will gradually lose the values that have made the justice system in this country so good. It's very strange and I would imagine that the same is happening to you as is happening to other public service bodies. I can definitely see it happening with us."

It was also stated:

"Well sadly it's going to depend on politics and I feel it's quite difficult to predict. As soon as there is a change of government there is a change of policy, a change of ideas. Without a change of government there's a change of prime minister, so I wouldn't like to predict. We seem to go in cycles of clamping down on punishment I suspect, lengthening prison sentences and perhaps recommending prison more often and then of course it swings the other way and it looks at a whole new way of managing offenders in the community. I really wouldn't like to predict which way it will go."

There is going to be more of the same: prisons overcrowded and pressure to keep more people out of custody, and so probation will be more overworked. Furthermore:

"I suppose with the set out of reports and things I see it as being unfortunately more computerised and more people in a big building somewhere rather than coming to court and actually physically being there to speak to people and help people. I mean I hope it won't happen but I see that it is more tick boxes than actually getting behind why somebody's committing offences."

Then again, "Well, I think pretty much the way it has been at present (and over the last five years) but it is becoming, and I'm sorry if I keep repeating it…. I don't want to say punishment as in sending people to prison but punishment in the community". There could be new community penalties; probation changing and moving back to a more social work-based service; laments for the dilution of contact between probation and court and the severing of these links. Also the introduction of NOMS and privatisation was seen as a retrograde step:

"I think you have all this highly trained pool of people and certainly the ones I come across seem very effective, and they should just be allowed to get on with the job and they shouldn't be sidetracked into punishment. If they want people to punish, use a different organisation and use probation for what they were originally set up for, leaving other people to do the punishment. So that is my opinion."

This constitutes yet another reference to the separation of care and control in the work of Robert Harris. Therefore a mélange of concerns were articulated in relation to time constraints and resources, chasing targets, pressures from government, constant change, bureaucratic routines, more punishment and the loss of professionalism.

Last word from the magistrates

Concerns were raised by magistrates when turning to the future about privatisation and contestability, more prisons being built, concerns about resources and staff run off their feet, and one implication was that members of staff did not "get a proper chance to build relationships with people who would certainly benefit". This is an insightful comment. Additionally disquiet was expressed in relation to softer sentences and "I have no confidence that the Ministry of Justice is going to do what society wants". But then again, "My concern is that it becomes too target driven as I've referred to earlier, that can be at the expense of a professional approach that might need more time. So I worry about professional standards being maintained as resources become tighter". Finally there was a concern to retain flexibility in circumstances of national standards and targets and the danger of too much central control. Therefore there were similarities between the concerns of magistrates and court clerks as they began to look ahead.

Conclusion

Bodies of social theory, in addition to personalist impulses and moral sensibilities, facilitate an exploration and explanation of what the modernised manifestation of probation has become since 1997 in the first four chapters of this book. By contrast this chapter provokes a challenging response by offering a perspective on what it ought to be as we listen to the views of solicitors, clerks and magistrates, but less so with barristers and judges. Consequently there is not always a seamless fit between the first four chapters and the current chapter, so much so that the concluding chapter will begin by extrapolating some of these material differences. In other words, there are a number of challenges to modernisation emanating from pre-modern traditions that should be explored in greater detail.

Notes

[1] It should be acknowledged that there is a paucity of published research on defence solicitors and magistrates' court clerks. By contrast there is more research-generated data on magistrates, barristers and judges: see Brown (1991); Gelsthorpe and Raynor (1995); Noaks and Wincup (2004); King and Wincup (2007); see also relevant Home Office research studies which have been published over a number of years.

[2] The first stage of this research project involved interviewing solicitors at 'Northtown'. For further details see Chapter 5 in Whitehead (2007) where these findings are presented in full.

³ Ethical issues are significant when undertaking empirical research and are touched on in the introduction to this chapter. For further information on this subject see, for example, Dohan (2003, p 241), when undertaking ethnographic research in the US.

⁴ For additional information on the ethnic composition of the magistracy see the following publication: *Magistrate*, May 2007, vol 63, no 5. Furthermore it should be acknowledged that there are just over 30,000 magistrates in post and it is said that progress has been made in relation to diversity issues. In 2002 the percentage of magistrates from black and minority ethnic backgrounds was just over 6%, but by 2006 this had risen to approximately 7.3%.

SIX

Modernising monstrosities and cultural catastrophes: probation trapped in a new order of things

Introduction

The first four chapters of this book introduced bodies of social theory as well as maintaining an interest in religious and personalist impulses that have left their footprint on the criminal justice system. These, in turn, were put to work as a collection of interpretative keys to unlock and by doing so bring into sharper relief developments in probation since 1997. When turning to the research findings in the previous chapter a frisson of tension has been injected into the narrative. In other words, modernising tendencies within the probation domain have, at certain points, been challenged by a number of respondents who continue to entertain what can be referred to as pre-modern inclinations. Consequently the first section of this final chapter will reprise this tension, which establishes a platform for some concluding reflections, as well as signposting a possible way forward.

The becoming of probation under New Labour

There have been a number of occasions since 1945 when the term 'modernisation' has been applied within the United Kingdom (Marr, 2008). Nevertheless it acquired an exalted cachet under New Labour and is synonymous with a political phenomenon that emerged during the 1990s, with borrowings from Clintonian Democratic politics in the United States. Previously it was acknowledged how the term has been applied to developments extending throughout the whole public sector, including the criminal justice system. At this juncture it is helpful to be reminded of some of these modernising features.

Modernisation signalled a discernible shift in criminal justice policy away from Old Labour tenets of adverse socio-economic circumstances providing an explanatory framework for offending which required compensatory social welfare, and a helping hand towards rehabilitation. Accordingly a new compass bearing was taken towards a more robust approach that enabled New Labour to enshroud itself in the clothes of former Conservative administrations, particularly those after 1979. But there is a residual contradiction in the soul of New Labour because even though criminal justice has been reconfigured in a more punitive direction, the Social Exclusion Unit, in addition to the Cabinet Office Strategy

Unit, acknowledges the links between difficult socio-economic conditions created by periodic downturns in capitalist markets and property offences, which continue to dominate criminal statistics (Newburn, 2007, p 55). This helps to explain why New Labour has concerned itself with child poverty and introduced the New Deal to help young people into work. It also established the Sure Start programme to benefit disadvantaged families.

More specifically, however, modernisation has manifested itself in fast-tracking young people who offend through the youth justice system, which has also taken a more punitive turn, reforming the Crown Prosecution Service and the police, and the introduction of ASBOs, which have contributed to criminalising lower-level forms of disorder. Modernisation also resonates with an increase in surveillance technology and a plethora of new criminal legislation (Auld, 2001; Carter, 2007). It should be observed that a change of penal philosophy signalled by the 2003 Criminal Justice Act implies that sentencing will become incrementally tougher for persistent offending. This undermines the just deserts approach of the 1991 Criminal Justice Act. There is a war being waged against crime, an atmosphere of zero tolerance pervades and the criminal justice system has been rebalanced, deliberately tilted, in the direction of victims and witnesses. By these developments New Labour has arrogated the epithet of being the natural party of law and order. As the next general election approaches, which must be held by 2010, there is little to choose between Labour and Conservative policy when it comes to thinking about criminal justice politics.

Yet there is much more to modernisation by noting profound cultural transformations in probation, which can be illustrated by the establishment of a national service in 2001. Moreover, centralisation and nationalisation were quickly followed by the creation of NOMS during 2003/04. It is the latter which created the conditions for a mixed economy of offender provision defined by the concept of contestability. These two developments in particular have done a great deal to re-route probation work in the direction of bureaucratic centralism and punitive controlism (Burnett et al, 2007). Accordingly, even though the language of rehabilitation remains part of NOMS, modernisation has repositioned the organisation towards the punitive-controlling end of the care–control continuum.[1] Arguably such far-reaching cultural transformations have disorientated the organisation and resulted in the loss of one identity and the forging of another. In fact modernising developments have turned probation and criminal justice into state-directed mechanisms to prosecute the war on crime. By doing so socio-economic adversities are more easily translated into criminal episodes as problems contingent on neoliberalism become individual moral failings illustrated by a lack of respect, which facilitates governing through crime (Simon, 2007; Rodger, 2008).

Additionally politicians and media outlets have elevated crime within the national consciousness to such a degree that it is presented as *a* if not *the* major national concern for which individuals are primarily accountable, rather than behaviours being a symptom of deeper problems associated with the deleterious effects of globalisation and capitalist economic arrangements. This means that the war on crime is directed largely against people from certain groups within society – vulnerable, poor, disadvantaged, the 'underclass' – rather than taking the fight to the differential impacts of neoliberal structures and attendant inequalities (Cavadino and Dignan, 2006; Reiner, 2007a; Wacquant, 2008, 2009; Wilkinson and Pickett, 2009). Therefore macro-structures themselves are hardly conducive to creating a climate of trust, loyalty and respect between people in local communities. But as in football so also in politics the Respect campaign is foregrounded, a front in the war strategy, which is presented as the solution to the way in which people behave, problems get defined and how they should be resolved (Pratt, 2007, p 121). Accordingly, probation has been modernised and culturally transformed to become part of these new arrangements. And yet there are voices of disquiet from within the criminal justice system.

Respondents' doubts and challenges

The significance of these research findings gleaned from solicitors, court clerks, magistrates and, to a much lesser extent, barristers and judges, is that *at certain points* modernising developments receive some support. By contrast there are a number of concerns at the way things have turned out. In fact there are doubts about and challenges to modernisation coming from a pre-modern direction that can be summarised as follows.

The *quantitative insights* reveal some interesting points of similarity between solicitors, clerks and magistrates when it comes to their working knowledge of probation, which should concern itself with understanding why people offend, an awareness of personal and social circumstances, promoting criminal and social justice and keeping people out of custody. Nevertheless there are differential responses to a number of other variables elucidated by consulting Table 5.3. It is clear that the politics of modernisation has created a climate of robust responses, bureaucratic targets, offenders as units of risk, rigorous enforcement procedures and an enveloping toughness. By contrast there is evidence for retaining the services of an organisation associated with benign rather than solely punitive instincts in response to complex human problems. Accordingly, there is more to probation and criminal justice than a punitive outlook, which means that these respondents are involved in a complex conversation with probation work. Briefly Table 5.4 is a more limited data set yet it provides further support for a number of pre-modern features among barristers and judges that challenge the becoming of probation under New Labour.

Next, interviews with clerks and magistrates reveal a rich source of *qualitative responses*. It emerged that the purpose of probation retains a rehabilitative element, complemented by providing a service to people requiring help, assistance, remedial education, as well as engaging with the dominant language of punishment. To some degree the information gleaned from interviews with respondents reinforces what are sometimes *mixed* messages emanating from the tick box data tables.

Importantly probation has a dual role because of its responsibilities towards the courts in addition to people who offend.

When turning to reports, a critical function throughout the history of probation, it has been suggested that there are worrying developments contingent on the simple, speedy, summary and new public management agendas. Until recently, and this point is worth emphasising, there was a Service Level Agreement for probation to produce 40% of its reports in the form of the fast delivery. By 2009 this had risen to 70% (National Probation Service, 2009). In a climate of recession (late 2008/09 and into 2010 in the United Kingdom) it may be extrapolated that there are mounting pressures to resort to the fast delivery report (FDR) as the default document in the magistrates' courts when the Ministry of Justice is trying to economise. The rationale of reports is to assist the courts to determine the most suitable sentence, which, logically, relies on furnishing the courts with *all relevant information* on the background of offenders. For nine clerks and nine magistrates the provision of 'background information' defines the rationale of reports. However, the focus on the fast delivery reduces the opportunity to do this, which potentially has serious implications for the pursuit of justice and reflections on fairness. This is a pertinent point for magistrates' courts, which deal with 95% of criminal cases. The FDR indubitably reduces costs and expedites answering *'What have you done?'* questions, yet contributes little to exploring the more sociologically probing *'Why have you done it?'* perspective. Interestingly 12 clerks and 11 magistrates do not anticipate problems with FDRs. By contrast eight clerks and six magistrates raised concerns by acknowledging that they only scratch the surface, can be rushed and are an example of chasing central government targets. In fact it is possible to tick all the boxes and achieve the targets yet fail to engage effectively with offenders, just as much as all the boxes can be ticked within the NHS yet fail patients.[2]

There are tensions between the pursuit of efficiency consistent with the new public management agenda, and achieving just outcomes. It is also clear that there is a noticeable shift in direction towards FDRs and away from full PSRs, as evidenced by the data contained in Table 5.9. Interestingly 12 clerks and six magistrates expressed concern that recent developments in the criminal justice system amount to putting the principle of business efficiency before the notion of justice. By contrast nine clerks and 10 magistrates articulated less concern about this growing tension.

There is also some evidence for the punitisation of reports at 'Northtown', supported by evidence supplied by central government (in the Teesside area business plan for 2008/09, see Teesside Probation Service, 2008). Fourteen clerks and nine magistrates perceived this was the case in relation to proposals for custody and punishment in the community. Then again other respondents were less convinced. Furthermore the notion of understanding (here I am utilising the Weberian notion of *verstehen* flexibly) is under pressure. Arguably the macro-context of neoliberalism is highly pertinent for the criminal justice system because it provides an explanatory context for some offending episodes. To some degree OASys lends itself to an exploration of offenders' lives, from personal and family factors to wider social circumstances. However, we have seen how the prevailing culture of FDRs, in addition to the triple 'S' and new public management agendas, undermines a detailed exploration of individual stories. Nine clerks and two magistrates said that probation was demonstrating *less* understanding of offenders, and cited reliance on tick boxes to support this claim. Alternatively 10 clerks and 14 magistrates indicated that probation was not diluting the contribution made to understanding people who offend. Additionally it was possible that there could be a return to the principle of understanding, as version 4.3.1 of OASys, released during the summer of 2009, implies probation staff will spend less time entering data into computers through the notion of layered assessments.

It is disquieting to note that even though NOMS has been in existence since 2003/04, so few respondents had any meaningful grasp of what it is, or its likely implications. Therefore, how will 'Northtown' react if their Probation Service is replaced, after 2011, by other organisations drawn from the public, private and third sectors? What will they think if, for example, Global Solutions is awarded the contract for offender services by the local Probation Trust and begins to provide reports to the courts instead of probation itself? This may not happen, but the point is that it is more likely to happen precisely because of the operational philosophy of NOMS. Consequently contestability is a central component of NOMS and received legislative legitimacy from the 2007 Offender Management Act. NOMS is critical to the future of criminal justice but only one clerk and four magistrates had heard of contestability.

When reflecting on the tension between *what probation has become* under New Labour, and the empirical findings on *what it ought to be*, it is possible to advance the position that a number of respondents restored a semblance of balance to the operational dynamics of criminal justice by holding onto, if not reinstating, pre-modern features. Back in 1993 Rutherford's book on *Criminal justice and the pursuit of decency* was published, based on interviewing 28 practitioners between 1988 and 1991. It is interesting to recall the comments by a Chief Probation Oficer who stated during interview that:

> I have no qualms that we are part of the criminal justice system. But our prime task is to be a social work service 'core', and that buys in a set of principles that we do not abandon because other bits of the criminal justice process find them uncomfortable. (1993, p 153)

Rutherford concluded that hope lay with practitioners if the criminal justice system was to be orientated around a set of principles that could be classified as decent and humane. However, since 1997, and particularly 2001, this has become increasingly difficult because of unbalancing tendencies.

The great *unbalancing* act at the heart of criminal justice

The insightful comments from a barrister with over 25 years' experience at 'Northtown' bear the weight of repetition when it was recalled that the:

> "Probation Service has changed beyond recognition over the course of the last 10 years. The shift of the Probation Service has left the criminal justice system unbalanced. There is too much emphasis on punishment and a void where there should be an agency dedicated to values of befriending and assisting."

We have seen how rebalancing criminal justice away from what, for example, can be described as an empathic *sociological* understanding of why people offend, towards victims and witnesses, has gathered pace (Home Office, 2006b). In an undated message to staff during 2008 from Jack Straw, Secretary of State, and Permanent Secretary Suma Chakrabarti (Ministry of Justice Priorities and Performance and Efficiency Programme), it was clarified that the primary purpose of the Ministry of Justice was to secure justice, protect the public and punish lawbreakers. There must be justice for the law-abiding and victims of crime and, as a starting point, it is difficult to demur from this stated policy. The message proceeded to comment that a further bout of modernisation could be required to realise these objectives, without saying what this might involve.

It may be suggested, after taking account of some of the research findings contained in Chapter 5, that rebalancing has unbalanced the criminal justice system. Barbara Hudson (1987) reminded us some time ago that the pursuit of justice should not always be equated with punishment when responding to offending behaviours. Additionally the position could be adopted that justice is not necessarily to be found patiently waiting at the end of modernising reflexes, constant change, expanding organisational bureaucracies or transforming probation into a power to punish. In fact justice may not be located in the direction of expanding the criminal justice estate at all, tinkering with penal policy, building new prisons or even reducing the cultural divide between probation and prisons. Instead dialogue surrounding criminal and social justice must take account of the circumstances of offenders including the macro-context of neoliberalism and its differential impacts on individuals, families and communities.[3] Therefore the lives of people who offend, and who subsequently appear before magistrates and judges, should be situated within a holistic explanatory context. By doing so it is logical to argue that there should be an organisation charged with the responsibility to explore and explain factors of relevance to those charged with sentencing responsibilities. Modernising tendencies have weakened this critical faculty, acutely illustrated by the changing nature of reports to courts. Accordingly rebalancing has unbalanced the system in the direction of punishment rather than enhancing the category of insightful understanding which is necessary for making careful judgements about offenders and offending responses. Arguably probation should be drawing attention to human casualties not compounding them on behalf of a more authoritarian and penal state; critically challenging the rationale of punitive excesses; being a signpost towards alternatives to custody and punishment rather than a weathervane which catches the prevailing political wind; and maintaining the professional capacity to engage with offenders in order to recount their life stories. However, modernising processes leading to cultural transformations have undermined these organisational functions.

Furthermore, rebalancing has unbalanced the relationship between probation and prisons. As mentioned earlier it is surprising that most court clerks, magistrates, but also solicitors, do not have a sufficient grasp of the implications of NOMS, particularly contestability. Additionally NOMS was restructured during 2008/09 to alter profoundly the two organisations by ensuring prison was the dominant partner. This new state of affairs can be illustrated more clearly as follows. First, there are currently 17 members of the Ministry of Justice Ministerial Team and Corporate Management Board in London. However, there is no probation representation at the highest strategic and decision-making level. Second, a parliamentary answer to Neil Gerrard MP on 21 January 2009 revealed that there were 113 former probation employees working within NOMS headquarters, compared to 3,445 prison service staff. In other words, probation accounts for only 3.17% of the total staffing complement in what is described as the 'new agency' (information contained in the NAPO briefing paper on 9 March 2009). Third, roles and responsibilities have been rationalised at a regional level by coalescing prison area managers and regional offender managers into the newly created post of director of offender management. Most of the 10 directors were appointed by February/March 2009 but only one appears to have a background in probation – Roger Hill – who left his post as director of probation, which was not in fact refilled, to become the first director of offender management of the South East region.

Therefore from the highest strategic level (NOMS headquarters), then into the 10 regions, and not forgetting that only approximately 50% of frontline employees are professionally trained, probation is under-represented in a modernised organisation dominated by prison. This is making it difficult, if not impossible, for probation to argue its case and to defend its principles and values within the criminal justice system, which of course is one of New Labour's finest achievements. Furthermore it should be clarified that the only point at which probation and prisons overlap is when prisoners are being prepared for release back into the community. Accordingly the primary tasks of these organisations are fundamentally different because the prison system is concerned with humane containment, and probation the supervision of offenders in the community. Consequently both sets of staff require different skills when working with prisoners in conditions of secure confinement and offenders on community orders in conditions of freedom. Of course there are points of interface, but the primary tasks are fundamentally different. Therefore bringing both organisations closer to each other within one organisational structure is an affront to logic, as well as being unwise and confusing, so much so that rebalancing unbalances the entire criminal justice system and because of this should be a matter of concern for all those involved.

A new order of things

There is no seamless fit between the philosophical discussion in Chapter 2 on Foucault's *The order of things* and its application to the history of probation, but it is possible to flex the thesis a little at this point. We have seen how McWilliams identified a number of discrete ideologies: 1876–1930s, a theology of saving souls; 1930s–70s, a 'scientific' form of curing by casework conducive to rehabilitation; and alternatives to custody during the 1980s. This continued beyond the 1980s with punishment in the community after 1991, and, more recently, bureaucratic managerialism. One of the important differences between these changing ideologies and Foucault's epistemes is that the former are not inexplicably discontinuous. At one level saving souls *is* discontinuous with punishment in the community – 1907 is not the same as 1991. However, members of staff with a religious disposition have always been associated with probation. By contrast bureaucratic centralism is a relatively recent institutional phenomenon. Therefore if Foucault operates within discontinuous epistemes, it is more accurate to say that probation is characterised by continuous *and* discontinuous features. It is also possible to analyse how different probation epochs have evolved (Whitehead and Statham, 2006), whereas Foucault is unconcerned to explain epistemic transformations beginning, as we saw earlier, with the Renaissance in the 15th century.

Even though one can explore and explain the period since 1997 with reference to 1979–97 (this should not be avoided), I have treated the period since New Labour came to power as a discrete entity for theoretically heuristic and explanatory purposes. It is clear that there is a new organisational architecture glued together by a cultural code tilted towards punishing offenders into conformity. Additionally it is suggested that a *combined theory* that utilises insights drawn from the work of Durkheim, Weber, Marx and Foucault is required to account for probation developments since 1997/98. Even though New Labour entertained the possibility of organisational reconfiguration early on during its first term of governmental office contingent on the prisons–probation review (Home Office, 1998), this did not materialise because probation remained a locally based service that presented obstacles to political objectives. By contrast after the creation of the National Probation Service in 2001, and then NOMS in 2003/04, such obstacles were systematically dismantled by a governance structure imposed by an authoritarian state that forced the organisation into an iron cage of centralised command and control. One dramatic illustration of this was to remove locally appointed Chief Probation Officers as the troublesome priests of the old order, and replace them with centrally imposed satraps in the form of chief officers, as civil servants, under direct political tutelage, no longer leaders of organisations but conduits and managers of party politics. Therefore seizing control of the organisation was the essential first step in the process of modernisation. In fact Windlesham (2001, p 245) described this process in terms of a diminution of delegated authority, local accountability and leadership, including trust in and respect for the profession.

Second, the political imposition of a structure of domination onto the organisation has, in turn, culminated in a culturally transformed structure of domination being imposed onto offenders. Some of these cultural shifts were neatly elucidated by the Secretary of State at the Ministry of Justice when he addressed an audience of trainee probation officers at the University of Portsmouth: from the language of clients to criminals and offenders; rehabilitation no longer dominates because it has become one sentencing aim among several; from advice, assistance and friendship to punishment, containment and control; probation as a correctional mechanism of the state not an adjunct of social services; persistent offenders will be punished with incremental toughness not proportionately to the seriousness of the offence; prison capacity expansion means 20,000 additional places by 2014; and community sentences must shed their 'soft image' problem (Straw, 2009). This represents the delivery of an uncompromising modernising message to those wanting to become offender managers in the new order of things through mapping a culturally transformed organisational logic. Additionally this new discourse, prosecuted with alacrity by the Ministry of *in*-Justice, constitutes the triumph of administrative banality over the cultivation of a sociological imagination. Moreover it is far from clear who required this reconfiguration beyond New Labour image makers because some of the research findings in Chapter 5 challenge this reconstruction.

Third, organisational modernisation and accompanying cultural transformations predominantly imposed from *without* but with some collaboration from *within*, notwithstanding resistance from NAPO and the Probation Boards Association, have occurred within a context of socio-economic change taking shape since the 1970s. Until the *crisis decade* a combination of post-war welfare and rehabilitation provided the possibility of compensatory support to people in need and trouble to steer behaviours in an acceptable direction. However, in the period since the late 1970s, which has seen Conservative and New Labour administrations endorsing neoliberal economics (from Keynes to Hayek, Friedman, Thatcher, Reagan, Major, Blair and Brown), a markedly different set of attitudes have strengthened their position in response to lawbreaking encapsulated by being tougher on crime than its aetiology. Moreover there is a renewed focus on the failings of individuals and families, more than them being failed by macro-structural factors imposing insecurities outside of their control. Accordingly the modernised organisation, as the new order of things, is less equipped to understand that the way people (this includes *all of us*) think, feel, behave and respond to situations, our changing moods, a hardening of sensibilities and lack of empathy that undermines self-respect and respect for others, can be shaped by material conditions under capitalist formations.[4]

Consequently probation has been ensnared in criminal justice repositioning, facilitated by decisions and choices selected by the political class and apparatchiks. Rather than probation being trusted by a mature government to develop professional competencies and values that facilitate an analysis of the impacts of changing material conditions on behaviours, the opposite has occurred. Modernisation, and here I adapt the discussion found in Rodger (2008), has to some extent dehumanised and desensitised the organisation and by doing so has become less capable of exercising empathy and those personalist sensibilities which help to maintain checks and balances within the competing forces of criminal justice. The neoliberal state responds to offenders more punitively rather than by ameliorative social welfare policies to compensate for structural and adverse material fluctuations. Probation as a state organisation has become part of the new approach to the NEETs (those not in education, employment or training), and the 'underclass' who are deemed to be anti-social because of lifestyle choices, personal inadequacies and a signal failure to take advantage of prevailing opportunities within a market-driven society. However, it would seem that 'the antecedents of that behaviour tend to be of little interest to those designing strategies to combat their deviant behaviour, certainly from the evidence of New Labour's respect agenda and anti-social behaviour strategies' (Rodger, 2008, p 69). In the new order of things punitive populism is the default response by the praetorian elite of New Labour towards people who offend. This compounds, and is related to, the 'violence from above' inflicted by neoliberal structures on the most vulnerable sections of the community in the first decade of the 21st century (Wacquant, 2009). Accordingly probation and the system of criminal justice has been modernised to respond more robustly with human casualties. At the moment of crisis when probation was needed to maintain organisational integrity in promoting criminal and social justice, it was bullied by the modernisers to pursue a different course. When it should have been exploring, explaining, facilitating an understanding of the deleterious effects of changes within capitalism on its clients, for example, it has collaborated with punitive and heavy-handed responses. When it should have held its line in the face of modernising pressures, it has been brought into line by New Labour politicians with little knowledge or experience of the history and traditions of probation work.

A 'what if' and 'if only' thesis

Ian Kershaw's book, *Fateful choices: Ten decisions that changed the world 1940–1941* (2007), is illuminating. These 10 decisions can be summarised as Britain deciding to fight on alone in the spring of 1940 rather than negotiating peace with Germany; Hitler's decision to attack the Soviet Union in 1940, given effect in 1941; Japan seizing her opportunities; Mussolini making the decision to grab his share of the spoils; Roosevelt deciding to lend a hand in the war; Stalin's refusal to take the German threat to his country seriously; Roosevelt eventually declaring war; Japan's decision to attack Pearl Harbour; Hitler declaring war on the United States;

and lastly Hitler deciding to eradicate the Jews from Europe. Kershaw makes the point that these decisions were made by a handful of people in Britain, Germany, Japan, Italy and the United States, but his main task is to explore those diverse and certainly complex influences that were brought to bear on these critical decisions. Intriguingly Kershaw poses the question: were the decisions taken inevitable, or were other courses of action feasible? Significantly, were there opportunities before the final and fateful decisions were taken to pursue alternative courses of action? He answers:

> In retrospect, what took place seems to have been inexorable. In looking at the history of wars, perhaps even more than at history generally, there is an almost inbuilt teleological impulse, which leads us to presume that the way things turned out is the only way they could have turned out. (2007, p 6)

Kershaw argues that this was not the case at all. Decisions imply choices and on this basis alternative decisions could have been made amidst the welter of variables, pressures and national and international contingencies that were at play in these exceptional times. Additionally, and here I resort to a complementary literary reference, James Joyce in *Ulysses* concerns himself with the nightmare of history in the way its hand lies heavily on us. Joyce, long before Kershaw and one might also refer to other great speculators of history including Vico, Hegel, Comte and Marx (Mazlish, 1968), is troubled by the thought that it could have been other than it was. What if Pyrrhus had not fallen or Julius Caesar knifed to death, asks Joyce? 'But can those have been possible seeing that they never were? Or was that only possible which came to pass? Weave, weaver of the wind' (1992, p 30).

It is possible to consider that other decisions could have been made not only where Kershaw's analysis is concerned but also in probation since 1997 and, of course, prior to this. For example the creation of the National Probation Service was not inevitable (arguments for a National Probation Service were being mooted as early as 1962 but rejected; Home Office, 1962); the Carter proposals in 2003 for the creation of NOMS could have been rejected (do not forget a step too far during 1997/98 but a step in time after 2003). Moreover there are alternatives to marketisation and contestability, reliance on computers, numerical targets, centralisation and bureaucratisation, including the management of 'problem populations' via punitive strategies, just as much as there are alternatives to neoliberalism (Saad-Filho and Johnston, 2005). Therefore a series of decisions were made by the political elite, subsequently implemented by apparatchiks *and probation managers*, but they were by no means inevitable. In fact it is possible to agree with Kershaw that things might have turned out differently; decisions imply choices.

David Garland cogently argues that today's crime control strategies should be seen as a response to late-modern crime issues associated with increased levels of insecurity, the decline of rehabilitation and diminution of a social welfare approach. It can be argued that the state is fighting back against those most affected by late-modern socio-economic conditions engendered by neoliberalism, primarily the urban poor, welfare claimants, minorities and offenders as the excluded 'Other' (2001, p 195). Within the context of this analysis probation has been *forced to adjust* to these changes to reflect the latest political, electoral and penal realities which have been emerging since the 1970s. Choices have been made which incorporate punitive retaliation and acting out to maintain the rule of law, social order and control. These choices have not been inevitable but perhaps more likely than others because of late-modern conditions and the problems they spawn. But 'what if' and 'if only' other choices had been made in the direction of more integrative social policies to reduce structural inequality (Wilkinson and Pickett, 2009), rather than a hardening of the state's penal arteries towards the individual? What if and if only probation had more cogently resisted these modernising overtures by defending its core values, organisational ideals and its professional integrity particularly before 2001? Why has probation, from the *inside*, allowed itself to be turned over within such a relatively short period of time into a phenomenon that hardly resembles probation? Why have respected social workers of the courts allowed themselves to be turned into punishment workers? Therefore, because modernisation has politicised and punitised the Probation Service, rather than enabling it to maintain its professional integrity and vestige of semi-independence, has the organisation been culturally transformed beyond all recognition? If this is the case then has it become necessary to look beyond the Probation Service itself for the restoration of balance and those values associated with a personalist ethic? These are deeply uncomfortable questions to pose and even more difficult to answer, but I present the following for reflection.

Is there any hope of salvation through the third sector?

Notwithstanding the many modernising changes that have been brought to bear on the criminal justice system, including the prison 'takeover' of probation following restructuring during 2008/09, the third sector is rapidly becoming an important feature of NOMS. In fact faith communities specifically, a component of the third sector as we saw earlier, have been singled out for special attention by central government. Even though a discernible punitive drift can be plotted in penal policy, could it be possible to detect the stirrings of constraining influences on the march from within NOMS itself but located outside the formal structures of probation? Arguably there remains the vestige of a personalist footprint within the probation domain because support, help, reform, decency and respect for the offender remain part of the lexicon of even the modernised organisation. However, it is no longer dominated by an ideology of anti-punishment and anti-custody, primarily because of overt politicisation that has created institutional, ideological and cultural complexity. Consequently one may have to turn to the third sector for the renaissance of those values that were traditionally associated with probation's historic mission to humanise criminal justice, and to rebalance the system in the direction of justice and fairness. But before getting carried away it is possible to theorise the involvement of faith communities in the third sector from a number of perspectives that adds a note of caution as we look ahead. Three possible approaches are selected for illustrative purposes at this juncture.

The new public management agenda and cost reduction

First, new public management (Whitehead, 2007, p 34), which emerged during the 1980s and 1990s in the United States and the United Kingdom, is associated with neoliberalism and the ideology of a minimalist government. Moreover it is an important component of the operational functioning of the public sector through its endorsement of value for money, economy, efficiency and effectiveness, audits and targets. Within the NOMS structure it also means allowing the public, private and voluntary sectors to compete with each other for the business of providing offender services. Accordingly those organisations awarded the contracts must be able to achieve government targets, for example a reduction in re-offending, but to do so as efficiently as possible consistent with the new public management principle and business mentality of maximum outputs for minimum inputs. In the current recessionary economic climate (of 2009–11) it is extremely attractive for the government to encourage the third sector to get more involved because the Ministry of Justice must save £1 billion by 2011. Therefore who better to turn to than the third sector! Accordingly faith communities operating within, alongside and perhaps even replacing functions currently performed by prison staff, in addition to working alongside but also replacing functions being performed by probation in the community, could have a very important part to play in the provision of services in future years.[5]

Legitimating the prevailing system: religion as a conservative force

Second, could it be possible that faith communities of the third sector will become the new *drainers* and *neutralisers* of the criminal justice system? In other words, will they perform, in fact be channelled by central government in the direction to perform, a similar function to probation consistent with the analysis of Peter Young (1976) considered in Chapter 3? This point can be expanded by returning to the Marxist concept of economic base and corresponding superstructure, and it is the latter which includes philosophical and religious ideas dependent on the former. Additionally one may recall that Feuerbach propounded a view of religion as a projection of human beings, and Marx drew attention to its illusory nature and the notion of religion as ideology. Accordingly religion is constituted by a set of subjectively held values and as such does not have a factual or objective basis in reality (Giddens, 1989). Essentially religion is construed as an intellectual product shaped by the economic system that benefits the ruling class as it functions to create false consciousness and mystification for those on the downside of class relations. What is more, religion as ideology, which effectively means ruling class ideas, is presented as being in the best interests of all.

According to this analysis, capitalism is not capable of meeting the needs of all its citizens because it is an economic system that produces an unequal distribution of property, power, wealth, capital and opportunity. Within this system human beings cannot fulfil their true natures because of alienating and dehumanising tendencies located within socio-economic structures. Therefore an illusory world is established through which human happiness is sought. Consequently religion's *ideological function* is useful for those in power because it supports the prevailing system; it offers the balm of comfort and prospect of support; it also offers hope, if not in this world then in the next, and in so doing masks its true function in legitimating but also diverting attention away from social inequalities, divisions and conflicts. It is the image of the velvet glove of religion containing the clunking fist of management, containment, punishment and state control, in order to maintain prevailing socio-economic arrangements. Is this the role being mapped out for faith communities and do they want to perform it?

Trojan horse of challenge and resistance

Third, it may be suggested that the new public management agenda is too crudely fiscal, and the second perspective too dystopian and politically conspiratorial, because they do not do justice to the nature of criminal justice practices. Consequently one should see the encouragement being given to the third sector, particularly faith communities, for what it really is – a genuine desire to reduce the punitive excesses of the state by plotting a new course towards humanitarian values of care and compassion, tolerance and support, including empathic understanding. In other words, if rebalancing criminal justice has taken the system too far in the direction of robust exclusionary punishments, and towards a greater concern for victims and witnesses, then it could be the case that the third sector will begin to redress this imbalance. This can be described as the Trojan horse of challenge and resistance located at the very heart of NOMS and offers the third sector an opportunity to make a material difference by reanimating the personalist agenda conducive to re-civilising and re-humanising the justice system. In fact one may have to look in this new direction rather than towards the modernised and culturally transformed probation organisation for this objective to be realised. Or could it be possible for what remains of the probation ideal to form alliances with the third sector that could indeed benefit both?

Conclusion

This book has been written to explore and explain, and in so doing to facilitate, a better understanding of what probation have become since 1997. It also allows the research findings to raise challenges and provoke doubts concerning wholesale modernisation and cultural change that have implications for criminal and social justice. A central thesis is that the Probation Service has become confusingly complex, primarily because modernisation leading to cultural transformations has turned it into an organisation that operates with a new language, a markedly different notation. In fact there are occasions when it is a vehicle for the politics of expressive justice, a symbolic spectacle, communicating a robust message into the social body on behalf of the state, rather than a measured analysis of all those factors involved in offending repertoires (Durkheim); but the organisation has also been coerced into a bureaucratic iron cage which has diluted its ability to engage with people who offend within a context of *verstehen* (Weber). It can also function as a politicised instrument for the expression of state power, of punitive regulation, over some of the most vulnerable and insecure people within conditions of late-modern capitalism (Marxist). Consequently it is less able to sustain a professional logic orientated towards anti-punishment and anti-custody, and by so doing humanise criminal justice practices according to a distinctive set of values. In the last analysis modernisation has created a new order of things, a new *social fact*, which is more useful for the exercise of state power than the pursuit of penological effectiveness (Foucault). Accordingly, probation has become embedded in a punitive episteme at a specific historical juncture on the back of developments since the 1970s, but especially so since the election of New Labour. This is the current state of things that a combined social theory helps to explicate, thus providing additional support for the position that 'criminal justice functions go well beyond the prevention and control of crime' (Castellano and Gould, 2007, p 78).

Nevertheless, combining the search for a deeper understanding of these issues, facilitated by theoretical application and empirical research, should not cease at this point. If it did then all too inadequately it becomes another academic exercise. Instead it is hoped that the work can clear away some of the rubble which has accumulated in order to encourage critique, challenge and change by allowing theories and research to make a difference. The nature of change I have in mind begins by restoring a semblance of balance to the criminal justice system, which means re-engaging with what were formerly referred to as probation values and ideals encapsulated within a personalist ethic. When Frederick Copleston reviewed the philosophies of Hegel and Marx (1963 [2003], vol 7, p 30) he clarified that the former wanted passively to understand the past. By contrast Marx wanted to understand the past in order to create change that would positively affect the future. Ideals and values rooted in personalism and formerly associated with probation are one thing, but they have to be put into effect to make a difference to the operational dynamics of the criminal justice system. Accordingly such ideals and values can be utilised to humanise the system by questioning the prevailing punitive epidemic and expansion of the prison estate, in addition to questioning an approach which looks no further than pinning blame on the individual offender instead of factoring in the adverse effects of political, social and economic structures.

During the early 1980s and long before the modernising excesses explored in this book occurred, Walker and Beaumont (1981) argued that an organisation was required to reduce the punitive excesses of the criminal justice system in

England and Wales, to minimise the use of custody and breach proceedings, and they state clearly that laws can be unjust and prison destructive. Moreover an organisation was required that could support the troubled and troublesome by delivering a social work service to individuals and families (Harris, 1977, 1980; Bryant et al, 1978; Bottoms and McWilliams, 1979; Raynor, 1985), in addition to excavating the deleterious effects of material inequalities for both rich and poor alike (Wilkinson and Pickett, 2009). Prior to all those events associated with modernising monstrosities and cultural catastrophes, probation had more potential than other organisations to fulfil this role, while not overlooking the qualifications considered in Chapters 3 and 4. However, the politics of modernisation has damaged the ability of probation to undertake these functions and provide the requisite leadership. But is the damage irreversible or a temporary aberration? If the former, has the point been reached to look beyond probation to the third sector? Has probation been reduced to an arm of the prison system, within an expansionary penal state, reaching into local communities under the guise of end-to-end management, in effect recycling the same offenders? Or has it the capacity, even after the events of 1997–2010, to renew itself by re-engaging with those pre-modern features that find some support among respondents? Answering these questions will determine the next phase of *criminal* and *social justice* in England and Wales. These questions are so pressing they should not be left only to the monologues of the political elite to shape a response. In fact, it is everyone's business.

Notes

[1] Some years ago I located what were referred to as different models of probation on a care–control continuum (Whitehead, 1990). First, a number of *academic models*, from the contributions of Robert Harris (1977, 1980) at the care end of the continuum, to Griffiths (1982a, 1982b) at the control-punitive end. Additionally I introduced a *bureaucratic model* associated with SNOP (Home Office, 1984), in addition to a NAPO *professional model*, and finally a *local area service model*.

[2] The introduction of an objectives and then target culture into the public sector during the 1980s/90s, which continued after 1997, has elicited numerous comments in the national press which can be illustrated as follows. First, we were told that a consultant gynaecologist quit the NHS 'over the tyranny of targets and tick-boxes' (*Daily Mail*, 8 June 2006). Second, Simon Jenkins, in *The Sunday Times* on 24 September 2006, headlined his article with the words 'Set a silly target and you'll get a really crazy public service'. Jenkins explored targets in education and the NHS, arguing that a public service and professional ethos had been replaced with a target-driven culture imposed by central government with corresponding adverse effects. Next Peter Riddell, in an article on treasury targets in *The Times* on 19 July 2007, exclaimed that 'No one will miss targets when they're gone'. The next two examples begin to raise deep concerns about the effects of targets when we read, in *The Times* again, 'Children taken from parents and adopted to meet ministry targets' (24 August 2007). Also in *The Guardian* on 3 April 2008, 'Police criminalising young to hit

targets, says charity'. And, *The Guardian* said, on 19 March 2009 (G2 section), 'A hospital is able to tick all the boxes, yet still utterly fail patients'. Finally the reader is invited to consider numerous illustrations of New Labour's controlling and centralising targets in *The Sunday Times*, 3 January 2010, p 15. This is an article by Jenni Russell on 'Labour's big fixation in strangling everyone'. For a critique of the target culture in probation see Whitehead (2007, Ch 2, pp 39–46).

[3] Castellano and Gould (2007) refer to three types of justice: procedural, distributive and restorative. Where the first two are concerned it can be argued that procedural justice refers to the processes and procedures adopted by organisations by which disputes are resolved. Therefore within a criminal justice context it may be suggested that the dilution of discretion and autonomy, particularly within the Probation Service, in addition to putting the procedural emphasis on the fast delivery rather than standard delivery report, may not enhance the cause of criminal and social justice. Furthermore distributive justice alludes to the economic system and the equitable distribution of material resources throughout society (which relates to the arguments advanced in Wilkinson and Pickett, 2009, already considered and referenced in this book).

[4] In 1994 a research-based text by Beynon et al was published: *A place called Teesside*. This is an interesting book because it describes the development of the iron and steel industry, including engineering and shipbuilding, in the 19th century; then the chemical industry makes its appearance in the early 20th century. In other words, Middlesbrough was a town that owed its origin to the Industrial Revolution and was shaped by the demands of capitalist production. However, there was a downturn in the town's fortunes during the depression of the 1930s, then again in the 1980s. Therefore the point is cogently made that it is not possible to explain social relations and complex human behaviours (including offending) without taking account of the changing fortunes of capitalism and attendant material conditions on individuals, families and communities within a town. For example during the 1980s local unemployment rates exceeded 20%, which were among the highest in the UK. This, in turn, injected insecurity and uncertainty that contributed to social deprivation. What capitalism gives it also takes away. Additionally for a penetrating scholarly analysis of many of these features within the context of neoliberalism, see Wacquant (2008, and particularly 2009).

[5] During 2008 and 2009 the Ministry of Justice made it clear in numerous documents that budgets would be cut during the next three years. Where the Probation Service was concerned, a briefing paper compiled by Harry Fletcher (NAPO, 2009) makes the following observations in response to Ministry of Justice projections. The probation budget for 2008/09 was £914 million; for 2009/10 it should be £894 million; subsequently there will be a further reduction of £50 million in 2010/11 and a further £50 million reduction in 2011/12. Therefore by 2012 the probation budget will be £794 million, which constitutes a total reduction of £120 million. Significantly the briefing paper provides a breakdown of the implications within 30 area services and it summarises that, 'The consequence of the cuts are dire and coupled with the recession are likely to have

a major impact on crime. The average cumulative cut is about 20%, and therefore most areas will have to cut frontline jobs' (p 6). Harry Fletcher, on behalf of NAPO, concluded that the Probation Service faced 'meltdown if the current cuts go ahead and crime soars in the recession' (p 11). Therefore these could be the conditions in which the third sector will flourish in the criminal justice system.

References

Albrow, M. (1970) *Bureaucracy*, London: Macmillan.

Auld, Lord Justice (2001) *Review of the criminal courts of England and Wales*, London: The Stationery Office.

Bailey, R. (1980) 'Social workers: pawns, police or agitators?', in M. Brake and R. Bailey (eds) *Radical social work and practice*, London: Edward Arnold.

Bailey, R. and Brake, M. (eds) (1975) *Radical social work*, London: Edward Arnold.

Barber, M. (2007) *Instruction to deliver: Tony Blair, public services and the challenge of achieving targets*, London: Politico's.

Bean, P. (1976) *Rehabilitation and deviance*, London: Routledge and Kegan Paul.

Bean, P. (1981) *Punishment*, Oxford: Martin Robertson.

Beirne, P. (1993) *Inventing criminology: Essays on the rise of homo criminalis*, Albany, NY: State University of New York Press.

Belsey, C. (2002) *Poststructuralism: A very short introduction*, Oxford: Oxford University Press.

Bendix, R. (1960) *Max Weber: An intellectual portrait*, London: Heinemann.

Beynon, H., Hudson, R. and Sadler, D. (1994) *A place called Teesside: A locality in a global economy*, Edinburgh: Edinburgh University Press.

Biestek, F.P. (1961) *The casework relationship*, London: George Allen and Unwin Ltd.

Bochel, D. (1976) *Probation and after-care: Its development in England and Wales*, Edinburgh: Scottish Academic Press.

Bonger, W. (1916, re-issued 1969) *Criminality and economic conditions*, Bloomington, IN: Indiana University Press.

Bottoms, A.E. (1983) 'Neglected features of contemporary penal systems', in D. Garland and P. Young (eds) *The power to punish: Contemporary penality and social analysis*, London: Heinemann Educational Books.

Bottoms, A.E. and McWilliams, W. (1979) 'A non-treatment paradigm for probation practice', *British Journal of Social Work*, vol 9, no 2, pp 159–202.

Bottoms, A.E. and McWilliams, W. (1986) 'Social enquiry reports twenty-five years after the Streatfield Report', in P. Bean and D. Whynes (eds) *Barbara Wootton social science and public policy: Essays in her honour*, London and New York: Tavistock Publications, pp 245–76.

Bottoms, A.E. and Stelman, A. (1988) *Social inquiry reports: A framework for practice development*, Community Care Practice Handbooks, Aldershot: Wildwood House.

Bourgois, P. (2003) *In search of respect: Selling crack in El Barrio* (2nd edn), Cambridge and New York: Cambridge University Press.

Box, S. (1987) *Recession, crime and punishment*, Basingstoke: Macmillan Education Ltd.

Brake, M. and Hale, C. (1992) *Public order and private lives: The politics of law and order*, New York, NY and London: Routledge.

Brody, S.R. (1976) *The effectiveness of sentencing*, London: HMSO.

Brown, S. (1991) *Magistrates at work: Sentencing and social structure*, Buckingham: Open University Press.

Brown, S. (2005) *Understanding youth and crime: Listening to youth?* (2nd edn), Buckingham: Open University Press.

Bryant, G.A. (1985) *Positivism in social theory and research*, Basingstoke: Macmillan.

Bryant, M., Coker, J., Estlea, B., Himmel, S. and Knapp, T. (1978) 'Sentenced to social work?', *Probation Journal*, vol 25, no 4, pp 110–14.

Buchdahl, G. (1969) *Metaphysics and the philosophy of science: The classical origins: Descartes to Kant*, Oxford: Basil Blackwell.

Burke, R.H. (2008) *Young people, crime and justice*, Cullompton: Willan.

Burnett, R., Baker, K. and Roberts, C. (2007) 'Assessment, supervision and intervention: fundamental practice in probation', in L. Gelsthorpe and R. Morgan (eds) *Handbook of probation*, Cullompton: Willan, pp 210–47.

Cabinet Office (1999) *Modernising government*, Presented to Parliament by the Prime Minister and the Minister for the Cabinet Office, London: The Stationery Office.

Cabinet Office (2008) *Engaging communities in fighting crime (Casey Report)*, London: Home Office and Ministry of Justice.

Cabinet Office and HM Treasury (2007) *The future role of the third sector in social and economic regeneration: Final report*, London: Cabinet Office.

Campbell, A. (2007) *The Blair years: Extracts from the Alistair Campbell diaries*, London: Hutchinson.

Canguilhem, G. (1994) 'The death of man, or exhaustion of the cogito?', translated by C. Porter, in G. Gutting (ed) *The Cambridge companion to Foucault*, Cambridge: Cambridge University Press.

Carter, P. (2003) *Managing offenders, reducing crime: A new approach*, London: Home Office and Strategy Unit.

Carter, P. (2007) *Securing the future: Proposals for the efficient and sustainable use of custody in England and Wales*, London: Ministry of Justice.

Casey, L. (2008) *Engaging communities in fighting crime: A review*, London: Cabinet Office.

Castellano, T.C. and Gould, J.B. (2007) 'Neglect of justice in criminal justice theory: causes, consequences, and alternatives', in D.E. Duffee and E.R. Maguire (eds) *Criminal justice theory: Explaining the nature and behaviour of criminal justice*, New York and London: Routledge, pp 71–88.

Cavadino, M. and Dignan, J. (2002) *The penal system: An introduction* (3rd edn), London, Thousand Oaks, CA and New Delhi: Sage Publications.

Cavadino, M. and Dignan, J. (2006) *Penal systems: A comparative approach*, London, Thousand Oaks, CA and New Delhi: Sage Publications.

Chadwick, O. (1990) *The secularisation of the European mind in the 19th century* (Canto edn), Cambridge and New York, NY: Cambridge University Press.

Charman, S. and Savage, S. (1999) 'The new politics of law and order: Labour, crime and justice', in M. Powell (ed) *New Labour, new welfare state? The 'third way' in British social policy*, Bristol: The Policy Press, pp 191–212.

Chui, W.H. and Nellis, M. (eds) (2003) *Moving probation forward: Evidence, arguments and practice*, London and New York, NY: Pearson-Longman.

Clarke, J., Gewirtz, S. and McLaughlin, E. (2000) *New managerialism, new welfare?*, London, Thousand Oaks, CA and New Delhi: Sage Publications.

Clarke, P. (2004) *Hope and glory: Britain 1900–2000* (2nd edn), London and New York, NY: Penguin Books.

Clay, W.L. (1969) *Prison chaplain*, Montclair, NJ: Patterson Smith.

Cohen, S. (1985) *Visions of social control*, Cambridge: Polity Press.

Cook, D. (2006) *Criminal and social justice*, London, Thousand Oaks, CA and New Delhi: Sage Publications.

Copleston, F. (1953 [2003 paperback edn]) *A history of philosophy, Volume 3, Late mediaeval and renaissance philosophy*, London and New York, NY: Continuum.

Copleston, F. (1959 [2003 paperback edn]) *A history of philosophy, Volume 5, British philosophy: Hobbes to Hume*, London and New York, NY: Continuum.

Copleston, F. (1960 [2003 paperback edn]) *A history of philosophy, Volume 6, The Enlightenment: Voltaire to Kant*, London and New York, NY: Continuum.

Copleston, F. (1963 [2003 paperback edn]) *A history of philosophy, Volume 7, 18th and 19th century German philosophy*, London and New York, NY: Continuum.

Copleston, F. (1966 [2003 paperback edn]) *A history of philosophy, Volume 8, Utilitarianism to early analytic philosophy*, London and New York, NY: Continuum.

Coser, L.A. (1977) *Masters of sociological thought: Ideas in historical and social context* (2nd edn), New York, NY and London: Harcourt Brace Jovanovich, Publishers.

Cousins, M. and Hussain, A. (1984) *Michel Foucault*, London: Macmillan.

Cowling, M. (2008) *Marxism and criminological theory: A critique and tool kit*, Basingstoke: Palgrave.

Crawshaw, P., Bunton, R. and Gillen, K. (2002) 'Modernisation and Health Action Zones: the search for coherence', in L. Bauld and K. Judge (eds) *Learning from Health Action Zones*, Chichester: Aeneas, pp 221–30.

Descartes, R. (1988) *Selected philosophical writings* (translated by J. Cottingham, R. Stoothoff and D. Murdoch), Cambridge and New York, NY: Cambridge University Press.

Dohan, D. (2003) *The price of poverty: Money, work, and culture in the Mexican Barrio*, Berkeley, LA and London: University of California Press.

Downes, D. and Morgan, R. (1997) 'Dumping the "hostages to fortune"? The politics of law and order in post-war Britain', in M. Maguire, R. Morgan and R. Reiner (eds) *The Oxford handbook of criminology* (2nd edn), Oxford and New York, NY: Oxford University Press, pp 87–134.

Downes, D. and Rock, P. (1988) *Understanding deviance: A guide to the sociology of crime and rule breaking* (2nd edn), Oxford: Clarendon Press.

Duff, A. and Garland, D. (eds) (1994) *A reader on punishment*, Oxford and New York, NY: Oxford University Press.

Duffee, D.E. and Maguire, E.R. (eds) (2007) *Criminal justice theory: Explaining the nature and behaviour of criminal justice*, New York, NY and London: Routledge.

Durkheim, E. ([1893] 1984) *The division of labour in society* (Introduction by Lewis Coser; translated by W.D. Halls), Basingstoke: Macmillan.

Durkheim, E. ([1895] 1938) *The rules of sociological method*, New York, NY: The Free Press.

Durkheim, E. ([1897] 1952) *Suicide: A study in sociology*, London and Henley: Routledge and Kegan Paul.

Durkheim, E. (1899) 'The two laws of penal evolution', *L'Année Sociologique*, vol IV, pp 65–99 (1899–1900), in M. Traugott (ed and trans) (1978) *Emile Durkheim: On institutional analysis*, Chicago, IL and London: University of Chicagor Press.

Durkheim, E. ([1912] 1915) *The elementary forms of the religious life*, London: Allen and Unwin.

Durkheim, E. (2002) *Moral education* (translated and with a Preface by E.K. Wilson and H. Schnurer), Mineola, NY: Dover Publications.

Easton, S. and Piper, C. (2005) *Sentencing and punishment: The quest for justice*, Oxford and New York, NY: Oxford University Press.

Eribon, D. (1989) *Michel Foucault*, London and Boston, MA: Faber and Faber.

Fairclough, N. (2000) *New Labour, new language?*, London and New York, NY: Routledge.

Fielding, N. (1984) *Probation practice: Client support under social control*, Aldershot: Gower.

Foucault, M. (1970) *The order of things: An archaeology of the human sciences*, London: Tavistock Publications.

Foucault, M. (1977) *Discipline and punish: The birth of the prison*, London and New York, NY: Penguin.

Freiberg, A. and Gelb, K. (2008) *Penal populism, sentencing councils and sentencing policy*, Cullompton: Willan.

Fullwood, C. (1994) 'Policy and management implications', in J. Stewart, D. Smith and G. Stewart with C. Fullwood, *Understanding offending behaviour*, Harlow: Longman, pp 166–74.

Garland, D. (1985) *Punishment and welfare: A history of penal strategies*, Aldershot: Gower.

Garland, D. (1990) *Punishment and modern society: A study in social theory*, Oxford and New York, NY: Oxford University Press.

Garland, D. (2001) *The culture of control: Crime and social order in contemporary society*, Oxford and New York, NY: Oxford University Press.

Garland, D. and Sparks, R. (2000) 'Criminology, social theory, and the challenge of our times', in D. Garland and R. Sparks (eds) *Criminology and social theory*, Oxford and New York, NY: Oxford University Press, pp 1–22.

Garland, D. and Young, P. (eds) (1983) *The power to punish: Contemporary penality and social analysis*, London: Heinemann Educational Books.

Gay, P. (1967) *The Enlightenment: An interpretation. The rise of modern paganism*, New York, NY: Alfred A. Knopf.

Gay, P. (1969) *The Enlightenment: An interpretation. The science of freedom*, New York, NY and London: W.W. Norton and Company.

Gelsthorpe, L. and Morgan, R. (eds) (2007) *Handbook of probation*, Cullompton: Willan.

Gelsthorpe, L. and Raynor, P. (1995) 'Quality and effectiveness in probation officer reports to sentencers', *British Journal of Criminology*, vol 35, pp 188–200.

George, V. and Wilding, P. (1991 edn) *Ideology and social welfare*, London and New York, NY: Routledge.

Gerth, H.H. and Mills, C.W. (eds) (1948) *From Max Weber*, London: Routledge and Kegan Paul.

Giddens, A. (1971) *Capitalism and modern social theory: An analysis of the writings of Marx, Durkheim and Max Weber*, London and New York, NY: Cambridge University Press.

Giddens, A. (1972) *Emile Durkheim: Selected writings*, London and New York, NY: Cambridge University Press.

Giddens, A. (1978) 'Positivism and its critics', in T. Bottomore and R. Nisbet (eds) *A history of sociological analysis*, London: Heinemann.

Giddens, A. (1982) *Profiles and critiques in social theory*, Basingstoke: Macmillan.

Giddens, A. (1989) *Sociology*, Cambridge: Polity Press.

Gilbert, B.B. (1966) *The evolution of national insurance in Great Britain: The origins of the welfare state*, London: Michael Joseph.

Glover, E.R. (1956 revised) *Probation and re-education* (2nd edn), London: Routledge and Kegan Paul Ltd.

Goodman, A. (2003) 'Probation into the millennium: the punishing service?', in R. Matthews and J. Young (eds) *The new politics of crime and punishment*, Cullompton: Willan, pp 199–222.

Grayling, A.C. (2005) *Descartes: The life of Rene Descartes and its place in his times*, New York, NY: Free Press.

Griffiths, W.A. (1982a) 'A new probation service', *Probation Journal*, vol 29, no 3, pp 98–9.

Griffiths, W.A. (1982b) 'Supervision in the community', *Justice of the Peace*, 21 August.

Gutting, G. (ed) (1994) *The Cambridge guide to Foucault*, Cambridge and New York, NY: Cambridge University Press.

Gutting, G. (2005) *Foucault: A very short introduction*, Oxford and New York, NY: Oxford University Press.

Haines, K. and Morgan, R. (2007) 'Services before trial and sentence: achievement, decline and potential', in L. Gelsthorpe and R. Morgan (eds) *Handbook of probation*, Cullompton: Willan, pp 182–209.

Hall, A.R. (1954) *The scientific revolution 1500–1800: The formation of the modern scientific attitude*, London and New York, NY: Longman.

Hall, S., Critcher, C., Jefferson, T., Clarke, J. and Roberts, B. (1978) *Policing the crisis: Mugging, the state and law and order*, Basingstoke: Macmillan.

Harper, G. and Chitty, C. (eds) (2005) *The impact of corrections on re-offending: A review of 'what works'* (3rd edn), Home Office Research Study 291, London: Home Office.

Harris, R. (1977) 'The probation officer as social worker', *British Journal of Social Work*, vol 7, no 4, pp 433–42.

Harris, R. (1980) 'A changing service: the case for separating "care" and "control" in probation practice', *British Journal of Social Work*, vol 10, no 2, pp 163–84.

Harvey, D. (2005) *A brief history of neoliberalism*, Oxford and New York, NY: Oxford University Press.

Haxby, D. (1978) *Probation: A changing service*, London: Constable.

Hay, D. (1975) 'Property, authority and the criminal law', in P. Linebaugh, J.G. Rule, E.P. Thompson and C. Winslow (eds), *Albion's fatal tree: Crime and society in eighteenth century England*, Harmondsworth: Penguin.

Hinde, R.S.E. (1951) *The British penal system 1773–1950*, London: Gerald Duckworth and Co Ltd.

Hobsbawm, E. (1994) *Age of extremes: The short twentieth century 1914–1991*, London: Michael Joseph.

Home Office (1895) *Report of the Departmental Committee on Prisons* (Gladstone Committee), Cmnd 7702, London: HMSO.

Home Office (1909) *Report of the Departmental Committee on the Probation of Offenders Act 1907*, Cmnd 5001, London: HMSO.

Home Office (1922) *Report of the Departmental Committee on the Training, Appointment and Payment of Probation Officers*, Cmnd 1601, London: HMSO.

Home Office (1936) *Report of the Departmental Committee on the Social Services in Courts of Summary Jurisdiction*, Cmnd 5122, London: HMSO.

Home Office (1959) *Penal practice in a changing society: Aspects of future development (England and Wales)*, Cmnd 645, London: HMSO.

Home Office (1961) *Report of the Inter-Departmental Committee on the Business of the Criminal Courts (Streatfield Report)*, Cmnd 1289, London: HMSO.

Home Office (1962) *Report of the Departmental Committee on the Probation Service (Morison Committee)*, Cmnd 1650, London: HMSO.

Home Office (1984) *Probation service in England and Wales. Statement of national objectives and priorities*, London: HMSO.

Home Office (1998) *Prisons–probation: Joining forces to protect the public*, London: The Stationery Office.

Home Office (2001a) *Criminal justice: The way ahead*, Cm 5074, London: The Stationery Office.

Home Office (2001b) *Making punishments work: The report of a review of the sentencing framework for England and Wales (Halliday Review)*, London: The Stationery Office.

Home Office (2004a) *Confident communities in a secure Britain: The Home Office strategic plan 2004–2008*, Cm 6287, London: The Stationery Office.

Home Office (2004b) *Cutting crime, delivering justice: A strategic plan for criminal justice 2004–2008*, Cm 6288, London: The Stationery Office.

Home Office (2004c) *Working together: Cooperation between government and faith communities*, London: Home Office.

Home Office (2005) *Rebuilding lives: Supporting victims of crime*, Cm 6705, London: The Stationery Office.

Home Office (2006a) *A five-year strategy for protecting the public and reducing re-offending*, Cm 6717, London: The Stationery Office.

Home Office (2006b) *Re-balancing the criminal justice system in favour of the law-abiding majority: Cutting crime, reducing re-offending and protecting the public*, London: The Stationery Office.

Home Office (2006c) *Delivering simple, speedy, summary justice*, London: Home Office.

Home Office (2006d) *Improving prison and probation services: Public value partnerships*, London: The Stationery Office.

Hough, M., Allen, R. and Padel, U. (2006) *Reshaping probation and prisons: The new offender management framework*, Bristol: The Policy Press.

House of Commons (2007) 'Parliamentary debates', Official Report, *Hansard*, Wednesday 28 February, vol 457, no 51.

Howard, J. (1777 [republished 1973]) *The state of our prisons*, Montclair, NJ: Warrington.

Hudson, B.A. (1987) *Justice through punishment: A critique of the 'justice' model of corrections*, Basingstoke: Macmillan.

Hudson, B.A. (2003) *Understanding justice: An introduction to ideas, perspectives and controversies in modern penal theory* (2nd edn), Buckingham: Open University Press.

Hughes, R. (1987) *The fatal shore: A history of the transportation of convicts to Australia 1787–1868*, London: Pan Books.

Hugman, B. (1977) *Act natural*, London: Bedford Square Press.

Hutton, N (2008) 'The Sentencing Commission for Scotland'/'Institutional mechanisms for incorporating the public', in A. Freiberg and K. Gelb (eds) *Penal populism, sentencing councils and sentencing policy*, Cullompton: Willan, pp 138–47 and 205–23.

Ignatieff, M. (1978) *A just measure of pain: The penitentiary in the Industrial Revolution, 1750–1850*, Basingstoke: Macmillan.

Jarvis, F.V. (1972) *Advise, assist and befriend: A history of the probation and after-care service*, London: National Association of Probation Officers.

Jarvis, F.V. (1974) *Probation officers' manual*, London: Butterworths.

Jones, T. and Newburn, T. (2004) 'The convergence of US and UK crime control policy: exploring substance and process', in T. Newburn and R. Sparks (eds) *Criminal justice and political cultures: National and international dimensions of crime control*, Cullompton: Willan, pp 123–51.

Joyce, J. (1992 edn) *Ulysses*, London and New York, NY: Penguin.

Katz, M.B. (1989) *The undeserving poor: From the war on poverty to the war on welfare*, New York, NY: Pantheon Books.

Kehlmann, D. (2007) *Measuring the world*, London: Quercus.

Kennedy, H. (2005) *Just law: The changing face of justice – and why it matters to us all*, London: Vintage.

Kershaw, I. (2007) *Fateful choices: Ten decisions that changed the world 1940–1941*, New York, NY: Penguin.

King, J.F.S (1964) *The probation service* (2nd edn), London: Butterworths.

King, R.D. and Wincup, E. (2007) *Doing research on crime and justice* (2nd edn), Oxford and New York, NY: Oxford University Press.

Le Mesurier, L. (1935) *A handbook of probation and social work of the courts*, London: National Association of Probation Officers.

Leeson, C. (1914) *The probation system*, London: P. and S. King and Son.

Leys, C. (2003) *Market-driven politics: Neoliberal democracy and the public interest*, London and New York, NY: Verso.

Lukes, S. (1973) *Emile Durkheim: His life and work: A historical and critical study*, Harmondsworth: Penguin.

MacRae, D.G. (1987) *Weber*, London: Fontana Press.

McIvor, G. and McNeill, F. (2007) 'Probation in Scotland: past, present and future', in L. Gelsthorpe and R. Morgan (eds) *Handbook of probation*, Cullompton: Willan, pp 131–54.

McLellan, D. (1976 edn) *Karl Marx: His life and thought*, St Albans: Paladin.

McLellan, D. (1986) *Marx* (2nd edn), Hammersmith: Fontana Press.

McNay, L. (1994) *Foucault: A critical introduction*, Cambridge and Malden, MA: Polity Press.

McWilliams, W. (1983) 'The mission to the English police courts 1876–1936', *Howard Journal of Criminal Justice*, vol 22, pp 129–47.

McWilliams, W. (1985) 'The mission transformed: professionalisation of probation between the wars', *Howard Journal of Criminal Justice*, vol 24, pp 257–74.

McWilliams, W. (1986) 'The English probation system and the diagnostic ideal', *Howard Journal of Criminal Justice*, vol 25, pp 241–60.

McWilliams, W. (1987) 'Probation, pragmatism and policy', *Howard Journal of Criminal Justice*, vol 26, pp 97-121.

McWilliams, W. (1992) 'The rise and development of management thought in the English probation system', in R. Statham and P. Whitehead (eds) *Managing the Probation Service: Issues for the 1990s*, Harlow: Longman, pp 3–29.

Mack, M.P. (1962) *Jeremy Bentham: An odyssey of ideas 1748–1792*, Melbourne, London and Toronto: Heinemann.

Magee, B. (2001) *The story of philosophy*, London: Dorling Kindersley.

Maguire, M. (2004) 'The Crime Reduction Programme in England and Wales: reflections on the vision and the reality', *Criminology and Criminal Justice*, vol 4, no 3, pp 213–37.

Mair, G., Burke, L. and Taylor, S. (2006) 'The worst tax form you've ever seen? Probation officers' views about OASys', *Probation Journal*, vol 53, no 1, pp 7–24.

Mair, G., Cross, N. and Taylor, S. (2007) *The use and impact of the Community Order and the Suspended Sentence Order*, London: Centre for Crime and Justice Studies, King's College London.

Marr, A. (2008) *A history of modern Britain*, Basingstoke: Macmillan.

Marx, K. (1867 [1976]) *Capital: A critique of political economy, Volume 1*, Harmondsworth: Penguin.

Marx, K. (1932 [1964]) *The economic and philosophic manuscripts of 1844*, New York, NY: International Publishers.

Marx, K. and Engels, F. (1845 [1947]) *The German ideology, Part 1*, New York, NY: International Publishers.

Marx, K. and Engels, F. (1848 [1967]) *The communist manifesto* (Introduction by A.J.P. Taylor), Harmondsworth: Penguin.

Mathiesen, T. (2006) *Prison on trial* (3rd edn), Winchester: Waterside Press.

Matthews, R. (1999) *Doing time*, Basingstoke: Macmillan.

Mazlish, B. (1968) *The riddle of history: The great speculators from Vico to Freud*, New York, NY: Minerva Press.

Merquior, J.G. (1985) *Foucault*, Hammersmith: Fontana.

Merquior, J.G. (1986) *From Prague to Paris: A critique of structuralist and post-structuralist thought*, London: Verso.

Merton, R. (1968) *Social theory and social structure*, New York, NY: Free Press.

Millard, D. (1979) 'Broader approaches to probation practice', in J.F.S. King (ed) *Pressures and change in the Probation Service*, Cropwood Conference Series No 11, Cambridge: Institute of Criminology, University of Cambridge.

Ministry of Justice (2008a) *Prison policy update: Briefing paper*, London: Ministry of Justice.

Ministry of Justice (2008b) *Punishment and reform: Our approach to managing offenders*, London: Ministry of Justice.

Ministry of Justice (2008c) *Working with the third sector to reduce re-offending, Ministry of Justice and NOMS, Securing effective partnerships*, London: Ministry of Justice.

Ministry of Justice (2008d) *Probation statistics quarterly brief, January to March 2008*, London: Ministry of Justice.

Ministry of Justice (2008e) *Value for money, delivery agreement*, London: Ministry of Justice.

Ministry of Justice (2009) *Probation statistics quarterly brief, January to March 2009*, London: Ministry of Justice.

Ministry of Justice and NOMS (National Offender Management Service) (2009) *Strategic business plans 2009–10 to 2010–11*, London, Ministry of Justice.

Morgan, R. (1997) 'Imprisonment: current concerns and a brief history since 1945', in M. Maguire, R. Morgan and R. Reiner, *The Oxford handbook of criminology* (2nd edn), Oxford and New York, NY: Oxford University Press, pp 1137–94.

Morrison, K. (1995) *Marx, Durkheim, Weber: Formations of modern social thought*, London, Thousand Oaks, CA and New Delhi: Sage Publications.

Mounier, E. (1952) *Personalism*, London: Routledge and Kegan Paul.

Muncie, J. (2004) *Youth and crime* (2nd edn), London, Thousand Oaks, CA and New Delhi: Sage Publications.

NAPO (National Association of Probation Officers) (2007) *Changing lives: An oral history of probation*, London: NAPO.

NAPO (2009) *Probation under stress: A briefing paper*, BRF06-09 (compiled by Harry Fletcher), London: NAPO.

National Probation Service (2009) *Determining pre-sentence report type*, Probation Circular 06/2009, London: National Probation Service.

Nellis, M. (1999) 'Towards "the field of corrections": modernising the Probation Service in the late 1990s', *Social Policy and Administration*, vol 33, no 3, pp 302–23.

Nellis, M. (2007) 'Humanising justice: the English Probation Service up to 1972', in L. Gelsthorpe and R. Morgan (eds) *Handbook of probation*, Cullompton: Willan, pp 25–58.

Newburn, T. (2007) *Criminology*, Cullompton: Willan.

Noaks, L. and Wincup, E. (2004) *Criminological research: Understanding qualitative methods*, London, Thousand Oaks, CA and New Delhi: Sage Publications.

NOMS (National Offender Management Service) (2005) *The reducing re-offending faith and voluntary and community sector alliance*, London: NOMS.

NOMS (2006) *The NOMS offender management model*, London: NOMS.

NOMS (2007a) *Believing We Can: Promoting the contribution faith-based organisations can make to reducing adult and youth offending*, London: NOMS.

NOMS (2007b) *Probation circular 12/2007: Pre-sentence reports*, London: NOMS.

Oldfield, M. (2008) *Probation resources, staffing and workloads 2001–2008*, London: Centre for Crime and Justice Studies, King's College London.

O'Neil, O. (2002) *A question of trust*, Cambridge and New York, NY: Cambridge University Press.

Orwell, G. (1933) *Down and out in Paris and London*, London: Penguin.

Outhwaite, W. (1975) *Understanding social life: The method called verstehen*, London: George Allen and Unwin.

Parenti, C. (1999) *Lockdown America: Police and prisons in the age of crisis*, London and New York, NY: Verso.

Pashukanis, E.B. (1978) *Law and Marxism: A general theory*, London: Ink Links.

Piaget, J. (1971) *Structuralism*, London: Routledge and Kegan Paul.

Platt, A. (1977) *The child savers: The invention of delinquency* (2nd edn), Chicago, IL and London: University of Chicago Press.

PMSU (Prime Minister's Strategy Unit) (2006) *Policy review: Crime, justice and cohesion*, London: Cabinet Office.

Porter, R. (2000) *Enlightenment: Britain and the creation of the modern world*, London and New York, NY: Penguin.

Pratt, J. (2007) *Penal populism*, Key Ideas in Criminology Series, London and New York, NY: Routledge.

Pratt, J., Brown, D., Brown, M., Hallsworth, S. and Morrison, W. (eds) (2005) *The new punitiveness: Trends, theories and perspectives*, Cullompton: Willan.

Radzinowicz, L. (1958) *Preface to the Results of probation. Report of the Cambridge Department of Criminal Science*, Basingstoke: Macmillan.

Radzinowicz, L. (1999) *Adventures in criminology*, London and New York, NY: Routledge.

Radzinowicz, L. and Hood, R. (1990) *The emergence of penal policy in Victorian and Edwardian England*, Clarendon Paperbacks, Oxford and New York, NY: Oxford University Press.

Raynor, P. (1985) *Social work, justice and control*, Oxford: Basil Blackwell.

Raynor, P. (2002) 'Community penalties: probation, punishment, and "what works"', in M. Maguire, R. Morgan and R. Reiner (eds) *The Oxford handbook of criminology* (3rd edn), Oxford and New York, NY: Oxford University Press, pp 1168–205.

Raynor, P. and Vanstone, M. (2002) *Understanding community penalties: Probation, policy and social change*, Buckingham: Open University Press.

Raynor, P. and Vanstone, M. (2007) 'Towards a correctional service', in L. Gelsthorpe and R. Morgan (eds) *Handbook of probation*, Cullompton: Willan, pp 59–89.

Reid, J. (2006) 'Check against delivery', Speech by the Home Secretary on offender management, HMP Wormwood Scrubs, Tuesday 7 November.

Reiman, J. (1998) *The rich get richer and the poor get prison: Ideology, class, and criminal justice* (5th edn), Boston, MA and London: Allyn and Bacon.

Reiner, R. (2006) 'Beyond risk: a lament for social democratic criminology', in T. Newburn and P. Rock (eds) *The politics of crime control: Essays in honour of David Downes*, Clarendon Studies in Criminology, Oxford and New York, NY: Oxford University Press.

Reiner, R. (2007a) *Law and order: An honest citizen's guide to crime and control*, Cambridge and Malden, MA: Polity Press.

Reiner, R. (2007b) 'Political economy, crime, and criminal justice', in M. Maguire, R. Morgan and R. Reiner (eds) *The Oxford handbook of criminology* (4th edn), Cambridge and USA: Oxford University Press, pp 341–80.

Ritzer, G. and Goodman, D.J. (1997) *Classical sociological theory* (4th edn), London, Boston, MA and New York, NY: McGraw Hill.

Roberts, R. and McMahon, W. (eds) (2007) *Social justice and criminal justice*, London: Centre for Crime and Justice Studies, King's College London.

Rodger, J.J. (2008) *Criminalising social policy: Anti-social behaviour and welfare in a de-civilised society*, Cullompton: Willan.

Rose, G. (1961) *The struggle for penal reform: The Howard League and its predecessors*, London and Chicago, IL: Stevens and Sons Limited and Quadrangle Books, Inc.

Rose, J. (1994) *Elizabeth Fry*, London: The History Press Ltd.

Roshier, B. (1989) *Controlling crime*, Buckingham: Open University Press.

Rusche, G. and Kirchheimer, O. (1939 [1968]) *Punishment and social structure*, New York, NY: Russell and Russell.

Russell, B. (1946 [1996 edn]) *History of Western philosophy*, London and New York, NY: Routledge.

Rutherford, A. (1993) *Criminal justice and the pursuit of decency*, Winchester: Waterside Press.

Saad-Filho, A. and Johnston, D. (eds) (2005) *Neoliberalism: A critical reader*, London and Ann Arbor, MI: Pluto Press.

Safranski, R. (2003) *Nietzsche: A philosophical biography*, London: Granta Books.

Sampson, R.V. (1956) *Progress in the age of reason: The seventeenth century to the present day*, London and Toronto: Heinemann.

Scheurich, J.J. and McKenzie, K.B. (2005) 'Foucault's methodologies: archaeology and genealogy', in N.K. Denzin and Y.S. Lincoln (eds) *The Sage handbook of qualitative research* (3rd edn), London, Thousand Oaks, CA and New Delhi: Sage Publications.

Scruton, R. (2001) *Kant: A very short introduction*, Oxford and New York, NY: Oxford University Press.

Sim, J. (2009) *Punishment and prisons: Power and the carceral state*, London, Thousand Oaks, CA and New Delhi: Sage Publications.

Simon, J. (2007) *Governing through crime: How the war on crime transformed American democracy and created a culture of fear*, Oxford and New York, NY: Oxford University Press.

Simon, W.M. (1963) *European positivism in the nineteenth century: An essay in intellectual history*, Ithaca, NY: Cornell University Press.

Smith, D. (1988) *The Chicago School: A liberal critique of capitalism*, Basingstoke: Macmillan.

Smith, D. (2006) 'Making sense of psychoanalysis in criminological theory and probation practice', *Probation Journal*, vol 53, no 4, pp 361–76.

Solomon, E. and Garside, R. (2008) *Ten years of Labour's youth justice reforms: An independent audit*, London: Centre for Crime and Justice Studies, King's College London.

Solomon, E., Eades, C., Garside, R. and Rutherford, M. (2007) *Ten years of criminal justice under Labour: An independent audit*, London: Centre for Crime and Justice Studies, King's College London.

Spitzer, S. (1975) 'Punishment and social organisation: a study of Durkheim's theory of penal evolution', *Law and Society Review*, vol 9, no 4, pp 613–38.

Statham, R.S. and Whitehead, P. (eds) (1992) *Managing the Probation Service: Issues for the 1990s*, Harlow: Longman.

Stedman Jones, G. (1971) *Outcast London: A study in the relationship between classes in Victorian society*, Oxford: Clarendon Press.

Stelman, A. (1980) 'Social work relationships: an exploration', *Probation Journal*, vol 27, pp 85–94.

Stewart, G. and Stewart, J. (1993) *Social circumstances of young offenders under supervision*, London: Association of Chief Probation Officers.

Stewart, J., Smith, D. and Stewart, G. with Fullwood, C. (1994) *Understanding offending behaviour*, Harlow: Longman.

Straw, J. (2009) 'Probation and community punishment', Speech to trainee probation officers at the Probation Study School, University of Portsmouth, 4 February (www.justice.gov.uk/news/sp040209.htm).

Sztompka, P. (1986) *Robert K. Merton: An intellectual profile*, Basingstoke: Macmillan.

Tarnas, R. (1991) *The passion of the Western mind: Understanding the ideas that have shaped our world view*, London: Pimlico.

Taylor, I. (1997) 'The political economy of crime', in M. Maguire, R. Morgan and R. Reiner (eds) *The Oxford handbook of criminology* (2nd edn), Oxford and New York, NY: Oxford University Press, pp 265–303.

Taylor, I., Walton, P. and Young, J. (1973) *The new criminology: For a social theory of deviance*, London, Boston, and Henley: Routledge and Kegan Paul.

Taylor, R., Wasik, M. and Leng, R. (2004) *Blackstone's guide to the Criminal Justice Act 2003*, Oxford and New York, NY: Oxford University Press.

Teesside Probation Service (2008) *Teesside area plan for additional funding: Business plan 2008–2009 (Draft 2)*, Middlesbrough: Teesside Probation Service.

Thompson, K. (1982) *Emile Durkheim: Key sociologists*, New York, NY: Tavistock Publications.

Thorpe, D.H., Smith, D., Green, C.J. and Paley, J.H. (1980) *Out of care: The community support of juvenile offenders*, London: George Allen and Unwin.

Tierney, J. (2006) *Criminology: Theory and context* (2nd edn), Harlow: Pearson Education.

Traugott, M. (1978) *Emile Durkheim: On institutional analysis*, Chicago, IL and London: University of Chicago Press.

Turner, B.S. (ed) (1996) *The Blackwell companion to social theory*, Oxford and Cambridge, MA: Blackwell.

Valier, C. (2002) *Theories of crime and punishment*, Harlow: Longman.

Vennard, J., Sugg, D. and Hedderman, C. (1997) *Changing offenders' attitudes and behaviour: What works?*, Home Office Research Study 171, London: Home Office.

Wacquant, L. (2004) *Body and soul: Notebooks of an apprentice boxer*, Oxford and New York, NY: Oxford University Press.

Wacquant, L. (2008) *Urban outcasts: A comparative sociology of advanced marginality*, Cambridge: Polity Press.

Wacquant, L. (2009) *Punishing the poor: The neoliberal government of social insecurity*, Durham, NC and London: Duke University Press.

Walker, M. and Beaumont, B. (1981) *Probation work: Critical theory and socialist practice*, Oxford: Blackwell.

Weber, M. (1904/05 [1958]) *The Protestant ethic and the spirit of capitalism*, New York, NY: Scribner's Press.

Weber, M. (1922 [1968]) *Economy and society: An outline of interpretive sociology*, 3 vols (edited by Guenther Roth and Claus Wittich), New York, NY: Bedminster Press.

Whimster, S. (ed) (2004) *The essential Weber: A reader*, London and New York, NY: Routledge.

Whitehead, P. (1990) *Community supervision for offenders: A new model of probation*, Aldershot and Brookfield, CT: Avebury.

Whitehead, P. (2007) *Modernising probation and criminal justice: Getting the measure of cultural change*, Crayford: Shaw and Sons.

Whitehead, P. and MacMillan, J. (1985) 'Checks or blank cheque? Justifying custody of juveniles', *Probation Journal*, vol 32, no 3, pp 87–9.

Whitehead, P. and Statham, R. (2006) *The history of probation: Politics, power and cultural change 1876–2005*, Crayford: Shaw and Sons.

Wilkinson, R. and Pickett, K. (2009) *The spirit level: Why more equal societies almost always do better*, London: Allen Lane.

Windlesham, Lord (1993) *Responses to crime, Volume 2: Penal policy in the making*, Oxford and New York, NY: Clarendon Press.

Windlesham, Lord (2001) *Responses to crime, Volume 4: Dispensing justice*, Oxford and New York, NY: Clarendon Press.

Windlesham, Lord (2003) 'Ministers and modernisation: criminal justice policy, 1997–2001', in L. Zedner and A. Ashworth (eds) *The criminological foundations of penal policy: Essays in honour of Roger Hood*, Clarendon Studies in Criminology, Oxford and New York, NY: Oxford University Press.

Young, A.F. and Ashton, E.T. (1956) *British social work in the nineteenth century*, London: Routledge and Kegan Paul.

Young, J. (1999) *The exclusive society: Social exclusion, crime and difference in late modernity*, London, Thousand Oaks, CA and New Delhi: Sage Publications.

Young, J. (2007) *The vertigo of late modernity*, London, Thousand Oaks, CA and New Delhi: Sage Publications.

Young, P. (1976) 'A sociological analysis of the early history of probation', *British Journal of Law and Society*, vol 3, pp 44–58.

Zedner, L. (2003) 'Useful knowledge? Debating the role of criminology in post-war Britain?', in L. Zedner and A. Ashworth (eds) *The criminological foundations of penal policy: Essays in honour of Roger Hood*, Clarendon Studies in Criminology, Oxford and New York, NY: Oxford University Press.

Zedner, L. (2004) *Criminal justice*, Clarendon Law Series, Oxford and New York, NY: Oxford University Press.

Zedner, L. (2006) 'Opportunity makes the thief-taker: the influence of economic analysis on crime control', in T. Newburn and P. Rock (eds) *The politics of crime control: Essays in honour of David Downes*, Clarendon Studies in Criminology, Oxford and New York, NY: Oxford University Press.

Index

Note: The letters t and n following page numbers indicate tables and notes.

A

accountability 4, 20, 89, 114
Adam Smith Institute 93
advise, assist and befriend 3, 101, 113–14, 118
Albrow, M. 41–2
Ambitions for Britain (New Labour manifesto 2001) 4–5
anti-social behaviour 5, 158
Anti-Social Behaviour Orders (ASBOs) 8, 150
Auld, Lord Justice 13

B

Barber, M. 90, 106n
barristers 111–12, 121, 122
Beaumont, B. 49, 95, 163–4
Believing We Can: Promoting the contribution faith-based organisations can make to reducing adult and youth re-offending (NOMS) 102
benefit sanction 86, 87, 106n, 116–17
Birtspeak 90–1
Blair, Tony 83–4
Body and soul (Wacquant) 59
Bonger, W. 45–6
borstal system 69, 98
Bottoms, A.E. 75–6
Bourgois, P. 94–5
Box, S. 115
breach policy 85–6, 87
breach reports 85–6
Britain forward not back (New Labour manifesto 2005) 8
British penal system 1993–1950 (Hinde) 68
Bryant, M. 74–5
bureaucracy 41–3, 87–91
bureaucratic technicians 43, 89, 105
bureaucratisation 89–91
business efficiency 11, 89, 131–6, 152

C

Cabinet Office Strategy Unit 149–50
capitalism 46, 47–9, 50, 71, 95, 139, 162
    and prisons 58–9
care and control 74, 75, 100
Carter, Patrick 6, 85
Case Con 48–9
cases, tiering of 9–10
Cavadino, M. 95
central governmental control 4, 89–90, 91, 108, 150
Centre for Policy Studies 93
Chakrabarti, Suma 154

Changing lives (NAPO) 100–1
chaplains 9, 68–9, 102
Chief Probation Officers (CPOs) 107–8, 156
Children Act (1908) 69
Children and Young Persons Act (1933) 69
Children and Young Persons Act (1969) 69
Churches Criminal Justice Forum 102
class structure 45, 71
class-based justice 44, 46–8
clerks *see* court clerks
Cohen, S. 98
community chaplaincies 9, 102
community correctional service 76
community orders 85–6
community payback 17
community sentences 8, 12, 13, 17, 106n, 157
Comte, Auguste 24
Confident communities in a secure Britain (Home Office) 7
Conservative governments 87, 89
    neoliberalism 93–4
    probation officer training 8
    punitive law and order, change to 1, 107
contestability 6–7, 91, 102–3, 120, 133, 143–4, 150, 153
control by central government 4, 89–90, 91, 108, 150
Coser, L.A. 39
court clerks
    NOMS, understanding of 142–3
    profile of 123
    views on changes in probation
        contestability 143
        efficiency/justice potential conflict 134, 135, 136
        fast delivery reports (FDRs) 129–30
        probation, future of 144–6
        probation, purpose of 125
        probation, understandings of 119t
        reports, punitisation of 136–7
        reports, purpose of 128–9, 152
        verstehen/understanding 140
crime
    Durkheim 28–9, 30–1
    media reporting 13, 47–8, 84, 150
    outrage at 84
    portrayal of 47–8, 150
    as social problem 76
Crime (Sentences) Act (1997) 86
crime and disorder reduction partnerships (CDRPs) 5, 20n

crime control strategies, contemporary 84, 159–60
criminal and social justice 16, 118, 119, 121, 131, 139, 154
Criminal Justice Act (1982) 1
Criminal Justice Act (1991) 107, 126, 150
Criminal Justice Act (2003) 6, 7, 11, 85, 134
  reports preparation 126, 128
  sentencing aims 20n, 124, 125
Criminal Justice and Court Services Act (2000) 4
Criminal justice and the pursuit of decency (Rutherford) 153
criminal justice system 1, 11, 155
  control of the poor 47
  expansion of 95
Criminal justice: The way ahead (White Paper) 5–6, 20n
criminalisation 8, 50, 60, 95
Crown Prosecution Service 150
cultural changes 4, 150, 155, 157
  see also research: modernisation and cultural change in probation
Culture of control (Garland) 92, 93
custodial sentences 12, 85
custody, alternatives to 107, 108
Cutting crime, delivering justice (Home Office) 7–8

D

delinquency, political construction of 59–60
Delivering simple, speedy, summary justice (Home Office) 11
Departmental Committee reports
  1909: 72–3
  1922: 73
  1936: 73
  1962: 73, 97
deprivation *see* socio-economic conditions
Descartes, R. 52
deviance
  Durkheim's typology of 29
  fully social theory of 47–8
Dignan, J. 95
director of offender management 14–15, 155
disciplinary normalisation 96–9, 105
discipline 58–9
Discipline and punish (Foucault) 58–61, 99
discretion 72, 101, 141
Division of labour in society (Durkheim) 30, 31
Durkheim, Emile 24–5, 61
  crime and punishment 28–9
  deviance, typology of 29
  division of labour in society 30–2
  moral education 34–5
  themes 26–8
  'The two laws of penal evolution' 32–4

E

Economy and society (Weber) 36, 37, 38, 42
efficiency 11, 89, 131–6, 152
The emergence of penal policy in Victorian and Edwardian England (Radzinowicz and Hood) 68
empathy 79, 119, 121
empirical research 107
  see also research; research: modernisation and cultural change in probation
empiricism 51–2, 53
enforcement 6, 7, 8, 9, 10, 112–13
Enlightenment 26–7, 51–2, 54, 97, 99
Evangelical Alliance 102
expressive justice 30, 84–5, 86

F

faith communities 9, 102, 103, 160–2
fast delivery reports (FDRs) 11, 127, 129–30, 134–6, 139, 140, 152, 153
  40% rule 129, 130–1, 132–3
Fateful choices: Ten decisions that changed the world 1940-1941 (Kershaw) 158–9
A five-year strategy for protecting the public and reducing re-offending (Home Office) 10
Foucault, Michel 51–4, 62, 96, 97, 156
  Discipline and punish 58–61
  The order of things 54–8
  themes 54–5
Fry, Elizabeth 67

G

Garland, D. 31–2, 84, 92–3, 98, 138, 159–60
Gerth, H.H. 39
Giddens, A. 40
government-speak 90

H

Hanson, David 14
Harris, R. 73–4
Harvey, D. 94
Haxby, D. 76
Hill, Roger 14
Hinde, R.S.E. 68
Hobsbawm, E. 93
Hood, R. 68, 70
Howard, J. 67
Hudson, B.A. 37–8, 50
human understanding (*verstehen*) 37–41, 88, 91, 138–42, 152–3
humanitarianism 67, 78, 100

I

Ignatieff, M. 66–7
Improving prison and probation services: Public value partnership (Home Office) 12
individual responsibility 2–3, 5, 93, 138
inequality *see* socio-economic conditions
Institute of Economic Affairs 93

J

Jarvis, F.V. 138
Joseph, Keith 93
Joyce, J. 159
judges 111–12, 121
justice, types of 165n
  see also criminal and social justice; social
    justice
juvenile justice 69
  see also youth justice

K

Katz, M.B. 94
Kehlmann, D. 39
Keynesian economic management 1, 93, 138,
  139
Kirchheimer, O. 46
knee-jerk reactions 84–5, 87, 105

L

language, changes in 90, 157
law enforcement agency 112t, 115–16, 117t
Lawyers Christian Fellowship 102
layered assessments 132
league tables 90
Leeson, C. 72
legislation 13–15, 20n, 71–2, 150
  18th century 68, 80n
  Children Act (1908) 69
  Children and Young Persons Act (1933) 69
  Children and Young Persons Act (1969) 69
  Crime (Sentences) Act (1997) 86
  Criminal Justice Act (1982) 1
  Criminal Justice Act (1991) 107, 126, 150
  Criminal Justice Act (2003) 6, 7, 11, 85, 134
    reports preparation 126, 128
    sentencing aims 20n, 124, 125
  Criminal Justice and Court Services Act
    (2000) 4
  Offender Management Act (2007) 15, 102,
    153
  Probation of First Offenders Act (1887) 71,
    126
  Probation of Offenders Act (1907) 72, 97,
    113, 126
  Summary Jurisdiction Act (1879) 71

M

macro-structural factors 5, 139, 151, 157
magistrates
  NOMS, understanding of 143
  profile of 123–4
  views on changes in probation
    contestability 143–4
    efficiency/justice potential conflict 134–6
    fast delivery reports (FDRs) 129, 130–1
    probation, future of 146
    probation, purpose of 125
    probation, understandings of 119t

reports, punitisation of 136–7
reports, purpose of 128–9, 152
verstehen/understanding 140–1
magistrates' courts, modernisation 11, 112–17,
  132
Mair, G. 85
managerialism 77, 88
*Managing offenders, reducing crime: A new
  approach* (Carter) 6–7
marketisation 6–7, 89
Marx, Karl 43–4, 61
Marxist tradition
  20th century perspectives 45–51
  themes 44–5
Matthews, R. 98
McLellan, D. 44
McWilliams, W. 50, 71–2, 75–6, 77–8
media reporting 13, 47–8, 84, 150
Merquior, J.G. 57
Mills, C.W. 39
Ministry of Justice 14, 154
mixed economy of provision 6–7, 9, 11, 12
modernisation 51, 95, 96, 149–50, 158
  1997–2001: 2–4
  1997–2009, significant developments 18t
  2001–05: 4–8
  2005 onward 8–16
moral panics 47–8
moral responsibilities 96, 134–6
Morgan, R. 101
Morison Report 97
Morrison, K. 38, 44, 45
mugging 48

N

NAPO 14, 15, 157, 165–6n
National Deviancy Conference (NDC) 48
National Offender Management Service
  (NOMS) *see* NOMS
National Probation Service 4, 6, 91, 124–5,
  150, 156, 159
National Standards 11, 20n, 89, 127, 139
natural sciences 24–5, 26, 38–40, 61
NEETS 158
neoliberalism 51, 96, 138, 157
  punishment as control 92–6, 105
New Deal 150
New Labour 1–2, 13, 19n, 87, 89, 158
  1997–2001: 2–4
  2001–05: 4–8
  2005 onward 8–16
  manifestos 2–3, 4–5, 8
  modernising methodologies 20n
  probation, changes to 149–51, 153
new order of things 156–8
new public management 1–2, 16, 88–9, 96,
  132, 138, 153, 161
NOMS 6–7, 8, 150, 153, 161
  and bureaucracy 89, 90–1

and contestability 6–7, 102–3
court clerks' understanding of 142–3
headquarters function 14
magistrates' understanding of 143
and punishment 9–10, 87
strategic business plan for 2009–11: 100
NOMS offender management model 9–10, 90–1
non-treatment paradigm 75–6
normalisation 96–9
Northtown *see* research: modernisation and
    cultural change in probation

O

offender assessment system (OASys) 10, 90,
    122, 127, 132, 152–3
offender group reconviction scale (OGRS)
    127
offender management 90
Offender Management Act (2007) 15, 102,
    153
Offender Management Bill 133
offender managers 9, 10, 97, 99, 103–4, 155
offender mitigation 139
Old Labour 2, 19n, 149
Oldfield, M. 85
oral history of probation work 100–1
oral reports 127, 129, 131, 134, 139
order of things, new 156–8
Order of things, The (Foucault) 54–8
Orwell, G. 61

P

Parenti, C. 95
penal policy 8–9, 19n, 84, 92–3
Penal populism (Pratt) 8
penal-welfare system, indices of change
    105–6n
persistent offenders, penalties for 6, 157
personal responsibility 2–3, 5, 93, 138
personalism 74, 77–8, 79t, 81n, 88, 99–102,
    103, 160
philanthropy 67
philosophy 51, 52–3, 63n
Platt, A. 71
Police Court Mission 70, 71–2
police court missionaries 70, 71, 73, 99, 125–6
Policing the crisis (Hall et al) 48
Policy review: Crime, justice and cohesion (PMSU)
    12
politics and power 45, 46–8, 60, 62, 66
positivism 53
poverty 95
practitioner research 107–8
    see also research; research: modernisation and
        cultural change in probation
Pratt, J. 89, 122
pre-sentence reports (PSRs) 11, 85, 126, 127,
    132, 134, 140
prison chaplains 68–9

Prison Fellowship 102
prison population 1, 13, 115
prison reform 66–9
prisons
    birth of 58–9
    capacity expansion 8, 157
    Carter review (2007) 13–14
    failure of 59–60
    and probation, unbalanced relationship 14,
        155–6
Prisons-probation: Joining forces to protect the public
    (Home Office) 3–4
Private Eye 90
private sector 9, 12, 14, 102–3, 133, 161
probation 8, 16, 98
    approaches to 23–4
    budget cuts 165–6n
    changes under New Labour 149–51
    dehumanised and densensitised 158
    early history 70–1
    future of 144–6
    oral history 100–1
    and prisons, unbalanced relationship 14,
        155–6
    purpose of 124–5, 151–2
    understandings of 118–22, 151
    values 21n, 65, 119, 121, 154
Probation Boards Association 157
Probation Circulars
    06/2009: 133
    12/2007: 127
probation ideal 21n
Probation of First Offenders Act (1887) 71,
    126
Probation of Offenders Act (1907) 72, 97, 113,
    126
probation officers 8, 115–16
    early 73, 126
    oral history 100–1
Probation Officers' Christian Union 101
Probation Orders 107
probation reports *see* reports
probation rules, breaching 86
Probation Service 3, 12, 16
    renaming of 4
Probation Service Christian Fellowship 101
probation service officers (PSOs) 85–6
Probation statistics quarterly brief (Ministry of
    Justice) 134
Probation work: Critical theory and socialist practice
    (Walker and Beaumont) 49
PSRs (pre-sentence reports) 11, 85, 126, 127,
    132, 134, 140
public sector 9, 12, 14, 102–3, 161
punishment 10, 43
    as control strategy 91–6, 105
    as expression of outrage 34–5
Punishment and welfare (Garland) 92

R

Radzinowicz, L. 68, 69, 70
rationalisation 42, 77, 88, 95
rationalism 28, 44, 51, 52, 53
Raynor, P. 70, 76–7
Reagan, Ronald 93
rebalancing criminal justice 154–6
Re-balancing the criminal justice system (Home
   Office) 10–11
recidivism 21n, 59–60
*Reducing re-offending faith and voluntary and
   community sector alliance* (NOMS) 102
rehabilitation 9, 10, 125, 150, 157
Reiner, R. 139
religion/religious impulses 67, 68–9, 99,
   101–3
  religion as ideology 161–2
  see also chaplains; faith communities; Police
    Court Mission; police court missionaries
reports 134, 139–41, 152
  breach reports 85–6
  cost of 132, 133
  fast delivery reports (FDRs) 11, 127, 129–30,
    134–6, 139, 140, 152, 153
    40% rule 129, 130–1, 132–3
  format 126–7, 133–4
  oral 127, 129, 131, 134, 139
  pre-sentence reports (PSRs) 11, 85, 126, 127,
    132, 134, 140
  punitisation of 136–7, 152
  purpose of 125–9
  social enquiry reports 76, 126, 139
  specific sentence reports 127
  stand-down reports 126–7
research
  1980s 107–8
  2006–07: 108–9
research: modernisation and cultural change in
  probation
  findings
    from advise, assist and befriend to
      punishment 112t, 113–14, 117t
    benefit sanction 112t, 116–17, 117t
    business efficiency before justice 131–6
    contestability 143–4, 153
    enforcement 112–13, 112t, 117t, 119t
    fast delivery reports and 40% rule 129–31,
      134–6
    NOMS, understanding of 142–4, 153
    probation, future of 144–6
    probation, purpose of 124–5, 151–2
    probation, understandings of 118–22, 151
    public protection 112t, 116, 117t
    re-offending risk management focus 112t,
      116, 117t
    report formats 126–7, 133–4
    reports, cost of 132, 133
    reports, punitisation of 136–7, 152
    reports, purpose of 125–9, 152

Service Level Agreement (SLA) 132–3
  from social work help to law enforcement
    112t, 115–16, 117t
  target-driven organisation 112t, 114–15,
    117t
  triple 'S' agenda 132
  verstehen/understanding 138–42, 152–3
  victims, more concerned with than
    offenders 112t, 117, 117t
  operational framework 109–12
    ethical issues 112
    qualitative methodology 110
    quantitative methodology 109–10
  respondents
    barristers 111–12, 121, 122
    court clerks' profile 123
    court clerks' views
    contestability 143
    efficiency/justice potential conflict 134,
      135, 136
    fast delivery reports (FDRs) 129–30
    NOMS, understanding of 142–3
    probation, future of 144–6
    probation, purpose of 125
    probation, understandings of 119t
    reports, punitisation of 136–7
    reports, purpose of 128–9, 152
    verstehen/understanding 140
    crown court views
    modernisation and cultural change 117–18
    probation, understandings of 120–2
    judges 111–12, 121
    magistrates' court views
    modernisation and cultural change 112–17
    probation, understandings of 118–20
    magistrates' profile 123–4
    magistrates' views
    contestability 143–4
    efficiency/justice potential conflict 134–6
    fast delivery reports (FDRs) 129, 130–1
    NOMS, understanding of 143
    probation, future of 146
    probation, purpose of 125
    probation, understandings of 119t
    reports, punitisation of 136–7
    reports, purpose of 128–9, 152
    verstehen/understanding 140–1
    solicitors 110–11, 112t, 119t
Respect agenda 8, 151
responsibility, individual 2–3, 5, 93, 138
Rules of sociological method (Durkheim) 26, 31
Rusche, G. 46

S

*Securing the future: Proposals for the efficient and
   sustainable use of custody in England and Wales*
   (Carter) 13–14, 85
sentencing 8, 13, 133–4, 139, 150
  aims of, Criminal Justice Act (2003) 20n

Service Level Agreement (SLA) 129, 132–3, 152
social enquiry reports 76, 126, 139
social exclusion 5
Social Exclusion Unit 19n, 149–50
social justice 16, 118, 119, 121, 131, 132, 139, 154
social sciences 37–9, 40, 61, 62, 97
social solidarity 29, 30–1
social theory 24, 61–2
   see also Durkheim; Foucault; Marx; Weber
social work help 70–1, 74, 75, 76, 78, 79, 115, 120
Social Workers Christian Fellowship 101
socio-economic conditions 5, 12, 47–8, 93–5, 139, 150–1, 157–8
solicitors 110–11, 112t, 119t
Sparks, R. 138
specific sentence report 127
stand-down report 126–7
state 46–8, 49, 51, 96, 97–8
state benefits, withdrawal of *see* benefit sanction
statement of national objectives and priorities (SNOP) 107
Straw, Jack 17, 154
Streatfield Report 126
structuralism 55–7
Summary Jurisdiction Act (1879) 71
Sure Start programme 150
surveillance technology 150
Suspended Sentence Order 13–14, 85

T

target culture 89, 91, 112t, 114–15, 164–5n
targets 106n, 122, 144, 146, 152
Teesside Probation Service 85, 136
Telegraph 12
Ten years of criminal justice under Labour: An independent audit (Solomon et al) 12–13, 21n
Thatcher, Margaret 93
therapeutic imagination 43, 88–9
Think First programme 98
third sector 160–2
three strikes legislation 86
tiering of cases 9–10
Titan prison establishments 13
tough on crime 5, 10
trade unions 94
transportation 66
triple 'S' agenda 11, 132, 153
Turner, B.S. 38–9
two contract model 74

U

unbalancing of criminal justice 154–6
underclass 151, 158
understanding *see verstehen*/human understanding
United States 71, 93, 94–5
Urban outcasts (Wacquant) 95

V

Value for money, delivery agreement (Ministry of Justice) 132–3
Vanstone, M. 70
verstehen/human understanding 37–41, 88, 91, 138–42, 152–3
victims
   of crime 7–8, 10, 77, 117, 150, 154
   offenders as 96, 120
voluntary sector 9, 12, 14, 102–3, 161

W

Wacquant, L. 59, 94, 95, 158
Walker, M. 95, 163–4
war against crime 5, 85, 86, 106n, 150
Weber, Max 35–6, 61, 88
   bureaucracy 41–3
   themes 36
   verstehen/understanding 37–41
welfare state 48, 93, 95, 115, 138
Wheatley, Phil 14
'Where next for penal policy' (Clarke) 8–9, 102
White Paper: *Criminal justice: The way ahead* 5–6, 20
white-collar crime 47, 50
Windlesham, Lord 4, 86, 157
Working together (Home Office) 102
working-class crime 47, 50

Y

'yob' culture 5
Young, J. 94
Young, P. 70
young offenders 69
youth justice 19n, 69, 150

Z

Zedner, L. 12, 43, 44
zero tolerance 86, 150